CUSTOMER FRIENDLY

The Organizational Architecture of Service

James T. Ziegenfuss, Jr.

University Press of America,® Inc.
Lanham · Boulder · New York · Toronto · Plymouth, UK

Copyright © 2007 by
University Press of America,® Inc.
4501 Forbes Boulevard
Suite 200
Lanham, Maryland 20706
UPA Acquisitions Department (301) 459-3366

Estover Road
Plymouth PL6 7PY
United Kingdom

Library of Congress Control Number: 2007922676
ISBN-13: 978-0-7618-3752-7 (clothbound : alk. paper)
ISBN-10: 0-7618-3752-3 (clothbound : alk. paper)
ISBN-13: 978-0-7618-3753-4 (paperback : alk. paper)
ISBN-10: 0-7618-3753-1 (paperback : alk. paper)

⊖™ The paper used in this publication meets the minimum
requirements of American National Standard for Information
Sciences—Permanence of Paper for Printed Library Materials,
ANSI Z39.48—1984

To Margee, Kate, Sarah, & Jamie
for their listening endurance.

TABLE OF CONTENTS

PREFACE

Before you begin reading, you may want to conduct an informal poll in your workplace or with your family. Ask colleagues and family members to recall a recent service fiasco—with the bank, the hospital billing department, the university registrar, the auto dealer's service department, the pediatrician, the airport. Is there anyone who could not recite a customer service problem, or give an example of customer unfriendliness? Many customers and many writers have already established that we have a problem. What we need today is information that will tell us how to design effective, customer friendly organizations.

The need for customer friendly organizations exists across fields—from transportation to banking to government to health care to education. Corporate leaders in competitive industries have long known of the importance of serving customers. Companies such as Disney and Southwest come to mind. Even public agency leaders increasingly recognize the need to offer better service to citizens. Across the public and the private sectors, many leaders, managers, employees and students would like to better understand how and why some companies achieve success as customer friendly organizations.

This book presents the organizational architecture of customer friendly organizations. How did some private companies and some public agencies become customer friendly—by accident or by design? I propose it is by design—a design that can be replicated.

Consider these questions. Why does a sales clerk go out of his or her way to help you find the jacket you want? Is it for the money he gains from the sale, or is there something more? Does this attitude flow naturally from good employee selection? Or, does the organization's design contribute significantly to the behavior of its members? Both academics and practicing managers know that design affects behavior. We just have not explored much of the intended architecture of customer friendly organizations. And we need to.

This book contributes to an understanding of how we develop high performance organizations—in this case, organizations that consistently deliver high quality service. It builds on the theory and application of systems thinking to organization design and organization behavior. The underlying model is adapted and has been used to guide a series of research and field consultancies over the past 20 years (reported in both journal articles and books). The model is conceptually elegant, yet offers easy comprehension for operating managers.

The book is written for professional managers and students of business and public administration. Other books describe customer friendly companies, but no books examine the architecture that leads to the performance. The book should interest any organization with customers. Lead "teaching cases" are taken from the fields of education, banking, transportation, manufacturing, hotel and lodging, and health care. They are fictitious cases built on real experiences with reports from newspapers, colleagues, friends and students woven in. The greater set of examples includes a wide range of private companies and public agencies such as the IRS.

The book is based on my research and consulting work of the past 30 years. I have researched and helped to design public and private ombudsman programs to respond to employee and customer concerns in fields ranging from banking to transportation to utilities. I have worked on quality improvement designs in the health care sector, including 15+ years as Associate Editor of the *American Journal of Medical Quality*. My previous work has been reported in three books on this topic—one on customer complaint programs, one on ombudsman programs, and one on organization designs that support quality management. I have also given executive education seminars on diagnosing customer service problems using earlier versions of the architecture presented here.

Chapter One opens with an account of a series of customer service catastrophes, followed by additional anecdotes outlining examples of service gaps. These stories build the rationale for addressing the customer service problem—a need that will resonate well with most readers. The second chapter reports on some of the customer service work to date, including attention to service improvements through product design, psychological climate and culture. The organizational architecture framework is presented as a network of five systems: product/technology, structure, psychological climate, leadership/management, and corporate culture. The "architectural support" for customer service is embedded in each of these five systems. *The customer friendly organization is thus "co-produced" by the interactive design of each of these internal systems.* The "holistic nature" of the architecture is illustrated by the cases and by actions that can be taken to improve service. Each of the subsequent chapters addresses one of the five systems both as an individual design challenge and with regard to its interaction with other systems.

Each chapter features a case illustrating that particular aspect of the architecture, with examples including a hospital, automobile plant, airline, hotel, university and library.

The book provides an extensive supply of stories about service success and failure. The teaching cases are fictitious composites—cases that could be true or should be true (in the case of missed attempts to provide high level service). No case represents an existing company. A wide range of industries are highlighted so that the reader may find examples from his or her own field. However, the reader is encouraged to consider how, for example, transportation or hotel management methods could be applied to education or health care.

The book can be used for several purposes: to continually improve the *degree of customer friendliness* in your organization; to radically *re-engineer* your organization to further support service to customers; and to help leaders, managers and employees to *design a vision of the future organization*—one that is more customer friendly than today.

A number of persons contributed to the thinking for the book. I have learned much about customer friendly action from several colleagues in particular: David Jones, M.D., at the medical quality journal; Justine Sentenne, employee ombudsman at Hydro Quebec; and Pat O'Rourke, patient ombudsman at McGill's Royal Victoria Hospital. The systems thinking orientation is due to my Wharton School faculty Eric Trist and Russell Ackoff. Finally I appreciate the research assistance of graduate students here at Penn State; and the editing of Yvonne Harhigh and Katherine Ziegenfuss Sharpe, and the manuscript preparation expertise of Steve Dahm.

From my own experiences it is clear that universities, banks, hospitals and other organizations could be far more customer friendly than they are. Family, friends and colleagues readily agree. It is my hope that this work will convince leaders that the architecture of their organizations can be purposely directed to support customer friendliness. In the end, this an extension of our work on quality and excellence, an extension that can help patients, students, buyers, citizens and clients throughout this country and across international borders.

Professor James T. Ziegenfuss, Jr. Ph.D.
Pennsylvania State University

CHAPTER 1

THE CUSTOMER SERVICE PROBLEM IN SIX CASES

My uncle would be able to tell me the secrets of customer friendly service, if he were alive. But I know what many of his opinions would be. On summer visits he would talk about his days with a large retail firm, where he started at the bottom and eventually worked his way to Vice President of Toy Purchasing. He died at age 94, the curmudgeon I remembered on my visits, but his spirit has helped me puzzle out this service architecture problem. His occasional comments provide a lighter view of a serious and important subject.

Is customer friendliness an *accidental* outcome? Or, is the quality of service *designed in* (i.e. is success or failure with customers built into the organization)? This simple, but powerful, question opens our inquiry. Let's begin with an assumption—that you want to keep current customers and add new ones. As a collective group of organizations, how are we doing? Consider this letter received from my uncle.

> *Dear Nephew,*
>
> *I hope you are well. I thought I would use this note to tell you of some recent "adventures" of mine.*
>
> *The other morning my car battery died and I had a flat tire. Called my Auto Association and the operator told me "We'll be there when we can get there." This Autocoach car is only one year old so maybe they stuck in a battery from an earlier model!*
>
> *I went inside to wait and decided to call the bank to fix an overdrawn check. But I couldn't get to a live person—I kept pressing those number choices for a while, but eventually gave up.*
>
> *And did I tell you I had to call the plumber to come back and fix the toilet that he fixed last week? It no longer runs continuously—it now leaks.*

After I finally got my car fixed, I headed to the doctor's office for my annual physical. Do you know I had to wait over an hour even though I showed up early? I just about memorized those posters on the wall, let me tell you. When I returned home, I found the cable man had come and gone, even though he was scheduled for yesterday. He was returning to remove the wrong cable box and to shift the cable he had stapled across the front siding of the house, which he said was more direct.

I couldn't even cut the grass because my expensive new lawnmower stalled out. The store said I have to "bring it in, we don't make house calls." Doesn't fit in my trunk, so maybe I'll just tie it to the bumper and drag it in!

Since the day was wasted, I went over to have a nice, quiet dinner at the Royal Court Hotel they just renovated. Unfortunately two tables away was a screaming youngster. The restaurant staff must have thought of her as dinner music because they didn't do a thing. I left before my dinner came.

Well, that's pretty much my day. Oh—one more thing— I received a "notice of an audit" letter from the IRS. I wonder if they are nice people.

All for now,
Your Uncle Arthur

Most of us do not have so many "customer unfriendly" experiences on the same day. But many of us have had them. As companies push to increase customer friendly service—while safeguarding existing levels of service—they will undoubtedly use existing strategies and methods. Unfortunately, these same old ways will not be sufficient. If we try to create a "customer service future" using the approaches of the past, we can expect to fail. The old models are obsolete.

Customer friendly service is an increasing concern for organizations that *provide* services and for groups that *advocate* for consumers. Increased competition raises anxieties about trade-offs. Do we enhance the bottom line through reductions in customer service? As service becomes a strategic issue, organizations will *compete* on the basis of service. Companies that offer high customer service will survive murderous competition. As an example of how far this concept has come, physicians are now reducing their patients' waiting times, an unlikely prospect just a few years ago.

Attention to the concept of customer service is now noticeable in strategic plans, advertising, and employee training. A growth market in strategies and techniques for improving service is emerging, with hundreds of disconnected offerings.

This book presents a systems approach to designing and maintaining customer friendliness with two main objectives. First, it frames the problem in an "organizational architecture" context. Traditionally, customer service was viewed only as a production and product delivery problem, often labeled "defective product." But the lawnmower clerk was surely not trained to insult a grandfatherly customer, nor was his attitude directly part of a "defective lawnmower". Successful executives and management scholars have long known that organization behaviors result from attention to all of the aspects of the organization—culture, structure, and management, as well as production and customer support responses. This book will illustrate why increasing customer friendliness is an organization-wide problem, using "organizational architecture" as a guide.

Second, specific methods and actions are presented for "designing in and improving" customer friendliness. The examples are action-oriented, while grounded in organization behavior theory. The cases offer suggestions for increasing customer service through changes in the organization's product and production, structure, human relations and management.

Why is this approach needed? At its simplest, it answers the question, "how can we insure that we best serve each customer each time?" But this approach also helps dispel two incorrect, yet prevalent assumptions about customer friendliness:

1. *That individual employees* are the *cause* of poor customer service—that my uncle's bad experiences were solely the fault of the person with whom he dealt.
2. That *isolated* actions are sufficient to increase the customer friendliness of the whole organization—fix that one product, salesman, or store and the company's customer hostility is gone for good.

These assumptions limit customer service improvement to a single employee or initiative at a time. If that type of individual approach would suffice, we would all work in customer friendly companies. The *necessary analysis* and *set of responses* requires a full review of the organizational context of individual action. Lawnmower services, automobile repair and banking transactions are created and delivered by large complex organizations, not just the salesperson or the bank teller. Public and private sector leaders need a practical approach to managing customer friendliness. Educators need a training tool for students in management and public administration. In the next 10 years, customer service will be one of the leading issues in management debates.

To date, little discussion has occurred regarding the underlying architecture of customer friendly companies like Disney and Southwest Airlines. Most customer service improvement work focuses on a single procedure or product orientation, e.g., how to improve telephone inquiries, the development of a customer complaint program, shifting to a 24-hour store schedule. Instead of a piecemeal effort, a systems approach integrates existing strategies and practices. We can think about an "architecture" for increasing customer service, designing friendliness into every aspect of the organization.

Systems thinking is a promising tool for addressing management and organization problems because it counters our tendency to isolate workers from products, from incentives, and from leadership. When we isolate parts—"one employee is the poor service cause"—we try to solve multi-faceted problems with single dimension solutions. Only an improvement process as multi-faceted as the problem can succeed!

Unfortunately, unconvinced of the need, many leaders will not invest in improvement. We should therefore begin by addressing the need for customer service.

WHY CUSTOMER SERVICE?

Uncle Arthur understood why outstanding customer service is important. So do many executives. But all of us, on occasion, forget. Competition in private business markets and for public sector resources is stronger than ever. The life and health of our companies and public agencies are at stake. Executives know that to stay in business they must:

- Convince customers to *become* customers
- Convince customers to *continue* to buy
- Convince customers to *increase* purchases of current products and services

- Convince customers to *expand to new and related* products and services
- Convince customers to *recommend* our organization to others

To entice customers to start, continue, increase, expand and recommend is the customer friendliness rationale for public administrators and private company executives alike. Many commentators and analysts have already recognized this need across industries and disciplines—from manufacturing to retail to education to health care.

The service failures reported by Uncle Arthur cut off repeat business. The ratios above show that over time, customer dissatisfaction can be devastating, but if we successfully satisfy customers, our businesses prosper in measurable ways. The stock market recognizes the importance of reaching out to customers with improvements in service responsiveness, conveniences, guarantees, and hours reflected in better stock prices. Conversely, when customers are negatively affected by reduced operating hours, closed service departments, limited guarantees and complicated telephone access, stock buyers take note and reduce their investment.

Executives leading the companies that produced my uncle's experiences would offer some defense, starting with a changing and hostile business environment. Although it's a tough business world, could this be an effective excuse for poor service?

Customer service failures have not escaped the attention of leaders. What has been done to date? Are there building blocks that will inform our quest for a customer friendly architecture? Six initiatives are common in many companies—all have contributed to our ability to realize customer friendliness.

1. *Product design and development has advanced through technology.*

How have companies used technology to enhance customer service? The innovations are numerous and cut across all fields. Consider:

- 800 numbers for inquiries
- Internet-based product information and delivery capabilities
- Automated teller machines
- Bar codes for package tracking

- Shrinking cell phone size and expanding capability
- Distance education

A standout example is Amazon.com. Customers can review extensive listings of books and other products, order at reduced prices, and receive quick delivery, losing only the ambience of the local bookstore. The ability to purchase quickly, conveniently and inexpensively from home is a stunning advance. At Amazon, customers can browse and order with speed. Searches are exact. Order confirmation is fast and reliable, reassuring the customer about the process.

2. *Workplace psychology and climate have been improved.*
Companies have also attended to the "psychology" of the workplace to improve customer service. Managers have long known that employee attitude is a significant component of "customer friendliness." In both public and private companies employees have:

- Attended customer service orientation
- Been empowered with the discretion to create solutions for service needs
- Been recognized for outstanding service
- Participated in customer contact forums
- Included customers in product design and process work groups

A public sector example of a work in progress is the Internal Revenue Service. When citizens complained vigorously about their treatment by IRS agents, public hearings produced some surprising findings. Audit staff were working under strong pressure to produce "financial returns" and often operated with the belief in "citizens as thieves." Leadership efforts focused on turning the attitude, changing the incentives, and in creating a "gentler IRS workplace."
Starbucks has already worked the "people side". New employees are taught the "star skills," guidelines for on-the-job interpersonal relations: 1. maintain and enhance self esteem; 2. listen and acknowledge, and 3. ask for help.[1]

3. *Product quality is the subject of continuous improvement by everyone in the company.*
The 1990's were considered the decade of the quality improvement movement. Following Japanese corporations, American exec-

utives invested heavily in developing customer satisfaction through improvements in quality. They have added guarantees, "no hassle" returns and continuous product improvement. From cars, to nutrition, to telecommunications, examples of product quality improvements are many. We can recognize product quality gains in Ford cars, Motorola products, and Xerox production processes, among others. Still, we can see that "getting it right each time, every time" is not yet a reality. There is more room for improvement in aligning incentives, in core product quality, and in responsiveness to service failures.

4. Leadership is the driving force of higher quality service.

As in other areas of customer service innovation, we have looked to leadership to establish goals, foster a climate of attention to customers and to regularly review progress. As quality experts Deming and Juran have noted without leadership we have nothing.[2, 3] Some visible leaders in customer service include Sam Walton of Wal-Mart, Herb Kelleher of Southwest Airlines, J.W. Marriott of Marriott and Lee Iaccoco of Chrysler.

As an example of commitment to customers, consider how Southwest corrected an unintended consequence of their 25th anniversary. So many customers flooded the telephones to secure their great celebration rates that existing customers could not get through. In response, Southwest mailed free tickets to all frequent flyers.

5. Data and information are vital to meeting and exceeding customer needs.

Most companies have figured out that they need information about how their customers use and evaluate their products. We have become increasingly sophisticated in assessing service. Many companies maintain data that helps them determine customer use patterns and comments, repeat business, geographic and demographic characteristics, and use of related products.

At many hospitals, managers have information on patient waiting times, and diagnostic and surgical outcomes to help them judge customer service. Banks, universities and airlines all benchmark their performance against leaders in their respective fields.

6. Customer contact now and forever is absolutely necessary.

Although some companies have been slow to increase their "first hand" customer contact, many more now understand why and how to interact with customers. From the 1980's recommendation to "stay close to the customer," executives have tried numerous customer contact and feedback strategies. This list is long and includes satisfaction surveys, focus groups, ombudsmen, customer membership on design teams, a day at the front lines, and "management by walking around."

A number of organizations already build close contact between executives, managers, employees, and customers. Fast food restaurants have executives at the counter several days per year. Physicians sit in the waiting room of a hospital. University presidents eat lunch and dinner with students. These are simple but effective ways to increase customer contact.

LESSONS LEARNED

How would we summarize the preceding efforts to improve customer friendliness? We have made real progress, and we could say that actions to date incorporate a mix of positive and negative characteristics. Customer friendliness efforts are now interdisciplinary (i.e. not focused on a single department), but are still disconnected, falling short of an integrated package of actions. Efforts now employ automated and Internet-based technologies, but still rely on people in the end, especially organizational leaders. Customer friendliness efforts currently hold tentative consensus; they are grudgingly, but not completely, recognized. For many executives, the quest to improve customer friendliness never ends. With a continuous improvement philosophy, we can make our public and private organizations even more customer friendly. How do we combine these disparate efforts with help from customers themselves?

First, let's consider a few more cases of failed service as we begin to put them in the language of organizational architecture.

1.1 THE CASE OF THE FRIENDLY IRS? A CUSTOMER HOSTILE PROBLEM

"In her book *Unbridled Power*, Shelly L. Davis, the IRS's official historian from 1988 to 1995, describes the agency as secretive, paranoid, and arrogant. She also asserts, despite IRS denials, that it keeps an enemies list of people whose "political activities might have offended someone at the IRS." Certainly the organization is insular. It has its own security force, which critics say spends as much time muzzling internal dissidents as protecting the agency from outsiders. About 350 IRS employees use pseudonyms because they're afraid of being threatened or assaulted. And who could fault them? In fiscal 1996 the IRS collected nearly $29 billion in delinquencies, issued 750,000 liens, and seized 10,000 properties.

Until recently, some revenue agents had a quota of taxes to collect from alleged deadbeats. One account from the San Francisco office put the figures at $1,000 an hour from personal audits and $2,200 an hour from business audits. The easiest way to meet those goals was to target poor people and small-business owners because they were less likely—and less financially able—to fight back. According to the Transactional Records Access Clearinghouse at Syracuse University, audit rates for people with annual incomes over $100,000 declined by a factor of four between 1988 and 1995, to 2.79% from 11.41%. The rates for individuals with incomes less than $25,000 nearly doubled, to 1.96% from 1.03%.

Tales of taxpayer abuse poured in: There was the New York priest hounded for thousands of dollars on his mother's estate because he had once filed the wrong form. The Virginia restaurant raided by IRS agents and closed for five months over what turned out to be a false tip about tax fraud. The California woman who fought the IRS for 17 years over a debt owed not by her, but by someone with a name similar to her husband's. The 6-year-old whose bank account was seized to help pay her parents' overdue tax bill (the IRS got $26). The Senate Finance Committee will hold hearings soon to disclose other hair-curling stories.

There's plenty to disclose. Take the case of Arthur S. Flemming, one of the most respected public servants of the 20th century he served Presidents Roosevelt, Truman, Eisenhower, and Nixon at senior levels and was awarded the Medal of Freedom, the nation's highest civilian honor. Flemming continued to fill out his own tax forms well into his 91st year. Perhaps inevitably, he failed to report all his income from various sources. Still, he kept the revenuers at bay by paying whatever they said he owed—until he fell and broke his leg. He died a month later, on Sept. 10, 1996, but he must have missed a payment during his convalescence. Soon thereafter, Flemming's wife of 63 years, Bernice, bounced a check for the first time in her life. The federal government, which her husband had served faithfully for so long, had seized Bernices's $800 bank account without warning her. "There was no attempt by the IRS to try to understand," bemoans Flemming's son Harry."[4]

In addition to this treatment of customers—fellow citizens—the agency also is working with an extremely outdated computer system. Vulnerability to unavailable data and missing support is only one aspect of the IRS technology problem. Their technical capability—storing, access, and use of data—is undercutting their ability to be "customer friendly." Because data is the centerpiece of their work, their production process is seriously flawed. This public agency illustrates the results of an architectural failure present in many of our public and private companies.

1.2 THE CASE OF THE HOSPITAL BYPASS, A PRODUCT PROBLEM

What happens when we enter a hospital for a serious ailment? We expect expert technical competency, an ability to produce and support high quality clinical service. Customer friendliness in a hospital is literally defined as professional competence in clinical work, the core product of the enterprise. Consider this elderly woman's experience.

Mrs. Rathbone was admitted to the hospital suffering from chest pains. At 63 years old, she had already had one coronary artery bypass operation on her heart. And it was difficult for her. She took almost a year to recover as she suffered from the pain and associated depression over her physical limitations.

On this admission, her physician declared her in need of a second bypass. She refused, citing her bad first experience. They insisted on calling in social workers and the family. The family was told she would not last six months without the operation and, that she had the beginning of Alzheimer's disease.

Mrs. Rathbone still refused. She left the hospital five years ago. Suffering from confusion and a respiratory infection, she was readmitted to the hospital several months ago. A CAT scan was done. When the family asked about the Alzheimer's, they were told there were no signs whatsoever.[5]

Experiences such as Mrs. Rathbone's cause doubt about the hospital's ability to do its primary work. Customer service means, first and foremost, high levels of professional competence and technical quality. A friendly attitude, parking spaces and good hospital food may enhance the overall experience. But the right diagnosis is a critical part of the product. A poor quality product is certainly customer *unfriendly*.

1.3 A CASE OF THE STUDENTS' BOOKSTORE, A PROBLEM OF INCENTIVE STRUCTURE

Students are customers of universities, although many faculty find the business label "customer" to be offensive. Colleges are not immune to the design and transaction flaws found in other organizations. The following story relates a failure in the structure of the student bookstore's incentive system.

Beginning in the fall semester, Tom and Mary found that the bookstore was out of law books for their class. Concerned about keeping up with the reading, the students were unhappy. They called Professor Smith to ask what happened.

Smith was surprised to hear of the problem because he always orders 40 books even though the class enrollment closes at 35. He said he would check on the problem.

When he contacted the bookstore manager(who works for Legal Books International) she said she only orders books to match the number of students on the registration list one week before the start of the term. But this method doesn't work very well, Smith told her. "Many students add the class at the last minute, or do so as a part of the drop/add process. And learning is easier if students have books," he added, trying to be humorous.

The manager said she would look into the problem. Meanwhile the students would have to call the bookstore daily to find out if their books were in. Smith said, "Wait! Isn't that somewhat inefficient? Why don't we call them?"

"No," said the bookstore manager. "We don't have time."

Smith replied, "We should actually mail the books to the students' homes when they finally arrive." The bookstore manager just rolled her eyes.

The next semester the problem was repeated. Smith called the bookstore to find out what had happened. The manager said that she had shorted the orders to match the enrollment. Unfortunately, registration was high—he reminded her of the numbers.

"Yes," she said "but we don't want extra books. When we have extra books we incur inventory and return costs that undercut our profits and my bonus as manager." The air cleared—the fog around the problem lifted. The manager worked for Legal books International and was responsive to their structure.

Professor Smith said, "you mean your incentives are tied to low inventory and return costs? So you purposely short the orders?"

"Yes," she said, "there is nothing I can do."

The bookstore's "unfriendliness" problem is designed into the structure of the partnership between the university and the law books corporation (a private profit making enterprise). Competing incentive systems (deliver books to students while reducing inventory and return costs) undercut a critical customer demand—books on time, every time, at the semester's start. Clearly, the architectural structure of incentive systems has the power to enhance or reduce service.

1.4 THE CASE OF THE DRY ATTITUDE, A PROBLEM OF EMPLOYEE PSYCHOLOGY

We all have had customer service adventures. Consider the problems encountered by this letter writer. Over several weeks, he suffered at the hands of a gas station attendant who refused to wash his window and a surly bank teller. While some customer service problems can be linked to business technology, many are problems of attitude—the psychological climate of the organization. The following is a story of deficient service in the little problems of daily life.

Upon returning from the dry cleaners, Fred noticed that two of his newly starched shirts were missing the stripes on their pockets. He returned to the dry cleaners to complain, he was confronted with the following:

"Could you tell me what happened to my shirts?" Fred asked.
"They are worn out," said the clerk.
"In only one spot on two shirts? I don't think so," Fred replied.
"It's a shirt quality problem, not our problem" she said.
"These are expensive shirts," Fred said.
"Are they really?" said the clerk.
Fred walked out.

Since he had been using this cleaner for 18 years he decided not to pursue the matter. He rationalized the rudeness and loss with the fact that the shirts were some years old. He did notice a new sign explaining loss of color, so other customers must have complained. It was, however, a second encounter that finished him off.

One evening Fred realized he needed to drop off his shirts at the dry cleaners. It was 7:45 p.m. but he knew they did not close until 8:00 p.m. When he arrived with five minutes to spare, he was surprised by the locked door but could see the young clerk at the counter.

A knock on the door produced nothing. A second and third knock enticed the clerk to look up. She pointed to her watch and mouthed the words; "We're closed."

He pointed to his watch noting that the time was not yet 8:00. She shrugged and refused to open the door.

Left with no recourse, he returned to his car but never returned to the dry cleaners again.

What organizational architecture creates this level of employee unfriendliness? Employee attitudes are a key ingredient of service. We recognize, but do not always act like the psychology of the workplace is a critical component of customer friendliness. Fred's experience is too common.

1.5 THE CASE OF THE WRONG RITUALS, A PROBLEM OF CEREMONY

How do we recognize managers' and employees' contributions to the company's performance, especially their contribution to customer friendliness? Consider this example of a senior management team's planning session.

"Let's talk about this upcoming "year-end" company meeting. We will be recognizing the outstanding performers as we have in the past. Employees at all levels seem to appreciate it...."

"Tom, remind us of the reasons why we are doing this, as we listed them last year."

Tom grabbed his notes and said, "There were two reasons for the ceremony, to reinforce the core values of the company, and to recognize the outstanding work that is critical to our success."

The four executives nodded in collective memory. The CEO followed up: "Mary, what are the most critical aspects of the business?"

Mary, Vice President Marketing, quickly replied: "building business and conserving resources."

But Matt quickly countered, "Aren't these the wrong topics for our annual celebration ritual? Why not give out quality and service awards?"

Silence.

Mary responded first. "Quality and service are not the most critical aspects of our business. Without sales and cost management, we are dead. The marketplace is brutal."

Matt retorted: "Without quality and service we don't deserve to be in business!"

Creating customer friendliness organization-wide requires a culture of core values, including celebrations and rituals that recognize and reinforce the company's interest in service. Absent "cultural consensus" about the importance of service, and without ceremonies of service celebration, company members are likely to see other values as critical—in this case sales growth and cost containment.

1.6 THE CASE OF CHASING THE LAST DOLLAR-AWAY, A PROBLEM OF LOST EQUITY

The hotel business is highly competitive. Hoteliers have been building large and small hotels, vacation resorts and interstate lodgings at a furious pace. Some hoteliers have taken a questionable approach to collecting every last dollar. Consider the case of a young engineer's attendance at his annual professional association meeting.

John's very busy company allows little time for "conference attendance." But an annual meeting advertised some new online education workshops that he and his company manager felt would be useful for both junior and senior colleagues. After pleading his case repeatedly, he was given approval to attend.

John checked into the resort hotel in Orlando, Florida on Sunday evening for the four-day conference. The clerk noted his arrival and expected departure date. On Tuesday, John's manager telephoned to say they needed him for an important project meeting on Thursday. He arranged to catch a late flight back on Wednesday evening.

When he received his bill, he questioned an unexpected $50.00 charge.

"It's an early checkout fee. You are leaving a day early," replied the clerk.

Since John had not traveled for a while, he was unfamiliar with this policy.

"Can it be removed?" he asked.

"No sir, all guests are charged when they change dates."

So John paid the fee, and upon return, told his manager. His manager became furious at what he considering gouging, and vowed not to stay at the hotel chain again. He notified the company's travel department to remove the hotel chain from the company's "preferred lodging" list. Since the travel department handled arrangements for 20,000 employees, this represented a significant loss of business for the chain.

This customer friendliness problem could be seen in several ways. The check out manager felt he did not have the authority to eliminate the charge. The hotel managers lost sight of the unpredictable nature of business travelers' schedules. The hotel chain opted to risk the long term equity of a large customer in favor of a small, short term "early check out fee." The hotel will feel the financial impact of what a customer and his company's management team perceive as "business unfriendly".

These cases illustrate that customer friendliness breakdowns have a wide variety of causes—product failure, incentive barriers, employee psychology, management values, and short term financial thinking. We could just ignore these "unfortunate incidents", but we owe it to our companies to ask why we invest in customer service.

THE CHANGING ROLE OF THE CUSTOMER

What role does the customer play? Over the last 10-15 years we have enlarged the customer's contribution beyond simple buyers. Public and private companies are beginning to recognize customer sophistication and knowledge, and to consider customers as partners. Managers have increased direct customer contact and used customers to improve product and production process quality. Some companies now cite customer satisfaction as a strategic goal.

The architecture of customer friendly companies recognizes the diversity of possibilities for customers like my uncle, those with failure experience, and those customers with good things to say. Leaders now think of five roles for customers.

- *Factfinder*—in this role, customers provide information on their buying habits and follow up behaviors, recount experiences with the company, and feed back compliments and complaints.
- *Educator*—customers educate companies about their needs, the friendliness of their buying experience, their uses and evaluations of the product and about future opportunities to serve.

- *Options Developer*—rejecting the old passive role of recipient, customers now provide input to product and service designs up front, offer suggestions on improvement and suggest new directions.
- *Co-producer/collaborator*—customers in many organizations literally co-produce the service or product, tailor-making the product to fit their needs (patients, students, computer buyer).
- *Advocate*—customers advocate for new uses, for innovation, and for expansion of the use of products and service, thereby promoting research and development. And they act as a sales and communications channel.

Many companies now use customers in these roles, some more directly and widely than others. For example, credit card users supply purchase data to various companies (fact finders). Movie goers create "buzz," educating producers, actors and film companies about the quality of new film releases (education). Beta testing of new software enables customers to recommend changes to software engineers (options developer). Students engaged in teams and joint projects help to create their own learning (co-producers, collaborators). And patients become promoters of new medical protocols from a minimally invasive heart bypass to use of a new Gamma Knife for brain tumors (advocate).

Another way to look at the customer's more recent role is as a partner in the company's "knowledge and idea building." Company leaders are searching for ways to add value to products to secure and please customers. Why not simply ask customers to help? We just do not do it consistently, or very well. Customer friendly leaders design the architecture so that customers contribute in this way. Some recent writers think of employees as knowledge brokers but we can add customers to the group (see chapter 3).

Who are Your Customers?

First, the obvious—customers are external buyers of products and service. But think about the public and private sector diversity of the following:

Agriculture
Automotive
Banking

Chemicals
Construction
Consulting
Education
Federal government
Health care
Insurance
Military
Petroleum
Real estate
Retail
Social service
State and local government
Telecommunications
Transportation
Utilities

Each of these industries presents an opportunity for "customer friendly" or "customer hostile" interaction. We all have tales to tell about department stores, transportation failures, governmental bureaucracy, unhelpful teachers, gasoline prices, etc. In addition to external customers, though, we also have inside customers.

Quality management advocates have taught us to think about "customers inside our organizations." Within organizations we must ask whether we are "customer friendly" between departments, divisions, and functional groups. In the bookstore example, the bookstore staff was not friendly to either inside or outside customers. Students (outsiders) were angry and underserved. But so were faculty (insiders), because the delivery of high quality teaching is certainly sabotaged by the absence of books. This book focuses for the most part on external customers. However, the friendliness notion transfers easily to the internal customer as well.

Barriers

If customer friendliness were easy, there would be no need for books and seminars on improvement, nor would there be so many negative stories to tell. Many barriers to customer friendliness exist. They include, but are not limited to:

- Insincere leadership
- Outdated technology

- Hostile employees
- Lack of employee directives to address issues
- Total focus on market share and profitability
- Lack of knowledge (know how)
- Inadequate user understanding
- No feedback loop (from customers)
- No understanding of cost of poor service
- Too few resources

Management both *designs in* customer friendly service and *leads* the company with policy decisions that support or undercut customer friendliness. The conference hotel's attempt to make a little more money and to dissuade guests from early checkout illustrates management's short sightedness and insensitivity to customers at the point of service. The limited financial gain is likely to be far outweighed by the accumulated ill will. Other leaders are unwilling to allow or encourage employees to make on-the-spot judgments about how to best serve the customer. Each barrier can be viewed as an architectural problem.

Summary

Employee attitude and workplace psychology contribute negative experiences in the small tasks of everyday life. Even when no grand debilitating experience is present, the death of service by a thousand small cuts can show up at the dry cleaners, the mower shop and the bank. Management is the architect of the company, creating structure and making decisions to foster quality. Without rigorous discussion of the customer service impact, management will choose the path that creates the easiest route for the company, not its customers.

What have these opening stories told us? Retail store employees are surly and unresponsive. The IRS, an example of a public organization with many architectural flaws, offers poor customer service nationwide and vies for most "customer unfriendly". In hospitals, some patients receive poor quality care—the essence of customer friendly service is the right product delivered in a competent, timely fashion. While tuition increases yearly, student customers have trouble getting books on time.

The creation of a culture that believes in true customer satisfaction should be the architectural foundation of a customer friendly company. Chapter two reviews the work that executives and managers have done to design and support a customer friendly culture.

CHAPTER 2

THE ORGANIZATIONAL ARCHITECTURE OF CUSTOMER FRIENDLY COMPANIES

> A man that has a taste of music, painting, or architecture, is like one that has another sense
>
> Spectator, 93; June 16, 1711

How do we create customer friendly organizations? Consider this exchange with my Uncle Arthur.

Nephew: "What's the secret to service?"

Uncle: "Ask some of your friends—see what they say before I answer."

Nephew: (days later) "OK, this is what they told me."

Bart (Plant Manager, Autocoach): "It's all about product. Customer friendly is another name for product quality."

Roger (CEO, Intercoast Airlines): "Products are not enough—employees need incentives—a reward system to encourage their customer friendliness."

Sarah (Manager, Royal Court Hotel): "It's not about incentives. Hire the right people with good personality and attitude."

Thomas (President, Federalist Bank): "Those points are true but the key is leadership. Leadership trumps all."

Elizabeth (Provost, Eastern University): "I think customer friendliness is in company culture—you need deep basic beliefs."

Uncle: "So, what do they have in common?"

Nephew: "I don't know, they all seem different to me."

Uncle: "Taken individually, they are each incomplete, necessary but not sufficient for customer friendly. The answer is all of the above—connected design and action."

Nephew: "Do you think companies are designed to be customer unfriendly, or do they just get to be that way?

Uncle: "I think it is a problem of design, of slippage and of sloppy behaviors."

~~~~~~~~~~~~~~~~~~~~~~~~~

Clearly, our companies have room for customer service improvement. Most of us understand that simply hiring another customer service representative will not be enough to build a world-class reputation for service. But it is harder to see the rich complexity of behaviors that produce an outstanding customer experience. Consider the case of the Westside Hospital, where the primary customers are patients. Richard, the hospital's president for 17 years, faces a troublesome problem.

Westside Hospital is a 450-bed suburban community hospital located in a small city of 300,000. The hospital operated for 75 years at the same location. During this time, the hospital has grown from 85 beds to a modern facility with the latest technology and a staff trained at some of the best schools in the country. The staff of more than 2500 includes 450 physicians and surgeons. Volunteers provide more than 80,000 hours of service per year. The hospital specializes in cardiovascular procedures, orthopedic services, oncology, rehabilitation and trauma care including related intensive care support. Ranked among the top 100 U.S. hospitals, Westside is located in a wealthy section of the city but one in which deterioration has begun to appear. Several outreach centers have been established recently to address tobacco use, breast cancer, obesity, and family violence. Along with the main facility there are five outpatient centers and 16 physician practices.

The management team has been intact for the past 10 years. They appear to operate smoothly with consensus on direction, policy and operations, and are the dominant force for health care in the community. The team was aware that community members were beginning to express some dissatisfaction with the hospital, but they were not concerned, as the issues were not apparent nor loudly expressed. Patients sometimes grumped about privacy, poor attitudes of staff members, costs of prescription medicine, safety during evening visits, too few nurses and side effects of medicine.

Management was surprised when a community group publicly presented a report blasting the hospital for inadequate services to the poor, citing delayed responses to trauma care patients and backups in the emergency room. And there were concerns about significant differences in infant mortality rates (by population) and low ratings by the state's Health Care Performance Report Card (on cardiac surgery). As the report became front page news, the hospital management team met immediately to analyze the situation and respond. Several issues surfaced. The staff confirmed that differences in infant mortality existed, although they did not know why. Nor did they understand the higher than predicted deaths in open-heart surgery. Second, staff had recently completed a patient origin study. The data indicated that most patients came from the higher socioeconomic districts.

Third, the team recognized that the staff refers most "poorer" patients across town to the city hospital. In particular, the CEO did not want to staff up the emergency services to meet the needs of patients without family care physicians and/or health insurance. Staff expressed frustration over visits to the emergency room for "simple" problems by these types of patients. Fourth, the team admitted that while in compliance with governmental guidelines, the staff composition was hardly rich in ethnic and minority diversity.

The public complaints quickly caused a political problem as well as a managerial one. The mayor called for an investigation into possible discriminatory actions by the hospital. A county commissioner suggested that the hospital had given up its charitable mission and should now be made to pay taxes.

The Chairman of the Board and Richard, the CEO, met to discuss the situation. A public complaint about poor service is serious. If they could diagnose the problem and put in a quick fix they could minimize the negative impact on the community. Richard discusses his view of the problem below. I have included in brackets some elements of the organization's architecture that seem to lie at the root of the problem.

Richard: "We can view this problem in several ways: as flawed medical care [product quality]; as inadequate staffing [structure]; as poor attitude on the part of emergency center staff [psychology], as failed strategy [management] and/or as questionable corporate values [the culture supports "dumping" poorer patients on the city hospital]."

Board Chairman: "If it involves product, structure, psychology, management, and culture, then we have every aspect of the hospital involved in this situation."

Richard: "Yes, our problems seem quite complex."

Staying customer friendly is a complex task. Each aspect of the hospital's problem is an element of and contributor to the patient's perspective on service quality. Defining the problem as a staff shortage would lead to an inadequate diagnosis and a response not rich enough to solve the entire problem. A better diagnosis requires a deeper understanding of the underlying elements of the customer friendly organization.

AN ORGANIZATIONAL ARCHITECTURE APPROACH

Examining the writings on customer service, two key points emerge: (a) we are just beginning to understand the organizational architecture supporting customer service; and (b) we have not yet established multi-dimensional approaches for increasing and maintaining customer friendliness. We view the problem most often as a marketing topic, stressing the need to analyze and respond to customer needs.[1]

Managers' solutions are often too limited in scope. In the Westside Hospital case, a few more emergency room staff may be necessary but adding them will not be sufficient to regain customer friendliness. Such a decision assumes that one type of action, i.e., changing a policy or procedure, will address the customer service problem throughout the organization. A customer's perception of poor service may be based on slow distribution of products, belligerent repair representatives, or even price. But the reasons for a breakdown in customer friendliness can be varied, including: not understanding the customer's needs, unavailability of supplies, outdated product tracking systems, poor quality of goods or services, and no performance standards and measurement.

This list broadly defines our points of potential deficiency—from poor market and needs assessment, to production processes, information system support, and even product quality.

Everyone at Westside Hospital is interested in providing high quality care. If asked, they will tell you they want Westside to be patient (customer) friendly. Their interest in customer satisfaction is shared by auto manufacturers, bankers, hoteliers, airline executives and university deans. At some level, we all want to know how to be customer friendly in our respective fields. The central question, then, is:

How does organizational architecture contribute to the creation and operation of customer friendly companies?

All types of businesses and services organizations are involved in this question. Until we understand the architectural nature of the problem, it is unlikely that we will realize effective improvement. To create a multi-dimensional, customer friendly organization, we must understand customer friendliness as an organization-wide phenomenon, including root structures and functions.

There are three elements to understanding this view of customer friendly organizations:

Systems thinking assumptions
Organizational models
Organization development and change processes

Designers and managers of highly friendly companies—Disney, Southwest—know intuitively that they must work from underlying values and assumptions about what conditions produce customer friendly behaviors in their companies. They must understand the company's architectural plan—a model that drives decisions and actions. They work formally or informally with a sense of how to develop and change their organizations—to become customer friendly, and or, to stay that way (see Figure 2.1).

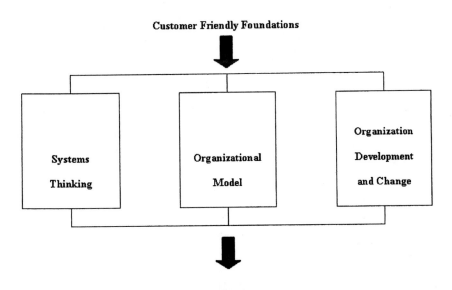

Customer Friendly Foundations

| Systems Thinking | Organizational Model | Organization Development and Change |

Figure 2.1 Customer Friendly Foundations

A SYSTEMS VIEW—THE CONNECTEDNESS OF SUBSYSTEMS

A historical perspective on organization theory suggests that systems thinking can help us to understand the design and use of diverse customer service improvement actions. What organization designs produce customer friendly companies? Historically, there have been several competing views. The main schools that have evolved in organizational theory—structural/functional (policies, procedures, job roles), human relations (individual psychology, group dynamics) and systems (product-people-technology inter-face), can be seen as separate dimensions of the same reality.[2] To-gether, each of these seemingly separate dimensions is a part of the whole architecture of the private company or public agency. Each explains a bit more about organizations, simultaneously expanding our understanding of how to design new customer friendly compa-nies and how to change those we have.

Consider the Westside Hospital case. Service problems are evi-dent, values are in question, and community support is threatened. Diagnosis of the problem is a necessary starting point. But the diag-nosis will be driven by our view of the organizational architecture. In Scott's historical review of our evolving knowledge of organization theory, three streams of thought about how organizations work were identified as classical, neoclassical, and modern theory.[3] Classical theory focused on formal organization. It was concerned with struc-ture—how organizational functions are divided, linked, delegated, reported on, and controlled. Policies, procedures and organization charts would be studied to find the causes of the Westside Hospital problem. Classical theorists would define the problem in terms of reporting relationships, job descriptions and reward structures.

Neoclassical theory extended our view of the classical theo-rists' one-dimensional picture by demonstrating the existence of an informal behavioral dimension. Neoclassical theorists believed that this informal behavioral dimension defined the organization, and that the classical focus on structure was derived from it. In this view, the Westside Hospital problems are centered in work group relationships, work and performance norms and individual and team perspectives required for friendly "service to all patients." The needed response is not a change in reporting structure but an "atti-tude adjustment" at the individual employee level. This might help, but it is still not a rich enough solution to create a customer friendly hospital.

These two competing dimensions—structure and human relations—meant organization theory was incomplete and lacking in integration. Modern organization theory, which emphasizes integration of the two competing dimensions, describes the organization as a system with diverse interrelating elements and subsystems. Systems theory, with its holistic orientation, its emphasis on the external environment (all actions and elements outside an organization) and on interrelatedness of structure, psychology and technology, represented a significant development. Viewing the organization in context—by including the environment and recognizing all parts as the whole—represented a new way of thinking about the Westside Hospital case. Systems thinking is labeled "sociotechnical" by some followers because of joint attention to product and social psychology. Systems thinkers believe that the formal and the informal structures and the external environment play a role in behaviors such as customer friendly patient service.

What are some key points about systems thinking? Russell Ackoff has often written about systems thinking and organizations[4] and offers the following:

> Synthesis, or putting things together, is the key to systems thinking just as analysis, or taking them apart, was the key to Machine-Age thinking ...
>
> Systems thinking reverses the three-stage order of Machine-Age thinking: (1) decomposition of that which is to be explained, (2) explanation of the behavior or properties of the parts taken separately, and (3) aggregating these explanations into an explanation of the whole. This third step, of course, is synthesis. In the systems approach there are also three steps:
>
> 1.Identify a containing whole (system) of which the thing to be explained is a part.
>
> 2.Explain the behavior or properties of the containing whole.
>
> 3.Then explain the behavior or properties of the thing to be explained in terms of its role(s) or function(s) within its containing whole.
>
> Note that in this sequence, synthesis precedes analysis. . .
>
> This orientation derives from the preoccupation of systems thinking with the design and redesign of systems. In systems design, parts identified by analysis of the function(s) to be performed by the whole are not put together like unchangeable pieces of a jigsaw puzzle, they are designed to fit each other so as to work together harmoniously as well as efficiently and effectively ... If

each part of a system considered separately, is made to operate as efficiently as possible, the system as a whole will not operate as effectively as possible . . .

The performance of a system depends more on how its parts interact than on how they act independently of each other.[5]

Over the past 45 years, systems approaches have been used in a variety of applications from computer modeling to city design to business management.[6, 7, 8] In recent years, systems thinking has continued to evolve so that it is now an accepted part of basic management and engineering training, crossing fields and industries. [9-12] Recent research has reported on its application to quality management, decision-making, reengineering, and marketing.[13-18]

Systems thinkers portray the "architecture" of an organization as part structure, part behavior and part integrating processes and would view the Westside Hospital problem this way. This approach has been in place for decades, but is still not fully accepted by practicing leaders and managers.

ARCHITECTURAL ASSUMPTIONS

This architecture of organization is the "target" for *diagnosing* problems, for *broad strategy* and for *specific action*s to improve customer friendliness and service. The five systems (product, structure, psychology, management, and culture) are the architectural sources of customer service. Early views of this architecture emphasized a simplistic view that a "customer service problem" results from poor products or lack of a clear reporting authority. In contrast, human relationists focused on motivation, group dynamics, and other psychological factors. Instead of seeing product design and delivery as the critical flaw, human relationists believe customer service is a "people problem" driven by employee's attitude, motivation and commitment. Each view of organizational architecture (school of organization theory) missed the key point—the path to customer friendly lies in addressing the whole architecture. The architectural approach rests on a set of assumptions about organizations, customers and strategies for change.

1. Holism: Customer service improvement will only be successful if we think about the organization as a whole. Sub-parts such as customer service departments are not sufficient for organization-wide change in behavior. Talking to the hospital's patient representative is like talking to a student advisor about the lack of text books in the school bookstore. The advisor may sympathize and even advocate for the students, but as long as bookstore staff are subject to competing incentives (bonus and return costs management), the core work of teaching will continue to be undercut (as illustrated in Chapter 1). At the Westside Hospital, denying access to emergency room care and the poor staff attitudes undercut the otherwise strong quality of service. A "clinical product" such as an emergency appendectomy may be of the highest quality. But when community citizens speak, what they discuss is the emergency staff's rude behavior—behavior for which there currently is no penalty.

2. Sociotechnical: Customer friendliness must consider the social psychology of the company/customer exchange and the technological quality of the products and services. The goal is balanced attention to the social and the technical dimensions of the organization.[19, 20] In Chapter 1, my uncle's new lawnmower was broken within days of purchase. But the clerk's attitude toward repair was disastrous. Which was worse—the technical deficiency of broken equipment or the staff's response of "tough luck, buyer beware"? How the Westside hospital management team responds—with thoughtful analysis, or anger and defensiveness—will color the community's view of the hospital. Leaders and staff cannot concentrate only on the technical assessment of heart surgery and infant services.

3. Multiple Systems as Co-Producers: Organization behaviors that support customer friendliness are produced by a combination of product design and production process, structure, psychological climate, management and culture.[21] The cause—effect equation is complex. Single systems are necessary but not sufficient to create customer friendly organizations. The lawnmower problem involved both product performance and service clerk psychology. Unless both are "fixed," a deficiency will remain. But the "fix" may be located in one or more of the five systems of the architecture. At Westside Hospital many aspects of the service problem were readily apparent. Product quality, leadership and culture were being questioned by the community. The board may quickly realize that to "fix" the problem they must go back to the hospital's root designs, the architecture that produces leader behavior, shared culture, and employee attitudes.

4. Subsystem congruence required. To create effective, consistent organization behaviors, the subsystems must be congruent with each other. For example, leaders may talk about "staying close to the customer", encouraging a psychological mind set of open communication. But if the leaders do not reward this contact [structural incongruence] and do not practice this activity [managerial modeling incongruence] the message and the effect will be undercut.

5. Macro/Micro Changes: Customer friendliness occurs when the leadership team of the overall organization targets high quality service and improvement at the board and executive level (strategic), and when individual work groups continuously strive to improve at the point of customer contact (operating levels). Executives can make a decision to build new branches, gradually improving performance by offering customers more services in closer locations. This action by board and executives will have implications for the "friendliness" of the organization as a whole (a strategic-level decision). Executives can also order an upgrade to a customer response telephone program in the Nashville office, and leave the design to the local team (strategic/operating combination that may lead to overall organization change in telephone service, but starts with a local site experiment).

At Westside Hospital executives can meet in private, collect and analyze data, and report about wholesale changes to the organization in response to the community's concerns. They can converse with the community in public town meetings. Simultaneously, small task groups can tackle the service problems in the heart and pediatric units, searching for technical and team coordination problems and opportunities for patient service improvement (operating level).

6. Strategic and Operational: Customer friendly performance is improved by making broad, long term decisions (strategic) and short term, practical ones (operational). Customer friendly architecture takes time to develop and is a long term commitment. But customers can also be served better tomorrow with short term, quick fixes. Deciding to drop a company or hospital's product line (cardiac or pediatric care) because of quality and delivery deficiencies is a strategic decision. Westside may feel that they can not compete with a larger hospital's Heart Institute, and may make a strategic decision to drop cardiac services. In the meantime, Westside may undertake operational action to improve the trauma center's accident response time through better communication. Westside also has a trauma unit that was cited and may require some immediate operational changes such as infection control. Customer friendly leaders use both strategic and operational level tools.

7. *Perceived and Substantive: Customers pay attention to the real quality of products and services.* Their perception of the total experience may enrich or undercut the technical "truth". Poor support services at a university—bookstore, registration, food—may erode students' confidence in the quality of the classroom experience (and the university as a whole).

At Westside Hospital, infant mortality and cardiac surgery problems may be caused by a data error, or even an exaggeration of normal complications that occur in any institution. But the perceptions must be addressed. Customers will extrapolate rude treatment at the emergency admissions desk to a generalized view of poor quality, clearly subtracting from the clinical team's efforts to provide urgent intervention such as surgery for head trauma or heart attack.

8. *Synergistic: Multiple systems support of the customer is synergistic in that it pushes value beyond the sum of the parts.* Strong product quality is enhanced by informed, personable salespeople, accessible customer service staff, ease of warranty use and feedback surveys. To use a public sector example, IRS employees' attitudes combine with the negative task (collecting taxes), the complex tax code and poor staff support to shape citizens' assessment of low quality service.

Westside Hospital appears to have low product quality (infant and heart services), inadequate staffing (emergency department), callous management (don't know or care about problems), bad attitudes (admitting clerks), and an interest in underserving certain groups in the community (low level discrimination). That synergy produces highly unfriendly service. With the hospital, the IRS, a university or any other organization, the snowball effect of customer hostility rooted in several architectural systems is dramatic.

9. *Incremental and Stretch: Customer friendly status is achieved and maintained over time with incremental and "stretch" goals.* Gradual improvements in existing processes are sought (incremental) while we also search for opportunities to "leap forward" to significantly higher service standards (stretch). We can search for ways

to improve IRS tax collection and audit processes or we can institute flat or sales taxes as a replacement (either offer the potential for dramatic changes). For citizens and politicians, changing to a flat tax would be a stretch indeed.

At Westside Hospital, executives can add a few more hours to the emergency room schedule and hire more staff (an incremental improvement). Or, they could create a family practice center operating next to the emergency room. The family practice would welcome patients from all of the community as part of the hospital's charitable service (in tight revenue times for hospitals this is a stretch). It would also free the emergency department to focus on its core mission—emergencies.

Systems thinkers view the organization as an open, sociotechnical system with customer friendly leaders paying attention to all the primary systems and their interactions. Some executives are already using this approach but without the jargon and certainly without the direct connection to the customer friendly concept.

An adapted version of Fremont Kast and James Rosenzweig's model of the organization as composed of five subsystems: (1) product and technical, (2) structural, (3) psychosocial, and (4) managerial and (5) cultural, is used to integrate our customer friendly thinking.[22, 23] As more of the systems become supportive of customer friendliness the level of the customer friendliness of the whole increases (See Figure 2.2).

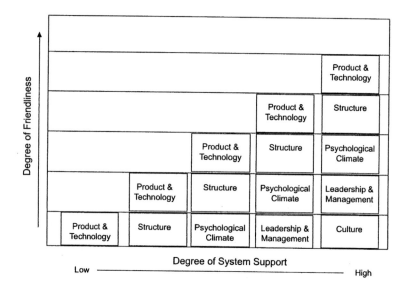

Figure 2.2 Architectural Support for Customer Friendly

Each organization has unique sociotechnical aspects. But if we could write one overarching statement, the formula would be something like this.

Customer Friendly Organization = product/technology quality +
structural incentives +
psychological climate +
leadership +
cultural values

Hospitals like Westside are different from schools, banks, and airline companies, but they are also different from other hospitals. The theory implies that at their root, all public and private companies have elements in common, namely the five systems. Each organization would have more or less of each formula ingredient—stronger/weaker service leadership, presence/absence of customer service incentives, and high/low product quality for example. Because the formula is not quantified, we must think of it as a conceptual tool that supports leaders' and members' thinking and behavior. This model has been used in a wide variety of studies.[24-32]

The extent to which customer friendliness is achieved is determined first by product and technology (poor product quality is always the most visible indicator of unfriendliness) followed by the strength of each element in the formula. For example, in the United States, recent Institute of Medicine reports have suggested that strong deficiencies exist in the quality of medical and health care.[33, 34] At Westside Hospital, the incentives for service may be in place, the psychological climate is good and everyone values the patient. But if heart patients and infants are dying from medical errors, it will be hard to make the case that Westside is customer friendly. Each subsystem has the potential to fatally undercut the customer friendliness of the whole. Absent service leadership might not fully sink the organization's product, but it can cause significant damage. We should learn more about the five elements of architecture—product, structure, psychological climate, leadership and culture.

1. *Product and Technology System:* Product and technology refers to the knowledge required for product design and delivery, including performance of core tasks, such as auto production, medical treatment, or teaching. The product and technology system is defined by the organization's task requirements and varies by activity, i.e., a hospital has different core technical activities from an automo-

bile manufacturing plant. The product and technology system means the marketing, design, production, delivery and support of products and services. Each type of technology influences the organization's structure and its psychology of individual and group relations.

Typically, the customer service problem is defined as technical in nature. State government reports citing low performance by the Westside Hospital in cardiac surgery and public concerns about infant mortality levels are questions of technical quality. The hospital response would include review of its cardiac surgery procedure (product design, production process, delivery system), including the level and quality of post-discharge support. Findings might result in different clinical approaches. Similar questions and actions would be taken for infant care. Clinical "products" would be redesigned so that staff could deliver the same type of services at higher quality levels.

When customers (patients, students, car buyers) complain, some managers address limited delivery and support service problems— telephone access, hours of availability, distribution speed.[35-37] This can effectively control low customer service, enhancing the company's customer friendliness. New technologies enable products to be delivered more efficiently (e.g., lap top computers support physicians at the hospital bedside). Technology evaluation groups that employ continuous quality improvement thinking can be formed to seek opportunities for incorporating technological advances in marketing, product design, production, delivery and support processes.

This focus on upgrading and redesigning products, production processes and delivery systems is necessary but not sufficient to create overall customer friendliness. It does not recognize the other aspects of the architecture—structure, psychological climate, leadership and management, and corporate culture.

2. *Structure:* Structure defines the way in which parts of the organization are differentiated and integrated. Structure is typically defined by organization charts, position and job descriptions, rules and procedures, authority and workflow. Structure is also the basis for establishing relationships between the technical tasks of product design, production, delivery and support and the psychological dimension and climate of the organization.

An organization's structure can contribute to the poor service problem, whether at Westside Hospital, an airline, bank or university. Incentives encourage employees to increase revenues, sometimes at the expense of customer friendliness. In the bookstore case presented in Chapter 1, employees shorted orders to meet inventory return cost constraints. Universities often admit more students than can fit comfortably into dormitories and classrooms, which increases revenue but creates other problems, e.g., expanding class size that reduces education quality and increases dissatisfaction.

In addition to growth, cost reduction objectives may also diminish customer service. Richard can curtail use of the hospital's emergency room and eliminate some infant services to reduce costs. But this will also reduce the range and depth of service to the hospital's customers, a structural dilemma common in many businesses. Organizations pursuing excellence attend to structure, meaning designing the structure is viewed as an architectural task.[38-40]

So, two aspects of organizational architecture that require attention to insure customer service are product/technology and structure. There are three other architectural elements.

3. *Psychological Climate:* Every organization has a psychological climate defined by employees' individual characteristics and by the interactions of individuals and groups. This climate includes, for example, behavior and motivation, status and role relationships, and group dynamics, along with employees' perceptions, attitudes, and expectations. This system is shaped by the production tasks, technology, and structure of the internal organization, establishing a climate within which everyone works.

At Westside Hospital, Richard faces a range of problems. One is the attitude of his emergency department staff. Occasionally, they have been overheard telling patients that if they have a problem they should take it up with the patient relations staff. Customer friendly leaders recognize the need to influence employees' attitudes and commitment toward customer service, creating a climate of "psychological friendliness."[41-44]

Delegating customer service to others erodes service responsibility. In many companies, the assumption is that customer service is someone else's problem. This psychological climate encourages "subcontracting" concern for the customer to a vague group of others, and to specialists. This mindset contrasts dramatically with the view that customer service is every employee's responsibility (an ingrained psychological set).

To create the psychological architecture of customer friendly, leaders address individual and group psychology—motivation, perception, group relations, and satisfaction. Psychology is only part of the design though, as managers have lead responsibility for much of this work.

4. *Management and Leadership.* The managerial and leadership system links the organization to its environment by setting goals, developing plans, designing the structure, and establishing evaluation and control processes. Traditional managerial activities include planning and development, leadership and control. Managers coordinate and integrate the goals, production processes, structure and psychological climate, fusing the four systems into a whole. Earlier, remember that Thomas, President of the Federalist Bank, said that "leadership trumps all" in creating customer friendly companies.

Coordinating customer friendly service is a managerial task. Managers and leaders apply customer service fundamentals and continuous improvement in the course of their managerial duties. Westside Hospital's CEO organized his team's response to the community's concerns. His effort to enhance customer friendliness involved employee communication, change, teamwork, and expanded and continuous contact with customers.[45-50]

5. *Culture:* The last of the architectural systems—culture—combines the goals and values of the members of the organization (e.g. physicians and staff) and the values from the broader socio-cultural environment (e.g. the Westside community). Culture is "the way we do things here."[51-52]

Organizations meet societal and community needs by successfully performing functions that support social system values, e.g., medical care with a customer friendly attitude. Designing customer friendly architecture involves asking whether we have established "corporate cultures" that value service and are sensitive to the need to maintain and constantly increase service quality. Too often, the service value is assumed to exist (many of us think we work in customer friendly companies but we usually have not spent sufficient time as a customer of our companies to know). Richard's hospital board and staff were surprised by the community's complaints—they thought they were a friendly hospital.

To combat this cultural aspect of the problem, leaders at Westside could initiate a "culture audit."[53] How? One method would be to hold dialogue sessions that explore executives' vision and values and force a confrontation of behaviors that supposedly support, but instead undercut, service. This tactic illuminates the problem that we have theories of our own behavior which may differ from how we are perceived—the Argyris dichotomy between theory and action, i.e., how we think we will behave and how we actually do.[54] For example, executives may loudly proclaim that the hospital is patient friendly, but be forced to acknowledge that the family clinic is closed on Saturdays and Sundays, when customers can most easily come for care. Executive rhetoric is not matched by service schedule. An internal discussion at Westside would first announce that the community's concerns are important enough to be talked about. But questions could arise about how much Richard and the other executives are in touch with the community, their pool of current and potential customers. Restatement of core values as a patient-focused organization may be an outcome. This has two benefits: education about the meaning of customer service; and reinforcement of a culture that is sensitive to customer service. The public presentation of substantive and widely promoted customer service awards could be added to advertise the customer friendliness of the hospital and motivate employees.

Although culture is an all-encompassing web in the architecture (see Figure 2.3), customer friendliness is not just a corporate

The Web of Customer Friendly Culture

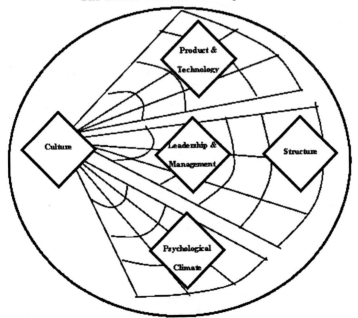

Figure 2.3 The Web of Customer Friendly Culture

culture issue. In this model, customer friendliness is co-produced by product quality, structure, psychological climate and culture. The degree of friendliness of the company rises according to the amount of friendliness designed into each of these systems (visually represented in Figure 2.3.

At a retreat for the board of trustees and the senior executives, Richard's Planning and Development Committee chair, a bank executive, presented their key findings. He said the committee concentrated on the tasks that they felt framed the service questions for the Westside Hospital. He began his presentation with the following:

"As the architects of our community's medical care system, we have the responsibility to create the structure, psychological climate, and culture of a customer/patient friendly hospital. We are being confronted by the community and we must address five questions."

- "First, does management have an effective *plan* for becoming and staying customer friendly, including "friendliness" as a component of the strategic plan?
- Second, will management *organize* to support customer friendly structures and behaviors to provide service at a higher level if necessary?
- Third, will management *develop* future leaders and employees who understand the need to increase and maintain customer friendliness and have the skills to do so?
- Fourth, will management *lead* the hospital, modeling behaviors consistent with the friendliness intent?
- And, fifth, what *control* mechanisms will management develop to monitor the level of customer friendliness (e.g., data and reward systems)?"

"Accepting this responsibility means that we will have to work with the whole organization to achieve success."

Richard understood the objective, but the task was daunting. Management had to create a culture that fosters and maintains friendliness. The point of the customer friendly organization is that all systems contribute to the friendliness. Consider the following prototype with key principles, applicable across fields.

CUSTOMER FRIENDLY PROTOTYPE

How do we know our organization is customer friendly? First, we have the highest quality products, backed by production technology that is constantly updated and improved. Our customers have easy access to products and services and have opportunities to offer feedback and submit complaints. For distribution errors or defective products we offer immediate and complete service recovery. Support technicians are readily available.

Second, our authority structure supports customer service using as few management levels as possible. To support customers, employees can work across functions and departments and through an open communication process.

Third, we offer a psychological climate that is based on individual, team, and interdepartmental communication and collaboration, strong motivation, attitudes of "customer first" and the highest levels of job satisfaction.

Fourth, our leaders and managers are selected and supported for their commitment to and ability to serve the customer. They are expected to design the architecture, execute its actions and plans and vigorously communicate our values of service. They educate our employees and spokesmen regarding our vision of customer friendliness.

Fifth, we have developed a culture based in support of our customers. The elements are visible in ease of contact, open communication and deep beliefs in our purpose as an organization—to serve the customer (buyers of our products, patients, students, guests, clients, users and travelers). Our culture is defined by the belief that no matter how good we are, we have an opportunity to be better. Our products and services, behaviors, and especially our leaders' actions illustrate this culture.

Let's return to Richard's hospital board and their executive retreat. The group found that the five systems model was useful in their discussion of how to address the community's complaints. However, after a day's discussion, Richard suggested that they hear from a critic before proceeding further. He scheduled Professor Harold Martin of the Eastern University Business School to talk with the group. At breakfast Martin was briefed about the previous day's discussions. His opening presentation was scheduled for an hour and was designed to offer skepticism about this approach to becoming customer friendly. Martin spoke generally about organization design and strategic improvement efforts, focusing his questions about this approach on the following six points which he adapted to fit the Westside Hospital case.[55]

Professor Martin: "This model of the customer friendly organization architecture is not without criticism," he began. Colleagues and commentators would offer the following cautions:

1."Knowledge of the five systems is incomplete, so they are somewhat "black box" (no one really knows what is in each)." There is limited research on the validity of these contributors to the design of customer friendly companies. The team at Westside Hospital could use the model just as a discussion tool, keeping in mind that it is a somewhat artificial, and not completely tested organization model. If this is acceptable, the group should proceed to use the model but with the following additional limitations.

2."The model fosters system by system attention with limited focus on the interactive effects." Because of the complexity in each subsystem, Westside Hospital planners should remember that in practice, all of the systems work simultaneously, and their interactions are key. When the Westside board commits to becoming more customer friendly—beginning with value statements and desired culture- they are also implying possible changes in incentives systems, product design, production and delivery system, attitudes, and degree of collaboration with the community.

3."The model is static in orientation, so the perspective can cloud our knowledge that customer friendly companies are social systems and as such are constantly changing." How the emergency room staff reacts one day may not reflect their daily attitude. While the board is launching task forces to investigate cardiac care performance and the shortfall in infant service, the clinical and administrative leaders of these areas may have already changed policy and procedure. And while those changes are made, others are in the design stage—ongoing efforts to continuously improve quality do not stop.

4."The intuitive clarity of the five systems model helps us to quickly see what must be done to become customer friendly, but it simultaneously undercuts recognition of how complex organizations are." At the hospital retreat, one physician listened to the presentation on culture change. In his practice, the three partners and small support staff move fast. He said: "If the community is angry, let's just change the culture around here." While his straightforward proposal may be on the mark, changing culture is a challenging, complex and long-term process. Executives and researchers can devote years to understanding what culture is and how to change it.

5. "The separating of the "whole" into five subsystems is necessary for the presentation but it is an artificial construction that can cause us to forget the nature of customer friendly organizations—as integrated wholes, product with structure with climate with leadership." At Westside, leaders are considering whether a culture change is necessary. But it is hard to separate out the potential effects of psychological climate, product quality (successful surgery) and leadership (determined commitment to serve the community). As we pay attention to culture or product we must constantly keep the other systems' effects in mind.

6. "Each of the system's variables are not yet specific and quantifiable and cannot take us easily beyond the qualitative judgment." When the first physician suggested we change the culture, a second physician asked: "How customer friendly is the culture now? How will we measure improvement?" This is a good question, yet hard to answer at the statistical level that physicians are accustomed to. Strides in measurement have been made, but each system is a construction of reality that is open to interpretation.

Professor Martin concluded, "Despite these concerns, I believe the model helps to promote a systems perspective of the problem and that it has the potential to sensitize management and policy leaders to the multi-dimensional aspects of becoming customer friendly."

How has system thinking and customer friendliness been represented in other fields? Westside Hospital could benefit from an understanding of the social architecture of Disney. Friendliness is a five system effort at Disney—high quality customer service achieved with a multifaceted approach. I have inserted our systems labels to link to the components of the Disney architecture : 1. listen and understand customers' needs (product/technology), 2. focus on value-added service throughout the organization (strategic leadership and culture), 3.employ user-friendly delivery methods (product/technology), 4. recover from customer defects with significant efforts (psychological), 5. empower front-line people (psychological), and 6.

celebrate outstanding service efforts (cultural).[56] Cultural values and psychological climate are apparent at the theme parks the company operates. Disney also has a strong product development and service approach and a definite reporting structure. Although Disney does not use the language of systems architecture, their leaders designed their organization with five-system support for high quality, customer friendly service.

THE ORGANIZATION DEVELOPMENT AND CHANGE PROCESS

Becoming customer friendly is an aspiration for some companies and already a reality for others. Systems thinking assumptions tell us that a built-in tendency to decay over time exists. Leaders of customer friendly companies must actively work to maintain their service levels. For organizations not there yet—the work to be done is often couched in the language of organization change and development.[57, 58] The process is simple to present but can be extremely challenging to execute.

Becoming and remaining customer friendly requires a continuous process of diagnosis, planning, action and evaluation in every social and technical system of the organization.

A continuous process means that hospital leaders like Richard would need to diagnose the organization's current state (on a scale of 1-10 how patient friendly are we?). Following the diagnostic work, leaders and staff plan interventions and changes that move the organization toward greater friendliness. Next, actions are taken to change the state of affairs. Finally critical indicators are evaluated to assess progress. This process parallels continuous quality improvement work of the last few decades, with a large exception. Much of the quality improvement work tends to be incremental. But to improve customer friendliness, three options for change are possible:

-continuous incremental improvement
-radical reengineering of the approach to serving customers
-development of an alternate vision of the company's future

In the Westside case, leaders could add more staff and slightly alter the schedule in the emergency room (incremental); develop an adjoining family practice to serve patients currently using the emergency room for primary care (radical reengineering); and/or they could form an alliance with another institution jointly offering emergency care in a new location (an alternate vision of the future).

The board asked Richard to summarize their new understanding of the community complaints and their plan to improve. His remarks, written in a memorandum and presented at a board meeting two weeks after the retreat, follow.

Memorandum

To: Westside Hospital Board of Directors
From: Richard, Westside Hospital President & CEO
Re: Patient services and customer friendliness

Below is a summary of our immediate intent to respond to citizens' complaints about service failure at the Westside Hospital. We are interested in understanding the problem causes and correcting them rapidly. Board and staff have been diagnosing the issues and are prepared to take five steps for a start.

1. Conduct a product service analysis. We will immediately evaluate the scope and quality of our services to infants and heart patients. We expect to use already available data, including the State Cost & Quality Council information, along with patient complaints filed with the ombudsman. Additionally, we will interview and survey patients from these departments.

2. Examine the changing structure of the community. We will reassess our patient base and the insurance reimbursement structure supporting patients from lower socioeconomic groups. We will develop a plan for responding to the changing demographics of the community.

3. Design and implement staff training. The training will target admissions experiences and will promote greater understanding of the impact of poor customer relations. Training will focus on general theories of patient friendliness, on diversity, and on specific skills such as interviewing.

4. Conduct a feasibility study for an on-site family practice. We will look into the feasibility of a family medicine practice that would adjoin the emergency room. This practice would serve patients who tend to use the emergency room for primary care, which is both expensive and distorts the emergency department's mission.

5. Conduct a hospital culture audit. At Westside we have always believed that we are patient-focused. The community has questioned this core value. Whether this is a correct perception is immaterial. We must renew our shared understanding of core values, our mission of community service, and our willingness to work jointly with representatives of a changing community. This review will begin at the board level and include every aspect of our service responsibilities, including recognition of the changing patient base, our tendency to quickly refer patients across town, and our resentment of recent attempts to eliminate our tax exemption status.

We recognize that initial actions will not make us more patient friendly overnight. If we think of these actions as the first in a series of steps that will eventually encompass the whole organization, we are making a good faith response to our customers. Thank you for participating.

~~~~~~~~~~~

Though specific customer friendly actions tend to focus on a single subsystem, the ultimate impact will depend on the effects and reactions that take place in all five systems (the connectedness of systems). Successful "friendliness" initiatives consider direct and indirect effects across all systems. The following chapters describe the systems in more detail and offer illustrations of how to create the architecture of a customer friendly company.

SUMMARY AND ARCHITECTURAL TASK: FIVE GRAND STRATEGIES

Customer service is a hot topic in organization and management circles and rightly so. Many executives see customer service as the emerging point of competitive advantage. Increased customer friendliness is a contributor to organizational survival and an improved bottom line. How customer service is improved is the question. In the Westside hospital case, the hospital director could assume that customer service is a one-dimensional problem—increase the staffing in certain services such as emergency. Without a broader starting point, limited diagnostic understanding is often the norm. In many companies, we continue to make selected, individualistic responses with limited impact. A new approach requires thinking based on two beliefs: that organizations are a set of closely linked systems which all must be changed to improve customer service; and that an organization can employ major strategies to design and increase customer friendliness.

Three assumptions underlie these beliefs: (1) Customer service is an organizational architecture problem, not a single employee or customer service department problem. (2) A systems-oriented approach that recognizes organizational complexity is required to change the whole organization. (3) Multiple actions will be needed to initiate and maintain customer friendliness.

Customer friendliness is a multi-faceted architectural problem that includes leadership, cultural, product, psychological, and structural components. Improvement actions can be systematically sorted using organizational architectural elements. The actions in the following chapters may not be terribly new. But now they are arranged in an architectural plan that encourages us to remember the fundamentals of high performance organizations.

This model organizes and links existing and innovative customer service improvement actions in an integrated architectural redesign strategy, making explicit what some friendly companies like Disney and Southwest[59] have been doing. This perspective of the design problem has several implications:

(1) An integrated architectural view of the customer friendly design task must be more widely disseminated.

(2) Expectations of widespread success from single system initiatives must be diminished or eliminated.

(3) "Packages of action" that build customer friendly architecture and include all components must be created and used.

(4) The complex and organization-wide nature of the customer friendliness problem must be considered in terms of time required for change, months and years, not weeks.

Here, then, are five grand strategies for increasing customer friendliness.

Strategy 1: Evaluate continuously, then redesign and reinvent the product and its delivery and support to improve customer friendliness.

Strategy 2: Change the structure to support customer friendliness.

Strategy 3: Create a psychological climate of service friendliness.

Strategy 4: Lead and manage the way to customer friendliness.

Strategy 5: Build a customer friendly corporate culture.

This architectural model—with assumptions and development process—holds across organizations and fields. One or more systems will require greater or lesser emphasis in each organization, depending on the unique attributes of that organization. Customer friendly leaders—executives, managers and employees—recognize that a complex multi-system problem requires strategies and actions developed and implemented in an integrated fashion.

This chapter presented an approach to a vital problem for leaders in the private and public sectors—how do we create and maintain customer friendly organizations? Each system in the architecture represents a "grand strategy" that will be expanded and developed with specific tools and structures. The next five chapters focus on each of the subsystems in turn, integrating both well-accepted and innovative approaches to improving customer service.

CHAPTER 3

THE PRODUCT SYSTEM: MARKETING, DESIGN, PRODUCTION, DELIVERY AND SUPPORT

AutoCoach is a manufacturer of a full range of automobiles for the North American and European markets. One plant and its allied sales dealership is the focus of the following case, which includes a new sport utility vehicle design and the problem of defective tires.

~~~~~~

Uncle: "What did your friend in the automotive field say was the key to being customer friendly?"

Nephew: "Bart is a plant manager. He said it was "all about the product, everything else is marginal. The design and performance of the car is all that counts."

Uncle: "He's right about product—but his answer is not complete."

~~~~~~

Many executives would answer the question in the same way— high quality products, delivered on time and supported well, are the answer. Customer *unfriendly* organizations certainly do this in reverse—poor quality and a lack of service support quickly ends the customer relationship.

In the last chapter, we considered the way in which hospitals can be customer hostile. The comments above about product remind me of physicians discussing their patients. Doctors often believe that when the surgery is successful and the patient regains all functions, nothing else matters. But when you talk to patients about their hospital experience, they relate stories about billing, nurse responsiveness, room cleanliness, parking, bedside manner and more.

Patients feel the transaction is composed of more than just the surgical product.

This chapter focuses on an auto industry case with Bart the plant manager and his colleague, Dan Taylor, from the dealership. Bart constantly refers to the architecture and processes of customer friendly companies in other industries. He feels each industry is too insulated, knowing that breakthroughs anywhere can be usefully transferred. He continually searches for lessons outside his field.

Autocoach is an international company founded in 1941 to support the war effort. Beginning with trucks and off road Jeep-like vehicles, Autocoach evolved into a major full product company with six different brands of automobiles. The company has more than 200,000 employees in hundreds of locations in North America, South America, Europe and Asia. Along with close ties between its manufacturing and sales operations, Autocoach also operates Autocoach Financing and Autocoach Rentals. As a major manufacturer, the company is ranked in the top 100 of the Fortune 500.

Let's examine customer service issues in the Autocoach Pittsburgh Plant and its allied sales operation, Taylor's Autocoach Sales and Service. The plant employs about 2000 persons, turning out 1000 cars per month. Over the years, the plant has struggled with threats of closures and layoffs, insuring competitive wages and benefits, working conditions, and shifting of jobs to low wage countries.

Autocoach executives are concerned about product quality. They recognize that their customers are focused on car style, durability, and reliability. Customers want safe, exciting vehicles that offer good value over many years.

Bart is an industrial engineer by training. His fascination with cars led him to join Autocoach in his first professional job. After 18 years and a master's degree in business administration, he was promoted to plant manager. A new model design team is based at the plant. Bart has very strong engineering skills since he worked in design, safety and quality control during his tenure with the company. A natural team leader—high school athlete, college student government, management fast track, community volunteer—Bart has great people skills. He enjoys resolving both technical and administrative issues in group settings. His staff feel comfortable in raising troublesome design and performance problems, even though they occasionally refer to him as the "mad memo man". While strongly loyal to corporate, he feels his real allegiance is to the car buyers and drivers, his primary customers. He wants his products to be simply the best.

Bart's team worries about auto industry pressures—for new designs, greater fuel economy, pollution free operation, crash safety, and, most recently, the security of tires that do not unravel.

The introduction of Bart and Autocoach brings us to the central question about products and organization design. To create a customer friendly company, how do we define the target of our architectural attention—narrowly or broadly? Here's what one expert tells us about this issue.

~~~~~~~~~~

Memorandum

To: Plant Management Team
From: Bart, Plant Manager
Autocoach, Pittsburgh Plant
Re: customer satisfaction

Please review the following excerpt from Professor Iaccobucci's work. We will discuss it at the next management meeting with the possibility of inviting her to visit with us in the future. Professor Iaccobucci writes:

> The question then is, what drives customer satisfaction? A company may modify the goods and services it offers but it needs guidance to know which alterations are most desirable and profitable. An important distinction that has developed in discussions of services, but is equally applicable to goods, is the difference between one's "core product" offering and one's "supplemental " (or sometimes, "value added") services. Examples of core products are: safe transport from one city to another via airplane, a physician's proper diagnosis and treatment, an attorney's sound legal advice, a hotel room with a comfortable bed and clean bath, the car to be purchased from an auto dealer, etc. Examples of supplemental are: a movie and meal on board the airplane, the physician's friendly bedside manner, the trust worthiness of the attorney, bathroom amenities and minibars in the hotel room, and the car dealership's financing.
>
> In studies of customer satisfaction in these and other industries, managers are frequently surprised to find their customers are judging them "on the little things" (i.e., on the supplemental). There are good reasons for this phenomenon. First, customers assume the core offering will be of high quality—it is a given. And while a

poor "core" will result in customer dissatisfaction, a good "core" execution is not sufficient for customer satisfaction.

A supporting reason is that, within and across competitors, there is typically little variability in the core product offerings—planes usually do arrive safely, medical treatment is fairly accurate, hotel rooms usually do have decent bedding, etc. With so few differences among competitors on the core product (or within a competitor across different purchases), this information is not distinctive and therefore not useful to a customer forming an evaluation. Furthermore, most consumers find the core of some services hard to judge (e.g., most do not have the expertise to judge an attorney's contracts and suggestions). What varies more, and is easier to evaluate, are the supplemental. Interpersonal skills differ greatly from physician to physician and attorney to attorney, and hotel room and lobby accoutrements also vary widely; all these things are easy to judge. Thus in an evaluation of a service experience or in a choice between service providers, supplemental services provide greater information to consumers and become those features of the product offering that drive satisfaction and choice.[1]

Two points here have architectural implications for Bart and his team, and for us. First, we must insure that the customer's assumption about product quality is right. We must design in and manage quality so that our cars (and our airplanes and other products) are safe and reliable. Second, customer friendly organizations must concern themselves with issues beyond the product—"supplemental," "peripherals," or in health care what is known as "amenities." Food, clerk friendliness, and parking all count in the formula that makes up customer satisfaction in a hospital.

Customer service in many companies has a limited definition focusing on the technology of the core products. The functional performance of the car, toaster, or television receives all the attention. In other words, service friendliness is thought to be primarily an improvement in product design, production process, delivery and support. The view is both accurate and too narrow. Customer friendliness *does* focus on the production and distribution process and on product quality. While this focus is *necessary*, it is not *sufficient.*

In another example, Bart's design engineers had to pay attention to cup holders, a humbling experience for engineers interested in speed, design beauty, and long term engine reliability. The message is that the customer makes a judgment about the degree of customer friendliness based on the whole experience of the product, not just on the "core" product's functioning or outcome. Bart's engineers must understand that the car buyer's satisfaction is driven not just by sleek lines and horsepower but also by the salesman at Taylor's Autocoach Dealership and the repair service response. For a surprisingly large number of technical people, this is a stunning and discomforting insight.

Customer friendliness is a derivative of the market needs analysis, the distribution system, periodic evaluation and redesign of products and access to quality support services. To understand "service friendliness," we examine the collegiality of work groups, the sophistication of service measurement approaches, and the degree of discretion in the work roles that support service. Rather than thinking of customer friendly as an outcome of the core product, we inject "friendliness" into all stages of the design, production, and delivery system. Summarized below are the results of a focus group led by Bart's staff for a sport utility vehicle design project.

...We expect that the auto manufacturer will consider our needs—to transport children to many recreational and sports events. We expect innovative design—from station wagon to mini-van to sport utility vehicle to hybrid. Combining gas economy and luxury is desired. We expect quality engineering and reliable operation—few breakdowns and repairs. We want quick delivery and available service. We increasingly expect buying "ease" through the Internet's comparative shopping and presentation of design options. ...

Most of us shop for cars by traveling to a dealer like Autocoach, looking for a car that attracts our attention and taking it for a test drive. At certain car dealerships, potential customers are given the opportunity to drive the car for several days, a try-out period. Additionally, some high-end car dealers advertise that if you do not have time to come to the dealership, they will come to you. The dealership drives cars to potential customers, allowing them to test the cars in their own neighborhood. Buyers can then order a car to their specifications, built with power, design and colors they select, without going to the dealership.

This approach to product demonstration is one possible innovative response among many. Customer friendly companies periodically review product design, foster teamwork among support personnel, and continuously consider whether they need different products. At the operating and strategic levels of the company, architectural design fosters or undercuts friendliness. The architectural intent in this system is visible in the attention to all aspects of the core products—marketing, product design, production processes, delivery and support; and continuous quality assessment and improvement.

Products—Marketing, Design, Production, Delivery, and Support

What are we trying to do as customer friendly company architects?

The architectural intent of the product and technology system is to understand customer needs, to design innovative, useful products, using production processes that lead to quality products, distributed and supported.

At Bart's Autocoach plant a poster displays the philosophy that drives their behavior:

"We pledge :
To ask our customers what they need
To design our products with customers
To produce our products with customers
To distribute our products with customers
To support and service our customers' purchases
To continuously assess and improve all of the above"

We will consider these topics one by one, but let's begin with one customer's trip to a car dealership.

"I decided to buy a new car to visit my grandchildren. When I went to the dealer, they told me I needed all this power, speed, comfort, and even computer capability. I said I just wanted transport. The salesman said, we only have "loaded cars", nothing else is in production. I ordered one, which came four weeks later, not one week later as promised. When I couldn't start it on the second day, I called their service department for an appointment which was scheduled two days later.

The customer had trouble with tailor-making the new car design, the reliability of the production process, and the follow up support, a three for one experience. Not all auto companies offer this level of service failure in one stroke. To insure that they do not, the architecture of customer friendly companies like Autocoach involves customer input at five critical points:

- marketing
- product design
- production process
- distribution and delivery
- support

These architectural points are linked, as we will see. In the example, the auto dealership staff did not understand the customer's minimal needs (marketing); offered an overly complex and luxurious product (design and production); delivered the product too slowly (distribution); and failed to be there when the customer needed help (support). In customer friendly companies, we design the architecture to prevent this experience and correct it rapidly when product or service failure does happen.

MARKET ANALYSIS: WHO NEEDS WHAT?

What are the *challenges* for the SUV design team? They must find out what their future customers need. Are the primary customers the "Colorado crowd"—constantly off-road, towing boats and horse trailers, with fishing, kayaking and biking gear in the back? Or are the primary customers actually suburbanites—highway drivers, focused on stereo sound, leather seats, and room for six kids, with only occasional parking on the soccer field grass? A SUV designed for ferrying kids is quite different than one designed for fjording streams.

Did marketing specialists discover that we needed a mini-van and then build it to specifications? Did marketing discover a renewed interest in sports cars and then build to specifications? Or, did design and engineering teams create the products and then the markets? The answer is both.

Customer friendly companies are engaged in continuous analysis, differentiating their markets to ensure that they are providing the needed products and services.[2] Failure to pay attention may have cost Detroit car companies their market lead.[3] In some traditional views, marketing has the functional responsibility for customer contact and needs analysis. In customer friendly companies, marketing departments exist but the marketing tasks—customer needs analysis, relationship building, continuous contacts and support—are distributed throughout the company. Thus, Bart's product engineers are expected to "know" the customer enough to act as a validity and reliability check on the marketing perspectives of corporate staff. In customer friendly companies, *the whole company* is the marketing department, enabling them to both discover and invent needed products in a partnership-like process.

"What do customers want" is the marketers central question. In cars, customers want style, comfort, gas economy, power, individuality, reliability, accoutrements, in any number of priorities and variations. We might hear: "damn the gas mileage, give me power" from a Hummer buyer but only minutes later the reverse; "damn the power, give me gas mileage" from a Ford SUV Hybrid customer. As products that have been in the design stage for many years roll out, gas prices increase and, for example, Hummer sales may go down.[4]

A strong marketing program maintains a closeness to customers' needs and believes that the linkage between customer needs and the company's product and service package is vital to company success. When Bart's team began discussing the design of a new economical SUV, they decided to move beyond their own industry, heeding the advice of an aircraft builder. Airbus Industries, maker of commercial jets, was developing a new jumbo aircraft, so Bart's team visited and listened. Here is Airbus Industries' view of how customers—airline companies and flyers—fit into the process.

"When Airbus started talking to airlines about a big airplane almost eight years ago, the customers responded with nonnegotiable demands. They not only wanted more seats but greater range as well, because most traffic growth is on routes from Asia to the United States and Europe.

Nobody wanted to rebuild airports to suit a new airplane. Airbus concluded that the A3XX would have to fit to an "80 meter box"— the maximum for wingspan and length. With a limit on length, the A3XX would either have a very wide cabin or two passenger decks. Dual decks proved more practical, neatly filling up an oval body measuring 6 meters wide.

The main deck seats 10 economy class passengers abreast, like a 747 but with more hip and elbowroom. The upper deck is as wide as Airbus' current A330/A340. To load and unload the A3XX in 90 minutes—another demand—the designers have provided extra-wide doors, a spacious "lobby" in front of the cabin, and a double width staircase between the decks.

Robert Lafontan, vice president for engineering on the A3XX, explains that several design considerations have caused the new airplane to end up with "a lot of square meters" in the wing. First, airlines want an aircraft that climbs quickly after take off, rather than being stuck among the thunderheads and puddle-jumpers until it burns off some of its fuel. The A3XX goal is an initial cruise altitude of 35,000 feet, with a maximum cruise altitude of 41,000 feet, or 4,000 feet better than current aircraft.

Second, Airbus wanted to cruise at Mach 0.85, or 85 percent of the speed of sound. Most Airbus jets cruise at 0.83, a little slower than Boeing rivals—the difference may not seem huge, but it means an extra 20 to 30 minutes on a long flight. Earlier arrivals show up first on airline computer reservation systems.

A third requirement was that the wing should be able to hold enough fuel for any future A3XX variant. It's possible to add extra tanks in the lower fuselage, but they displace money making freight.

And finally, wake effects were a key issue. Airports are not going to welcome a giant airplane if it trails invisible vortices that can tip smaller aircraft out of control. Such a plane would force air traffic controllers to leave long intervals between landings, which limits airport capacity."[5]

What did Bart's team learn? In preparation for product design and as a part of the design process, Airbus consulted a wide range of customers. Corporate buyers, frequent flyers and airport managers all have relevant data to add to the product design. They are brought in early. In some sense the product is "co-designed" by product engineers and customers, a concept that is underappreciated.

Bart's team decided that, like Airbus, they wanted traditional marketing data combined with access to customers. Spending time with SUV drivers was to be a regular and natural part of the process.

Bart organized a team of marketing staff, design engineers, production engineers, and sales/service staff to assess SUV customer needs. They used surveys, focus groups, personal interviews, test drives, and competitor product analysis to learn about customer perspectives. The team found that customers for a redesigned SUV had the following needs:

- safety (from rollovers and tire failure)
- fuel economy
- ease of use (doors, seat movement)
- power
- unique design
- reliability and quality
- resale value
- service access and honesty

While Bart's team wanted flexibility to use common platforms in manufacturing, customers want personalized, individualized vehicles.[6]

Bart told his group that new products sometimes result from attention to customer needs.[7] He cited the example of a rent-an-umbrella scheme, described below. The "product design" and "marketing" combination is simplicity itself.

~~~~~~~~~~

"The introduction of the "rent-an-umbrella" scheme stemmed from the very nature of customer-orientation. Through observation, staff noticed that customers were stranded in shopping areas in the event of an unexpected downpour. So, Giordano decided to render an umbrella service to its customers through a scheme whereby the store outlet will rent umbrellas to people for $10 per umbrella which is refundable when the umbrella is returned to any store outlet in any condition at any time. According to Danny Tan, this scheme is very popular among customers. Currently, Giordano has collected $15,000 in deposit for the 1500 umbrellas, which have not been returned to date. This may be viewed as a promotional gimmick, whereby the bright colors of the umbrellas with the bold Giordano's logo brighten otherwise gloomy rainy days. With customers using these umbrellas all over Singapore, the umbrella scheme serves as a form of outdoor advertising. However, Mr. Tan emphasized that the sole purpose of this scheme is to help those customers in need and not to take advantage of the situation.[8]

~~~~~~~~~~

Customer friendly companies view *serving customers' needs* as the objective. Marketing, in its fullest sense, is the discovery and confirmation of customer needs. Since Bart's customers come from both high and low socioeconomic backgrounds, use vehicles for business and for recreation, are interested in both luxury and efficiency, this task can be complicated.

PRODUCT DESIGN:
OUR PRODUCTS ARE FRONT EDGE IN STYLE
AND QUALITY

The design team faces a *challenge*: appearance is aligned with function, and multiple functional needs surfaced from the marketing team and in data from previous customers. How beautiful should the SUV be? Is boxy acceptable for overall appearance or is there a demand for a sleek workhorse? The design work must consider the dirt and scuff potential of hauled goods as well as the need for a walnut dashboard, leather interior and a Bose sound system. Are primary colors acceptable or do we need metallic paints in neon colors with xenon head lights?

For Bart's team, design means the elegance of an old Jaguar sports car, the family-friendly contribution of the mini-van, and the rugged off road usefulness of the sport utility vehicle. Designers and customers pay attention when Aston Martin announces that it will produce a new, cheaper model of the sports car used by James Bond, when companies talk of connecting the Internet to cars, and when new hybrid electric/ gas cars are developed (e.g., Toyota's hybrid success in America and its recent movement into China).[9] Customer friendly is first of all about product design.

Before we consider the elegance of Bart's Autocoach products, think about the flip side. Unfriendly designs in other fields have included: "assembly required" furniture, VCR recording instructions, and computer program commands, among many others. Ease of use, functional effectiveness, beauty, and all-age group applications contribute to "customer friendly" designs. Some design "winners" outside the auto industry include: the function of the umbrella, the simple practicality of the paper bag, and the transformational contribution of the telephone. Design highs and lows in Bart's auto business span the range from the Ford Edsel disaster, which was rudely rejected by customers, to the mini-van and sport utility vehicles, which have been greeted with warm acceptance, excitement and many purchases. In the automotive field, hybrids[10] and shared platforms for design choice[11,12] are now manufacturing necessities. Companies without certain models add them (Saab adds an SUV and a subcompact to its line).[13] Nissan adds new models, one including diesel engines.[14]

Customer friendly leaders always ask, do we offer the right products, at the right price, at the right time? The most obvious innovation in customer friendly product design systems is the Internet. This technology has enabled companies to invent new products and new delivery systems (e.g., electronic auction, car rental and airline ticket purchasing) and has enhanced the ability to deliver customized goods. Russell Ackoff offered a good description of the design process:

"Design is a cumulative process. It is usually initiated by using a very broad brush. Therefore, the first version is a rough sketch. Then details are gradually added and revisions are made. The process continues until a sufficiently detailed design is obtained to enable others to carry it out as intended by its designers."[15]

Characteristics are stirred in until a "witches' brew " produces the design in somewhat magical fashion.

Bart and his engineering teams constantly use computer assisted design software with state of the art hardware. But they too have had their installation and start-up problems. Computers are a product type with a huge gap between developers' views of customer friendly and customers' views of customer friendly. Computer companies are learning about customer friendly product design very slowly. It wasn't long ago that computer manufacturers moved consumers fully to the point of "plug and play," a techie's manifestation of customer friendly. Many of us remember the manuals that offer the ridiculous combination of "straightforward, simple" instructions for hardware and software operations. In fact, the unfriendliness of product design in the computer business and other fields spawned a book series—The Idiots and Dummies Guides. Available on dozens of topics, the guides are clear evidence of the shortfall in user friendliness.

The wide range of Idiot and Dummy Guide titles can be considered data, illustrating manufacturers' failure in customer friendly product design across fields. Customers are "dummies" because they fail to figure out the customer unfriendly products and services.[16]

What do customers want from car design? They want the beauty of Jaguar, the status of Mercedes, the performance of BMW, the cost and reliability of Honda, the availability and American manufacturing of Ford, and the nostalgia of Volkswagon's Beatle. Bart's design teams involve customers at every point of the process, including production.[17] What do they get in return? Bart thinks the payoffs for Autocoach are many: greater communication across functions; more ideas generated; greater trust; promotion of systems thinking; and stronger consensus on the ultimate design. Customer involvement reveals issues that threaten to block customer acceptance in the marketplace.

Customer friendly designers think ahead by using customers to do some of the thinking. For example, auto enthusiasts love manual shift. But environmental and safety laws are telling production engineers to shift to automatics.[18] Bart's SUV design team will address comfort and style, as well as regulatory requirements.

PRODUCTION PROCESS

The SUV team faces production challenges. Costs of new models are high, plants must be set up to meet demand, different customers want different variations in style, color, and capability. Manufacturing leaders want shared platforms and production flexibility to cut costs. Production engineers are told to push for high quality, but the sky is not the limit, pricing targets are. Recalls are not desired or expected, even with new models.

Customers are the direct beneficiaries of a high quality production process. In recent years, continuous quality improvement and reengineering have helped companies more efficiently speed new high quality products and services to customers. Bart's team at Autocoach is deep into quality philosophy and considered submitting an application for the Malcolm Baldrige National Quality award, a prestigious recognition of commitment to and execution of quality.[19] Entire careers are devoted to, and many books and articles have been written about production engineering and process improvement. The point is that customers can contribute to process improvement and simultaneously generate customer satisfaction.

Process gains have helped reduce the cost and increase the quality of Japanese and American cars,[20] desktop computers, televisions, cell phones, computer chips, and more. In auto manufacturing, flexible plants,[21] lean production process[22] and made-to-order parts[23] illustrate recent production improvements. The result for customers is often greater and quicker access to higher quality products at lower prices. And more production improvements are ahead, thanks to new technologies such as robotics,[24] flexible production lines[25] and replacement materials such as aluminum.[26]

The whole production process can be improved. Consider this case of fishing boat building that Bart passed on to his team. The team was working to make the plant's assembly line faster and more efficient, a never-ending quest that is eventually passed on to customers. Customers want both speed *and* quality.

~~~~~~~~~~~

Memorandum

To: Production Process Team
From: Bart, Plant Manager
Re: production innovation

Please read the following clips regarding production process breakthroughs. We need to work toward this kind of leap.

"By all accounts, the gamble has already proved worthwhile. For 25 years, the Genmar factory at Little Falls, Minnesota, has used the same caustic, grubby process to churn out Wellcraft and Glastron fiber-glass run-abouts. Men and women in blue coveralls layer or spray fiberglass over each hull. Half-finished boats are scattered around the warehouse, overshadowed by stacks of used molds. The stench of styrene is over powering. The manual layering process is so imprecise that each hull is different; imperfections have to be corrected by hand.

Next door, at a VEC test site that has produced 1,000 hulls in the past year, the air is clean. It's quiet. Three technicians in smart yellow shirts and blue jeans supervise two VEC cells. One man watches a monitor that shows injection flow, temperature and pressure levels. If something goes wrong, an alarm rings in Little Falls and at the VEC solutions center, 1400 miles south. Kirila's experts regularly tap into the Little Falls plant via the Internet to adjust production settings and troubleshoot problems.

Every 35 minutes each cell produces a new hull; next door it takes eight hours and at least twice as many people to finish one. Each completely recyclable plastic mold produces a dozen boats; next door it takes a mold per boat, and each year thousands of used molds have to be buried in landfills. Each VEC hull is so strong that Genmar has announced a lifetime warranty instead of the normal five years.[27]

~~~~~~~~~~~

Bart asked his team to think about the auto plant application of this thinking, beginning with the close relationships with suppliers. He knew that Honda was also working hard to create supplier relationships that guarantee smooth manufacturing operations. New plants and reliable suppliers help to deliver both speed and quality to customers, a key pressure from competitors. General Motors is also moving in this direction, as discussed below.

"Blue Macaw—that's the exotic code name for one of General Mortors Corp's most closely guarded secrets. It's an auto factory, possible the most modern in the world, built near the town of Gravatai in the Brazillian state of Rio Gande do Sul...... It's a mouthful, but the word "factory" alone would not do justice to this collection of 17 plants. Sixteen of the buildings are occupied by suppliers, including Delphi, Lear, and Goodyear. Their job is to deliver pre-assembled modules to GM's line workers, who then piece the cars together in record time. Modular assembly is not a new idea. But according to John Caseca, an analyst at Merrill Lynch & Co. in New York, Blue Macaw "pushes the concept of the modular further along then anywhere else in the world."[28]

Production in customer friendly companies is directed toward defect-free outputs—at the highest end, a six sigma effort (3.4 defects per million.[29] High performance cars, competent students, airline safety, and successful surgery are all customer-friendly production results.

First, quality management is essential to the architecture for recruiting new customers and retaining existing ones. Second, quality also defends against potential litigation and in some states may help avoid a criminal probe of your company's low quality products.[30] Bart's Autocoach plant is part of a major national manufacturing effort. The following comment underscores the significance of analyzing and understanding quality production in small and mid-size companies.

"The client company, like many businesses, does not have millions of customers. However, the concept of zero defects can be applied to any company regardless of the number of customers by using the percentage that falls outside the limits. For a company with only 1,000 customers and ten employees (or stages) who have an impact on customer satisfaction, the difference between +/- three sigma (499 dissatisfied) and +/- four sigma (60 dissatisfied) is 439 dissatisfied customers or nearly 44 percent of the company's customer base. The chance of operating a business with no dissatisfied customers reduces dramatically as the number of employees who come into contact with customers' increases or the number of aspects impacting satisfaction increases. It also reduces when the customer is made to go through a process with many stages. Therefore, there is a need for simplified processes with fewer stages. Process simplification is essential to reduce the number of defects and thereby increase customer satisfaction.[31]

The complexity of the production and delivery process is obviously important. A local book printing and publishing company is less complex than Bart's automobile plant. However, neither simplicity nor complexity would allow us to label a company "customer friendly" if 44% of its customers are dissatisfied. Few managers fully recognize the power of quantifying this issue. Bart wants to make sure that every manager and employee understands the implications .

Work groups who control the core activity of many companies must be sensitized to and targeted on the quantification of customer service. Individual employees are not *solely* responsible for customer service; work teams are. Production and delivery systems are too complex to let the responsibility for customer service rest with individuals.[32] In some companies what was thought to be an individual service is now a team effort. Autonomous work teams have long been used in the automotive industry. In place of endless production line piecework, teams build whole cars.[33] When Bart's group goes out to lunch they can observe first hand the workings of a production team, delivering service in collaboration.

At T.G.I. Fridays, the waiters and waitresses learn during training that they are to work as a team. When orders are ready, wait staff can bring out food and beverages for their colleagues' tables. They are taught to watch for opportunities to help each other with the "shared task"—food and beverage service to the customer. Disregarding old disincentives (tips to individuals) they have developed a team approach to services.[34]

We can easily find other examples—operating rooms of physicians, nurses and support staff; sales and service collaboration at automobile dealerships, and legal teams preparing for a trial defense. Thus, it is not only the technological prowess of the assembly line, but also the psychological climate, including teamwork, that makes the production process customer friendly (see also Chapter 5 Psychological Climate).

DISTRIBUTION: ON TIME EVERY TIME

The SUV design team faces the usual distribution and delivery *challenges*—especially hitting new model release dates and insuring that there are enough vehicles to meet nationwide demand. What incentives dealers receive to move new vehicles quickly and what impact will these incentives have on existing inventory? Are parts suppliers also ready for national distribution? Early buyers must be quickly satisfied by rapid repairs.

One of Bart's friends works for Firestone. Firestone's recent tire recall debacle was of particular concern to the SUV design team. Among other issues, Firestone had a distribution challenge driven by product failure—how to quickly get replacement tires to customers all over the United States. We will discuss Firestone further, but as for product distribution, anyone who has waited for back-ordered products—computers, cars, clothes, and furniture—knows that logistics is a critical component of customer service.[35] The writers Gilmour and Hesket list eight ways of defining the distribution and delivery problem, which Bart promptly passed on to his logistics team. Think of the list as some of the *unseen architecture* of the distribution system.

~~~~~~~~~~~~

Memorandum

To: Distribution Task Force
From: Bart, Plant Manager Autocoach
Re: measuring our distribution status

We have been struggling with how to determine whether we are successfully distributing our product on time every time, and whether we are receiving an equivalent level of service from our suppliers. Here are some measures to be considered. Two author/researchers, Gilmour and Hesket, list eight indicators that I have adapted to our plant's situation.

- the elapsed time between receipt of an order at the supplier's warehouse and shipment of the order from the warehouse, e.g. how fast we get fuel pumps from our subcontractor
- the minimum size or maximum assortment of items in an order which a supplier will accept from the customer, e.g. you all remember the exterior paint limitation

- the percentage of items in a supplier's warehouse out of stock at any given point of time, e.g. the fuel pump shortage we thought we fixed
- the proportion of customers' orders filled accurately, e.g. audio system component orders are often faulty
- the percentage of customers, or volume of customer orders, which are served (whose orders are delivered) within a certain time period from the receipt of the order at the supplier's warehouse, e.g. how long our suppliers usually take to fill an order
- the proportion of goods that arrive at a customer's business in saleable condition, e.g. our damage and repair costs on parts from subcontractors
- the elapsed time between a customer's placement of an order and the delivery of the order to the customer's business, e.g. the problem we solved with just-in-time delivery, now supported 24 hours a day
- the ease and flexibility with which a customer can place an order, e.g. we are now fully computer linked to our prime suppliers for stock replenishment and general inventory control.[36]

Attention to these issues will cut costs and improve the quality of our internal system, producing a positive impact on the bottom line.

~~~~~~~~~~~~~

Increasing the timeliness and ease of distribution from suppliers boosts perceived and real service at the plant and improves customer satisfaction. Cars are produced and delivered on time. Along with Bart's plant, there are many other examples. At the dramatic end of the continuum, the emergency room must respond quickly to parents with injured children in an atmosphere of uncertainty about task and work flow. If distribution systems are not working well, customer service may not be recognized or, in the worst case, even needed.

Distribution to locations specified by customers is a competitive advantage as illustrated by Dell's response to a bank upgrading its computer technology. For Bart's team, fleet purchases of autos for lease may be a similar example. Mr. Benaron, one of the bank's managers, was leading the purchasing team. Here is his story.

"Last summer, Benaron decided the bank needed a computer overhaul. He wanted to purchase 2,700 Pentium II PC's and 800 servers. Dell was in the competition. "At first it was between Dell,

IBM and HP but IBM dropped out because it couldn't match the price," says Benaron. The HP and Dell bids were nearly identical, he said, except for one critical detail. The HP reseller would only ship the order to the bank's headquarters, whereas Dell would deliver ready-to-boot machines to each of its 450 branches. At no added cost. "That was the clincher," says Benaron, who estimates Woolwich saved over $750,000 by going with Dell. Oh, by the way: Benaron just got a nice promotion."

Distribution and support can be blended. How often do employees refer to a "customer" who is "stupid" about start-up use? While Bart's plant engineers are not responsible for transfer of the new auto to the customer, they must insure that the delivery process includes enough information and support to satisfy the customer. Otherwise, each car should come with a "Dummies Guide." In customer friendly companies, employees make their products user friendly—even at the customer's location. Listen to one commentator.

"Acer America Corp., a personal computer manufacturer, is making PC set up even easier for customers with a new Desktop Set-up and Orientation Program and extended on-site service hours.

With the Desktop Set-up and Orientation Program, Acer's Aspire computer customers can schedule an appointment with an Acer representative who will come to their homes, lead them through the set-up of their system, and give them a 30-minute customer orientation.

Set-up includes unpacking the equipment, connecting the cables and power surge strip, testing the equipment via Acer diagnostics, powering up the system and bringing it to the Windows main menu, and installing the print driver.

The Acer representative will also provide a 30-minute customer orientation, which includes bringing up the Windows Program Manager and Acer Computer Explorer programs on the computer screen, registering the computer, verifying the system's configuration, guiding the customer through Windows, teaching the customer how to use sound activation to open software titles, and setting up the voice messages, speakers, microphone, and CD-ROM.

To further improve its customer service, Acer has also expanded its hours for on-site service and support. In addition to Acer's 24-hour, seven-days-a-week technical support and product information World Wide Web site, Acer Aspire customers can now receive onsite help Monday through Saturday from 8 a.m. to 5 p.m. by calling technical support."

Customer friendly companies respect the customer's view by looking for design changes, even in the distribution and delivery stage. Autocoach offers the choice of audio and VCR installations right at the dealer. Bart worries that his engineers have too little contact with service and sales personnel. The SUV design team wants to correct that. When Bart's team asked what customers wanted with automobile sales services, they found that a mix of design, access and financing issues were important:

- Internet information and pricing
- Dealer location
- Car availability
- New car preparation costs
- Warranty service
- Pricing
- Dealer networking for cars

Although plant managers have limited control of these issues, Bart's team will work to promote friendliness from the factory floor, keeping these in mind (e.g. by cost cutting, on time delivery, high quality). The goal is constant learning from the customer's early use, with the recognition that follow-up change is desirable.

SUPPORT: STAND BY ME

The last *challenge* for the SUV design team is to ensure that the dealerships are ready to support the new vehicle. Service philosophy requires responsiveness and integrity. How quickly are repair issues addressed? Are all warranties honored without aggravation? Is every service request handled correctly? The customer grapevine, helped by the Internet, fills with feedback rapidly, eliminating honeymoons for new models.

The final aspect of product and technology is support service. Service failures do occur: it's what happens next that is crucial. Service recovery is vital to satisfaction.[38-40] In customer friendly companies, technical assistance staff, testing and employees who follow-up make a reliable and very valuable contribution to the customer's experience. Lets turn to medicine for a lesson for Bart's team.

A surgeon's successful appendectomy seems to be the product of a single person, or small group in the operating room. Seen as an isolated transaction, it may appear so. But the patient/customer experiences much more than the "operating room product". Successful diagnosis based on appropriate tests led the surgery team to the right target. Follow up advice and care may be critical to full recovery. The pre- and post-hospital work is equally valuable. Customer friendly leaders see this in every customer transaction, regardless of the business they are in.

What lessons can Bart and Dan Taylor's sales dealership learn? Bart and his team feel that producing a car with a sophisticated level of design and engineering is the utmost in customer service. But given the hospital story, Bart's work is necessary but not sufficient. Dan Taylor's Dealership will have much to do with the customer's ultimate judgment. And, it will not end with the sale but will include the customer's experience at the dealer after the sale. How many customers relate their car quality and repeat buy decisions to the service department?

Bart and Dan came up with a teaching case, cobbled together from several dealer experiences with "so called" pre-certified cars. Consider the customer's view.

Four months ago, Thomas Washington purchased a pre-certified SUV for use in camping and other weekend activities. After his purchase, he discovered that the engine specifications were different than the salesman's presentation. The SUV had lower horsepower than promised and Tom worried that it would not pull his boat easily. After three weeks, Tom's check engine light came on, signaling an oil leak. Thanks to an additive, the leak stopped—at least for a while. Two weeks later in a heavy rain the electrical system malfunctioned while Tom's family was camping. The car would not start and towing from the rural location was expensive.

The second month, the clutch went, along with the transmission, during what was a routine off road trip. The cost was $3800. The dealer denied responsibility and an argument ensued. The dealer said he and the manufacturer stand by the quality of the vehicle and the certification process—but they did not stand with cash.

How Autocoach addresses this massive service failure is critical to retaining customers and recruiting new ones.

. Too often, leaders inadequately tap the knowledge of service teams. Bart has difficulty obtaining data from the dealers about performance and service problems, even though he is sensitive to how the customer's view will be shaped by follow up service. Obtaining parts for warranty work and repairs is a constant pressure. Technical obsolescence in the parts supply chain is a current and future problem. Here's a case where information is used.

"AutoZone, the largest auto parts dealer in the U.S., emphasizes strong customer service, supported through store-level information systems. Along with a corporate culture that stresses customer service, the linchpin of AutoZone's success in this area has been a company-developed information system called WITTDTJR, for "what it takes to do the job right." The system is focused solely on enhancing the customer experience.

More than 29 million warranty records are kept among stores. While WITTDTJR can only access a warranty at the same store in which it was originally recorded, future plans call for any store to be able to access all warranty records.

Inventory Look-up and Reservation—a satellite system with a dish at every store—was installed in 1994, linking all stores through a hub in Memphis. In addition to credit card and check authorizations, the system enables a store to check the inventories of neighboring stores for an out-of-stock part.

Remote Customer Phone Bank—The satellite network also provides inventory look-up capabilities to a call center in Memphis, opened last year to support customer phone traffic to the highest volume stores. When customers call a high volume store, the calls are routed to the call center. This is done over an 800 number; the customer dials the local store and the call is automatically routed.

The call center is staffed by "Phone Pros" who use the satellite system to tie into WITTDTJR to look up parts, quote prices and check inventory—all as though they were local AutoZones. The Phone Pros use the inventory look-up and reservation functions to remotely place an item on hold for a customer. As a result, employees in these high volume stores are free to help customers in the store.

Automated Replenishment—Developed in-house, the system automatically orders inventory, saving managers 12 or more hours a week with ordering functions."

In the auto parts business, the customers can be individual car owners or mechanics from a range of dealerships and garages. Both groups lobby for ease of use and AutoZone pays attention. Team building between dealer services and plant production employees is key to keeping service breakdowns—like parts shortages—from becoming a barrier to real and perceived assessments of product quality. Customer friendly leaders listen to service representatives and ask for suggestions on increasing effectiveness. Service staff know how to build friendliness based on their daily interaction with customers and their problems. And, they know how to build a knowledge base.

Bart sent around a list of knowledge sharing benefits to help convince his management team of the value of this data development.

~~~~~~~~~~~~~

"Some of the benefits companies have achieved in their knowledge sharing activities include:

- Improved problem-solving
- high-quality technical expertise and best practices to non-technical front line staff and, in many cases, directly to the customer
- consistently correct solutions for the same types of problems;
- increased first-call resolutions—enabling the front line staff to answer more of the calls the first time, without the need for technical experts;
- reduced cost per call—through more rapid problem resolution, usage of less expensive personnel and fewer escalations;
- reduced calls to the support desk—getting it right the first time reduces repeat calls; also, making the knowledge available to customers directly allows many to solve their own problems;
- reduced field service costs—solving problems remotely can eliminate field visits for products that sometimes require on-site support;
- movement to a less technical, more customer—oriented frontline staff—in addition to lowering costs, this allows a company to better leverage technical skills on new product development and focus frontline activity on those skilled in customer interaction and relationship building;
- accelerated training—accessing knowledge becomes part of everyone's job, essentially providing an on-the-job training facility, and enabling new employees to become productive faster;
- increased staff satisfaction—front-line staff can solve more problems independently, and gain confidence in their abilities; they can also expand their expertise to other products or services;

- increased customer satisfaction—customers get answers faster and more accurately; customer satisfaction contributes to customer loyalty and to potential additional sales."[41]

These payoffs should interest both Bart's team and his corporate superiors. How can they use the suggestions? Many are dealership opportunities.

Bart's team expects Dan Taylor's Autocoach Dealership staff to respond with increased knowledge of how other dealers solve problems, e.g. with tires, with brakes, with sound systems. Dan's dealership staff would have greater discretion and fewer repeat calls from customers (same problem—not fixed again). To achieve customer and staff satisfaction, Dan will need to invest in staff training and greater computer access (e.g. sharing of common car defects/problems across dealerships).

QUALITY MANAGEMENT—QUALITY AS A NEVER ENDING QUEST

Firestone and Ford have had experiences that Bart's team does not want to have, ever. A new SUV must be safe. A large part of product-related customer friendly architecture is quality management. Customer friendly companies *manage* quality in every aspect of their product system—marketing, design, production, distribution, and support. Quality management policy and practice now includes a range of philosophies and techniques.[42-45] Both Ford and Chrysler have active quality efforts.[46, 47] Donald Petersen, Chairman of Ford, put it this way: "Our systems for learning about customers and their wants and needs also are undergoing continuous improvement. We want to know our customers so well that what they define as quality is what we deliver. We want our products and services not just to meet customer expectations but to exceed them." Advocates of the various quality management models are competing for dominance, defining their strategy as the one best approach. But each has a place in the quality management repertoire because they all contribute to system redesign. Consider three popular models: continuous quality improvement, reengineering, and visioning.

When we think of customer friendly quality management inclusively, we mean methodologies (such as continuous quality improvement and reengineering) and preventive integrated actions (new visions). The vision enables us to describe and purposely design our desired future. Quality management leaders have already found that all three approaches are part of a package of tools to improve auto performance and travel for customers.

Continuous quality improvement can be viewed generally as the never-ending search for improvement in procedures and outcomes. In practice, the work uses a diagnosis-planning-action-evaluation cycle based on data collection and analysis to effect continuous incremental improvement to existing practice. For example, Bart's design and production teams have long been concerned with two problems—gas mileage and pollution emissions. The teams have continuously improved their traditional engines' performance. SUVs first averaged 14 mpg, then 17, then 21 miles per gallon. Using engineering performance data and teamwork, incremental gains have been made. Lower emission levels and higher mileage have resulted over the last 10 years. Customers are economically better off and many have appreciated the environmental benefits. Contrast this with another quality management model.

Reengineering is a radical and dramatic change in an existing process resulting in a "leap forward" in approach and practice.[48] Bart's teams have had a hand in working on electricity- and gas-powered hybrid cars. New combinations of power sources is one example of reengineering; a more dramatic one is the emergence of all-elecric cars. In these redesigns we are attempting to address the "mileage/pollution challenge" in a significantly different way.

Visioning, another quality management model, differs from continuous quality improvement and reengineering. Visioning is the creation of a desired quality future (a more customer friendly future) that may imply continuous improvement to existing practices, radical changes and new approaches, and a reformulation of the conditions that create the problem in the first place. Bart's team is focused on how best to improve mileage and reduce pollution. Along with continuously improved procedures and radically new approaches to engine performance, they could vision a company-led community-wide effort to reduce pollution (e.g., with mass transit, commuter pools, bicycle paths and residential/ office parks where we can walk to work). In addition to reactive steps (redesign existing engine models in response to environmental groups' criticism), quality improvement can be proactive (investment in alternative technologies, support for planned growth and roadway improvements).

This visioning approach takes a whole systems perspective in recognizing contributing factors such as: missing information and education, driver behaviors of solo-commuting, and low public support of mass transportation and environmental protection. We would use more fuel-efficient cars, new mass transit, electric cars, bicycle paths, and car pooling to create a vision of "economic and environmental friendly future." As Juran has noted—poor quality does not happen by accident but is designed in.[49] Given our present behaviors—love of large inefficient SUVs and solo travel—low fuel efficiency and high pollution is *designed* to be a part of our personal and community future. Incremental and radical process improvements in auto design and production can be accompanied by "stretch goals" of significantly improved transportation options.

Bart wanted a state of the art quality management effort to lead the way at Autocoach. What must he include? Five elements are critical to customer-friendly quality management: information systems; benchmarking; feedback; internal regulation and report cards. These elements are derived from general principles and contribute to product quality in practical ways. Bart needed to start with a common understanding of what the quality and customer service mission was about. John Tysse of Dow Chemical put it this way:

> This renewed emphasis on quality, on product performance, and—most importantly—on satisfying our customers, has paid off. Within the new culture, which we call QSPP (Quality, Service and Product Performance), our commitment to our customers is based on four principles:
>
> 1) Quality means conformance to mutually-agreed-upon specifications;
> 2) Conformance to these specifications must be proved by statistical evidence of process control;
> 3) Partners must identify and quantify conformance to these specifications and set priorities to eliminate any cause of noncompliance; and
> 4) The goal is to prevent defects by doing it right the first time."[50]

This combination of philosophy and values, standards, methods, and measurement returns great benefits to customers.

What prevents product failure disasters—the ultimate in customer unfriendliness? Some companies choose central quality control, managed predominantly by headquarters. *Redundancy* established in the product design stage enables work teams to create customer service control at the work group level, with back up by headquarters and by outside organizations. For example, clinical teams in hospitals monitor their own data on surgery outcomes, which are also monitored by the hospital's quality management group, and by external accrediting agencies. Product quality control coverage is tripled.

For Bart, the Firestone tire case is a recent example of quality control failure in the auto industry. Because of this breakdown, legislative efforts are now directed at creating quality redundancy. It took a massive failure (via product and design defects) to convince us that Firestone was not customer friendly enough to review and act on its own data.

Bart recognized that the various quality control functions should complement, but not duplicate each other. Each aspect of plant-level quality monitoring should not be automatically replicated at headquarters, or by external regulators. Information generated by plant and dealership staff should be linked to the external regulatory system (reviewing tire performance and customer satisfaction), complementing each other. Bart regularly receives reports from Dan's Autocoach Dealership that detail service problems (e.g. on retractable seats, moon roof leaks, and engine hose failure). Dialogue between plant and dealership employees can produce data on outcomes and help employees reach out to touch customers emotionally, demonstrating that they do care.

INFORMATION SYSTEMS

Bart's team knows that customer friendly organizations have the ability to collect information on customer needs and experiences—the ability to listen.[51] The basic concept is not new. Concerned with determining how comprehensive Autocoach's data system was, Bart sponsored a survey that concluded the following.

"A Forum study of Fortune 500 companies shows that data [on customers] pours in via the obvious, almost universally used conduits: 96 percent of respondents track comments and complaints mailed by customers, 92 percent use customer focus groups, 88 percent do phone surveys, and 83 percent mail out questionnaires.

Tactics little used but highly effective, according to companies using them, are site visits—going to visit your customers, and hosting visits from your customers. Front-line workers, senior executives, and people in between should partake, Forum says. Another effective but underused tactic is the customer panel discussion, again with workers at every level of the vendor company listening.[52]

Although many companies acquire and use some data, limited information system components and their continuous and effective use are points of weakness.[53, 54, 55] This is an architectural problem and continuing challenge for Bart's team and others. The issue is turning data into knowledge.[56] The issue is not just collecting the data, but the *quality* of the information. Berry and Pasasurman ask these questions to test data quality: Is the information "relevant, precise, useful, in context, credible, understandable, timely?" The architecture must answer these requirements.

The most important information system elements in a customer friendly architecture are the following :
- integrated data design
- benchmarking data
- feedback capability
- internal regulation autonomy
- precise "report cards"

How do these elements relate to Bart's SUV design team's efforts? First, Bart wants the team to work with both manufacturing data and sales/service data. Existing vehicle models' performance is benchmarked against the best SUV standards in the industry. Strong feedback from existing customers and from "testers" is used. Corporate has given the design team considerable freedom. Detailed report cards will be developed from early purchasers' experiences.

Integrated Customer Data

Bart and Dan, like many customer friendly leaders, wonder where to start. Autocoach could start with these issues raised by another industry leader.

"To begin with, consider some simple questions: (1) How many customers bought from you last month? (2) How many of those were first-time customers? Of the others, how many bought in their normal or regular pattern, and how many were out of the pattern—on either the high or low side? (3) How many customers stopped buying from you or sharply reduced their volume this year? Do you know why? What reports do you get routinely that tell you customer-specific information? Do any of them give you pattern information that might give you either defensive or offensive clues about what you should be working on?

Naturally, this sort of questioning doesn't tell you what your customers' specific values are. You have to apply common sense, industry knowledge, a fair amount of factual analysis, and a healthy dash of intuition to determine those. But we've found at Nashua that managers in businesses with blind-spot potentials simply can't focus consistently on customers without reinforcing behavior from the system around and above them. That means the stimulation of customer-based questions from bosses, and specifically creating customer-based slices of what is usually a large management information pie."[57]

~~~~~~~~~~~~

These basic questions only begin the discussion. For autos, the issues encompass a full range of concerns. Follow up information, analysis and the linking of various data streams provide the ultimate understanding about what customers feel and experience. Do customers like the power, the sound system, and the cargo space? As the tire problems arose, basic feedback questions could have led Firestone to look deeper and to act faster. Bart wants an early warning system that avoids inconvenience and certainly prevents multiple tragedies.

Bart's team learns that Xerox has been working on this problem for several years now. The data elements of their system include:

- *periodic Xerox customer surveys*
- *periodic Xerox & competitive customer surveys*
- *post installation & cancellation customer surveys*
- *customer query/complaint data*
- *customer panels/user/focus groups*
- *customer visits*[58]

There is not "one best way" to organize and collect customer data. Many digital and electronic tools have been developed.[59, 60] Bart's team thinks the effort involved in developing information is significant and are unsure what they get in return for all the data mining.[61] We can tell them that the benefits from this "customer intelligence" affect management practices and decisions. Customer intelligence:

- Encourages and enables management to incorporate the customer voice into decision-making.
- Reveals customers' service priorities.
- Identifies service improvement priorities and guides resource-allocation decisions.
- Allows the performance tracking of company and competitor service over time.
- Discloses the impact of service quality initiatives and investments.
- Offers performance-based data to reward excellent service and correct poor service.[62]

Several elements of customer information systems are considered especially important: benchmarking, feedback, information flow and report cards.

BENCHMARKING:
WHAT ARE THE COMPETITORS DOING?

To "design in" continuous improvement of service, customer friendly leaders search widely for ideas and practices.[63] Benchmarking is the label used for this "inside/outside" search for ideas and tools. Bart's team has used benchmarking for several years to track factory productivity and quality, comparing his plant to others in the Autocoach company. Dan looks at competitor dealers.

Some large customer friendly companies search *inside* their organizations, believing that isolated best practices in divisions, regional locations, and foreign countries can be used effectively by the whole company. For example, the Autocoach plant in Nashville uses robotics like BMW in ways that have not been accepted at Bart's Pittsburgh plant. They also have heard of the use of composites in new Corvettes.[64] Given the Firestone experience, Bart wants his team to have examples of product failure surveillance systems, the best models in use in any industry.

Customer friendly companies complement their internal hunt for ideas with an *external search* for best practices among competitors and even to companies outside their industry.[65] Bart's team collected information on Honda's supplier management. Some staff were also interested in what GM was doing in a Brazilian plant labeled the most modern in the world.

Executives at Autocoach headquarters also feel they could learn from producers and sellers outside their industry. Both Dell and Amazon have found ways to connect with customers, gaining business through the Internet. The question is "who is the best at electronic ordering? And can that model be adapted for use with cars in factory and dealership environments"?

Bart outlined the process to keep his team moving on this method.

~~~~~~~~~~~~~

Memorandum

From: Bart
Re: quality and benchmarking

Please include the following benchmarking process in future efforts, as part of an our continuing policy to implement best practices within the company. The benchmarking process is not complex and will differ somewhat by location. According to the strategic leadership team, a typical process might include the following elements.

- Define objectives and process targets
- Specify performance measures
- Identify the best-in-class performances
- Compare the best-in-class to your own department
- Develop action steps for adaptation or adoption

This process is applicable to every area of our company. Many of you know I serve on the Northside Hospital board. The hospital board has struggled with problems related to "lodging" in the health care industry. Along with medical care, hospitals provide hotel services—beds, linens, food, and response staff. In the last few years, we have looked to hotel chains for models, benchmarking outside the health industry. Using data from Marriott and Hilton gave us some innovative ideas. At Autocoach, we should also pay attention to other manufacturing environments.

~~~~~~~~~~~~~

FEEDBACK: THE WORD RETURNS

After sending the benchmarking memo, Bart wondered when he last used the data in his management team discussions.[66] Customer feedback was discomforting, especially for his design engineers. Complaint programs were viewed as threatening to management and their potential for providing important information was too often overlooked.[67, 68] Too many times the failure to distribute and use customer information is the crux of the problem. The mechanisms and art of feeding back customer data are critical to the customer friendly architecture.

Harrison summarized the characteristics of good feedback processes used in organizational change and development.[69] Adapted (with some substitutions) to fit customer friendly design, Bart and a consultant used these seven points to work on the feedback question ("how to give and get feedback," as one engineer said).

Bart hired the firm Hooper Watkin Welham (HWW) on recommendation from corporate. This national consulting firm conducts management and organization design projects across the country. Bart was clear about the assignment—to help he and his team solicit and use customer feedback in marketing, product design, production, delivery and support. The new SUV project and the Firestone disaster were to be the focus.

The HWW team said that they would build a one-day education session around the Firestone case. They had been using this example because it was a high profile public case with both positive and negative feedback events. During the session, HWW said, "Feedback is effectively "designed into" the company architecture when nine conditions are met." These nine are the organizing principles of successful customer friendly feedback.

1. *Clarity of Purpose: Data can be used for development or for judgment.* To use the customer data for continuing product and organizational development, the data presenters and the "manager audience" must recognize that the purpose is *formative.* How do we build a customer friendly SUV including style, performance and economy? Learning and change to improve customer friendly processes is the goal. A judgmental purpose (*summative*) offers a figurative grade of "pass or fail" and is designed for accountability. Customer feedback on Firestone tires as it appears in litigation and "front page" negative stories is not intended as help, but as a judgment of failed product quality. A misunderstanding of purpose will not serve the audience, or the presenters. At Firestone, the customer feedback may be used to help plant managers and leaders redesign tires. Or, it can be used to launch and/or defend against litigation, very different uses.

2. *Clear and Specific Data. Data presented must be clearly relevant to the group or unit that is the recipient.* For example, in Bart's hospital board role, he heard that patient satisfaction data collected for the whole hospital is rarely useful at the department level unless enough patients are sampled to represent that particular unit. Yet many times, clinical teams are asked to review satisfaction data in aggregate. In aggregate, it may have seemed there was no significant problem at Firestone, but using plant by plant feedback, one could see that tires were defective in at least one case. And country-level data was ignored. Firestone's Brazil and Egypt plants' experience with failing tires were not thought to be relevant to the United States. Furthermore, the data needed to be more specific, meaning tire types, conditions, (road, weather, speed), vehicles, and plant of manufacture.

3. *Descriptive, Not Evaluative. Useful feedback describes what is happening but does not offer an evaluative judgment (unless that is the intended purpose).* Presenters must not rush to judgment without some interaction with employees. Some Firestone management may have reacted with suspicion, suspecting internal or union sabotage. We do not want quick emotion, just the facts. This is particularly true if the design team wants to try some innovations in the new SUV (e.g., the capability to remove the rear housing, producing a pick up truck).

4. *Timely. How close to the action being reviewed are the data describing the events?* The golden rule is quick feedback, meaning monthly, quarterly or semi-annually. Much customer service quality data is a year old or more, by which time behaviors and environment may have changed. Old data are useful for historical and longitudinal purposes but they do not support behavior change in the near term. And old data can simply prove your errors. At Firestone, the data indicated problems starting in the mid 1990s.

5. *Limited. How great is the scope of the data? This characteristic requires that we tailor and focus the data to fit the specific needs of users.* Data relevant to technical support callbacks do not include company financial trends, turnover, industry trend information, and so on. Although those data are useful to executives, tech staff need feedback about types of calls, response time and most troublesome problems. Any new SUV design would have to address

rollover tendencies. Firestone undoubtedly rushed to generate all kinds of comparative data on tire and vehicle safety and reliability and to use what existed, wherever it was. Staff likely assembled a deluge of tire comparison figures, crash test data, National Highway Traffic Safety Agency data and more.

6. *Comparative. One side of the benchmarking debate argues that it emphasizes followership, not leadership.* But employees want to know how they compare with others and with their own past performance. A lack of comparative information deprives recipients of knowledge about their progress, or lack thereof. Without information, employees cannot answer the question "are we improving" relative to our performance and to our competitors? Autocoach designers need to find out whether their SUV design would have more of a tendency toward rollover and tire failure than rival company's designs. This is a customer safety question first but also an important competitive issue. Each company in a swamp like Firestone's hurries to say that all tires are somewhat faulty. Thus, their fault is lessened by the general state of the industry. All tire companies could use this data to move safely out of individual trouble, or to sink as a group (e.g., the tobacco companies).

7. *Participative Interpretation. This condition rejects the notion that complete analysis can be conducted without customer and employee involvement.* Joint interpretation occurs as analysts, customers, and employees discuss the meaning of the data and decide on follow-up action. Design and production engineers, managers, executives and front line service managers needed to interpret the Firestone data. In the ferocious publicity of the Firestone case there was scarcely room for reasoned analysis, at least in public. But in private, Firestone engineers and managers must carefully look at the data to understand what is going on. The "front page nature" of this feedback means that the participative analysis will be done after the public conclusions are made. Many internal analysts are still not sure what the tire design flaws were, even after much feedback of accident data.

8. *Safety and security. Receiving performance feedback is both a technical and a psychological event.* We must first collect and analyze the data correctly (technical event). Second, because evaluations generate anxiety, presenters must be sensitive to the psychology of the process and offer language and behavior that protects

employees. Design teams have "heavy psychological investments" in their designs. Crude trashing for style or safety reasons is insensitive and not supportive of innovation efforts (for new SUV designs or for addressing product failure). Firestone employees were hardly in a position to receive the feedback in a safe and secure climate. The extreme opposite prevailed in the Firestone case—customer hostility, political and legal threats, calls for the company's demise. Employees and managers predictably acted with fear and with technical uncertainty, and for a time, did not act at all.

9. Practical and Action oriented. To be useful, the data should suggest some followup action and should be practical enough to be used by field staff. Elite statistical analysis must be interpreted for employee—customer implications. "What do the data tell us to do?" is the bottom-line question. Firestone leaders at first acted in the worst possible way—denial of a problem, protection of data, and delay. Yet the feedback from customers was clear and demanding. It was not until significant national publicity had tarnished the company that leaders became open about the data they possessed and acted fully with promises of restitution.

Bart's team learned much from the Firestone case that they plan to incorporate into the new SUV design process and product. They came into the session believing in customer feedback and left with a stronger sense of its necessity. Their next team meeting was driven by the question of how to generate and use this feedback across the Autocoach plant. Customer friendly leaders must recognize that the "art" of feedback is one of the critical parts of the customer friendly architecture.

INFORMATION FLOW: THE ENEMY IS ME

"Customer friendly" companies use data to support customer service—as part of the "product." What happens when the regulation of this data flow fails? In customer friendly companies, teams often rely on company-wide data systems, an "internal process" that moves feedback to employees. Bart's design team needs this data as a foundation.

Consider the problem with Firestone. The National Highway Safety Administration and litigators discovered and publicized the problem, but Firestone and Ford experienced a breakdown in their internal regulation. Outside regulators are rarely able to generate enough timely data to help customers in the short term. Although "external customer service auditing" is the fad, internal vigilance is increasingly seen as the most effective means of control. Without work team commitment to service quality control, external mechanisms are too limited and too late.

SERVICE REPORT CARDS: WE NEVER MEASURE

In "customer friendly" companies, employees and managers regularly report on service progress. Most companies haven't achieved the definitive data set and flow of information, but basic data are necessary, no matter how crude. The use of "customer friendly" indicators—an internal service report card—ensures that employees measure "customer friendliness." Dan Taylor's dealership needs clear and complete feedback from their customers regarding their "after the sale" experience. Bart's team is interested in developing internal report cards, as it was obvious that Firestone did not have them, or at least did not use them.

Recently, companies have touted their exploratory report card efforts as a step forward in quality management, helping leaders inside and consumer advocates. The JD Power surveys of auto quality and Consumer Reports Magazine are leading examples of external reviews. Report card advocates purport to help customers make selections among companies, although the design of reports can be subject to debate. The reasons to develop and use report cards include:

- Enhance competition among companies
- Provide the capability to compare (with data to do so)
- Enable public and consumer accountability
- Stimulate development of higher quality services and organizations.

Underlying the reports are two core and opposing assumptions: (a) policing is required to keep companies honest and quality high, and (b) organization development can result from report card use. Although the architectural intentions are honorable, report card developers still have some nagging questions to address. There are at least five major problems that Bart's team will have to overcome to make these report cards successful.

Only product performance is considered. From a technical perspective, customer friendly frequently means product performance *only.* The targets and the methods involve the product—Bart's SUV team would focus on performance, style, reliability, parts and expected/unexpected defects. But customer friendly "whole organization architecture" also targets administrative operations from human resources to information systems. Customer friendly is moving beyond the focus on product and so should report cards. Bart's team will propose that their report card have data about the plant's administrative processes and the dealership's "employee turnover, absenteeism, job satisfaction" (unnerving some leaders, no doubt).

The missing standardization of methods and instruments. A comparison across companies and institutions requires standardized methods and instruments. Although progress has been made, many organizations use different metrics and individualized approaches to sample selection. We produce numbers, but they are not comparable. Bart's team will better use the data use if they can compare it to other Autocoach plants and other companies' plants.

Single dimension feedback. What has often passed for report card data is a single stream of information with uncertain reliability and validity. In education, teachers know that grades, by themselves, are too thin a measure of performance. Teachers use number grades *and* commentary; they request parent-teacher conferences; and some even develop student portfolios. The teacher's report card data are complex, more so than, for example, simply counting the number of defective products coming off an assembly line. Bart's team must produce a well rounded report that will withstand criticism from inside and outside.

Meaning of the data. When leaders and customers have report card data, how fast do we leap to a judgment about customer friendliness? Perhaps in some extreme cases where few repurchases are made, complaints are high, and many defects occur, the data are unequivocal. But many comparisons are fuzzy. Bart's team was left with little doubt that Firestone had a problem. But the root cause— road conditions, inflation pressure, type of vehicle, design flaws in the tires—still had to be sorted out.

Use and purpose—the uncertain linkage to continuous quality improvement. Report cards have taken on "policing" trappings in some organizations—bad data get people fired. This constrasts directly with many leaders' philosophy about quality. The psychology of continuous quality improvement reflects a different starting point. Whereas traditional quality involved action focused on weaknesses (policing, blame-fixing, problem correction), continuous quality improvement begins with the assumption that no matter how good the product and operations are, they can always be better. The assumptions and accompanying psychology reject "adequate and good" in favor of "continuous improvement now and forever". Firestone is caught in the trap. Data collected and analyzed will be used against the company in court. The report card concept is likewise a double edged sword, useful inside for development and outside for litigation.

Action needed. One additional aspect of "report cards", answers the "what happens next" question. After all of the effort to develop and analyze the customer data, leaders and employees must take action. They can agree to *increase, decrease, maintain, start or stop* products, product processes, delivery systems and support. In customer friendly companies action is sought. One of Bart's first follow up actions was to encourage change, which, he said, would be tracked by Hooper Watkin Welham and discussed at their next visit.

Management is involved in whole organization quality improvement. Traditional quality control was directed at production—managers could observe but their activities were not the subjects of the work. When the customer friendliness of the whole organization is involved, managers must lead and respond to the process, making improvements in administrative processes as well as engineering (e.g. financing, funding for technology, scheduling, and manpower planning).

Quality management leaders have begun to embrace the philosophy and practices of continuous quality improvement. Will report cards represent a step forward or a leap backward in architecture? The value of report cards is in announcing that customer friendly is important enough to measure and that service, along with cost, is a key to decision making.

SYSTEMS INTERACTIONS—CONNECTED ARCHITECTURE

Autocoach encompasses 37 plants and and 74 dealerships. At the annual meeting, Bart spoke about the lessons learned.

Bart's Presentation:
The Lessons of the Firestone Ford Tire Case

Thank you for inviting me to speak to this annual meeting of Autocoach Plant Managers and Dealership Owners. When I began to think about topics, new product design, the current fascination with luxury sports cars (which we don't yet build at my plant—please take note, corporate) and the new hybrid SUV/pick up trucks all came to mind. But the headlines intervened. Firestone-Ford is still news in our business. As important as this issue is to the media and to our customers, it is equally important to us as product designers and advocates.

Car customers buy quality from the auto industry, they trust us, and they expect performance and reliability. Have we let them down? If so, how did this happen when Ford in particular has worked so hard to be customer friendly and quality focused in the last 10 years?

My team has been working on the case as part of our management development program. With help from Hooper Watkin Welham we have explored the use of customer feedback data. But we also delved more deeply into the case. We found a breakdown of systems thinking, a focus on parts of the company not the whole, and some "designed in" product and service failure. The design and product engineers should not be blamed solely because they are not the companies' architects. Let me explain.

There are four points of interaction between the product system and other major components of the organization—"architectural connectedness" if you like the fancy language. Here are four insights I guess we knew but did not see—or at least had to hear about again. Our products are cars and trucks. We now remember that:

- product interacts with incentive structure
- product interacts with employee psychology
- product interacts with leadership
- product interacts with company culture

If we use the Firestone-Ford case, what are the questions for us at Autocoach? I know that many of you serve on hospital and other boards; these questions apply there as well.

Did we forget that product quality is influenced by personal and corporate incentives? In customer friendly companies, product quality and service are tied to rewards and incentives (structure). At Firestone Ford the profit incentive, with individual country and personal bonuses, may have been directed toward selling and moving products, not highest quality products, just products.

Did we forget that psychological climate influences how much employees care about product quality and how they react when massive failures appear? Products are distributed and supported with positive employee attitudes (psychology). "Fast to blame, slow to fix" seemed to be the crisis management method—at least at first. Deny the problem and limit disclosure of the facts was their lead strategy, driven in part by internal climate, and certainly by outside attacks (and fear of overwhelming litigation and liability). We do not think this is the behavior customer friendly leaders intended their climate to foster. In fact, the closed nature of internal data sharing about tire deficiencies may have hampered corporate-wide understanding of the failure size and ultimate risk.

Did we forget that leaders make companies customer friendly? At the first public presentations of the case, the Firestone leadership seemed to be "absent without leave." Do we promote AWOL as crisis management behavior in response to customer concerns? Tire recall was slow and inadequate in its initial offering. Ford leaders, after a slow start, understood that they needed go to public, demonstrating their continuing concern for their customers' safety, trust and good will.

Did we forget that product quality is a core value of our company? At Firestone, forgetting this core value could have resulted, literally, in the company's death. Product quality and customer satisfaction are core values and ever present in the company's vision (corporate culture). How will Firestone leaders re-establish product quality in employees' and customers' minds? While some employees will be loyal to the company regardless, many will wonder how their work led to unnecessary crashes and deaths.

Here at Autocoach we believe in, talk about, and act on our commitment to quality. I do not believe that the Firestone Ford case has revealed the presence of evil people, instead, it demonstrated failed company design. Customer friendly leaders must insure that quality is designed in, maintained and supported in the face of failure. A key point of this architecture is that the product system alone does not create a customer friendly experience. Customer friendly is produced by the interactions of product with structure, psychological climate, leadership, and culture. At Autocoach we know this. We just need to remember to act on it, perhaps with the notion that our company depends on it.

~~~~~~~~~~~~

SUMMARY

Many employees say that being customer friendly is beyond their control, meaning actions that they take are controlled by the "organization at large." This chapter focused on how we design the organizational architecture to support the product. Here we talked about cars, but we could use health care, education, banking, hospitality or any other industry.

When American companies first began to talk earnestly with customers in the 1980s, the conversation focused on complaint handling. Listening to complaint after complaint and searching for variances from standards was the norm. Now, customer friendly companies engage employees' active thinking about customer friendliness, challenging employees to diversify their tools and methods for dialogue—including surveys, focus groups, personal contact, and data review.

Customer service is part of the design and offering of products and services and the availability of such. Wal-Mart is successful because it has large stores with thousands of products sold at excellent prices all the time. "Customer service" in this context is thought of as the presentation of quality products at outstanding prices, thereby providing accessibility at diverse socio-economic levels.

Building customer friendliness requires innovation in product design, attention to market needs, ongoing evaluation and redesign of production processes, delivery and support services. Key elements of the architecture include the following:

- markets and marketing analysis (who is being served and who is not)
- product design
- appropriate product portfolio (change of product and service mix)
- production process review
- distribution mapping (customer service and availability evenly distributed)
- support services (allied staff and operations)
- quality management

This chapter has highlighted the architecture of customer friendliness in the product and technology system of the organization. While this "product system" has received much attention, it is only one part of the architecture. The structure of the organization, the level of psychological commitment to customer service, the way in which the organization is led and managed, and the culture of the organization all contribute to customer service improvement. These systems are the subjects of Chapters 4 through 7.

CHAPTER FOUR

THE STRUCTURE OF CUSTOMER FRIENDLY

InterCoast Airline is a 50-year-old national airline based in Nashville, Tennessee. The airline's CEO, Roger is determined to make Intercoast even more customer friendly by focusing on the organization's structure.

~~~~~~~~~~

Uncle: What did your friend Roger say about customer friendliness?

Nephew: Roger is an airline executive who sees everything in terms of frequent flyers. He said, "Incentives are the key. We reward customer friendly employees and punish those who are not."

Uncle: Many executives agree. The structure of the incentives and how they are applied is very important. But this aspect is only a part of the architecture.

~~~~~~~~~~

A story in chapter one revealed that a college bookstore's incentive to control inventory and book return costs sabotaged service to students and faculty. Bookstore managers reduced new semester orders so low that students had too few law books when classes started. The bookstore incentive *structure* impeded student learning and faculty classroom management. We will see in this chapter that airlines also pay attention to incentives and structure as a part of the customer friendly architecture.

Roger is CEO of InterCoast Air, an American airline operating since 1956. InterCoast employs 22,000 people in positions ranging from pilot to flight attendant to maintenance engineer to purchasing manager. Intercoast Airline began as a small feeder line supporting service between Nashville, Atlanta, and Chicago. With careful management and a focus on regional operations, the airline grew, adding coast to coast services in the 1980s. Still headquartered in

Nashville, major operations also are in four other American cities. The airline flies a mix of smaller planes and the popular Boeing 737-200 aircraft, offering more than 900 flights in 40 markets. Its major hubs are Nashville, Atlanta, Chicago, Detroit, and San Francisco. Regular flights offer passengers easy linkages to international flights to Europe and Asia. The airline offers strong recruiting and education programs and is known in the industry as a good place to work. Working for the company for 17 years, Roger had prior experience with an international carrier, and his initial training as a military pilot, to which he added an MBA from Wharton. He assumed the position when the founder retired.

When asked what some of the customer issues were, Roger answered: "Use the US Department of Transportation's categories; they are all issues we are concerned about." What's on that list? Roger replied, "Flight problems such as cancellations and delays, oversales (bumping); reservations, ticketing and boarding; fares, refunds, baggage, service problems such as rude employees and poor cabin service; disability access; advertising, tours and other odds and ends such as smoking, cargo and frequent flyer complaints." Some of these items involve structure.

Structure in organizational architecture is seen and not seen, loose and tight. When structural controls on performance are too tight, innovation and idiosyncratic attention to customer needs die. In the airline business, we think about the structure of schedules, the structure of hub locations, the pricing structure, and so on. When we create the *structure* of a customer friendly company we continue to follow the architect's path.[1] Although we have limited evidence about the link between structure and service, we believe that certain structures enhance "friendliness" and that customer service is a competitive advantage.[2] Managers proceed based on what they "think" will contribute to customer service, making adjustments as they test their experience against their viewpoint (learning). Roger believes, for example, that frequent flights at hub locations offer customer convenience. The structure of the airline is literally determined by this belief.

Roger asked his marketing group to investigate customer views of "quality service." He knew that premium and discount markets were different but was unsure about the specific needs of each. Holding 10 focus groups and conducting 40 personal interviews, the team found airline passengers are most concerned about four aspects of airline travel: on time arrival; safety; costs; and baggage.

At least one comment made it clear; for Gary Leff, it's no contest. Low-fare carriers rarely match the majors on offerings that matter most to him, the 29-year-old finance director says, and he won't be tempted when [Ted] expands flight to his hometown airport, Washington's Dulles. He'll fly Continental to earn flier miles and get business-class upgrades not only for work trips, but for vacations too. "I'm not interested in having fun," he says. "I'm interested in getting where I'm going with the least amount of discomfort."[3]

How do we arrange an organization's parts to increase their contribution to customer service and negate any undercutting? Changing structure is a rearranging of organization parts by attention to the common characteristics of architecture: formality, hierarchy, authority, centralization, complexity, standardization, specialization, and personnel. All of these structural characteristics potentially affect customer service—either positively or negatively.

In all fields, we search for a structure that will encourage and channel our efforts to be customer friendly. The architect's structural intent follows.

Architectural Intent

To create a structure that fosters high quality customer treatment. This means insuring that potential barriers such as formality and specialization do not interfere with seamless, integrated service. Personnel are available and professional and have the authority to improve friendliness (authority is decentralized with minimum complexity in review and control).

Here we are focusing on airlines but this "structure" is present in hospitals, automobile plants, banks, hotels, and universities, as discussed in other chapters. The structural characteristics of a customer friendly architecture include but are not limited to the following: overall design, size and location, formality, complexity, hierarchy and authority, centralization, standardization, personnel complement, specialists, rewards and incentives, and professionalism. Each of these characteristics contributes to a total structure that becomes either customer *friendly* or customer *hostile*, as experienced by two types of airline travelers. As a group, the structural elements help to co—*produce* customer friendly travel.

InterCoast Airline strives to serve *business* and *leisure* travelers. Susan and Mary are partners in a consulting firm, Instrat, an information systems service group. Their business is based mostly on the East Coast, but their needs are important: on time arrival with luggage. They want early morning departures and many Friday flights to insure weekends at home. They would appreciate Jet Blue's leather seats and 24 live satellite TV channels,[4] and United's inflight email.[5] Some day they may even want premium service including private jets.[6] For now, they often use air-hotel-car packages and most important, the airport clubs.

Richard and Lois are less demanding. As leisure travelers they have flexible schedules. They are more concerned with cost and safety, although they too want their luggage to join them. Their plan is to visit as many of America's historic hotels as they can. They took their first flight on their honeymoon 50 years ago and are still thrilled by the excitement of flying, the experience of being in the clouds and the adventure of new places. They miss the airline meals—only for their presence not their quality. Le Petite French Sandwiches do not appeal.

Can a no frills, low fare approach—now quite popular among airlines—serve both groups? Many airlines are trying both directions. Business-oriented Midwest Airlines added low fares for leisure travelers.[7] And Continental has added "Elite for a Day" status to full fare passengers.[8] Only some leisure travelers need flat beds,[9] faster group boarding approaches,[10] in flight cafes,[11] premium wines,[12] and e-tickets.[13] How does the structure support the general and unique needs of each of these travelers?

CUSTOMER FOCUSED STRUCTURE:
A PASSENGER FIRST OVERALL DESIGN

The basic design of organizations is customer focused, or not. If organizing principles are to target customers, what are some of the choices? Several traditional ones include organizing by function, product, geography, or type of customer. Leaders of customer friendly companies feel that "friendliness" increases if the company is structured to focus on distinctions—business versus leisure travel, autos versus trucks, national versus international, young versus old. Customers' needs can be served better by careful, grouped attention structured purposely by leaders and managers.

Airlines organized by *function* create positions, teams, and departments according to their respective specialized activities. Some typical departments are: engineering, scheduling, human resources, and finance. Staff working together build expertise and support each other, eventually enhancing service to the customer.

Most organizations have some degree of structure by *product*. In Roger's airline business, one division is business versus leisure. But in addition to these categories, service can be further divided—domestic air travel versus international and so on. All activities in a product dominated structure are directed toward one type of product, reducing communication between product lines and focusing attention on single product users.

Some companies structure by *geography*—West Coast, North America, international. Airlines have hubs and spokes for concentrated service and domestic and international operations. The intent is to insure that customers in those locations have an easy connection and that the location allows employees to account for local cultural and regional variations. Labor costs and materials may be lower with a geographical focus (shorter or no delivery distances). Marketing staff are based closer to the customer.

Finally, some companies organize service and support by *customer*—frequent business flyers, women and children's medical service, senior citizen services. The concept is that customers' needs are different because of age, usage, product function, and so on. Attention to the customer's characteristics, to the product, and to location enhances service quality and efficiency. Many organizations use some combination of designs.

As CEO of Intercoach, Roger sits on the state university advisory board and has just gone through a reorganization of the entire university system. He knows that some organizations manage their product and service offerings with a combination of structures. During the reorganization, he learned, for example, that Penn State University has 22+ campuses around the state. Some campuses—the law and medical schools—have very specific customers. Some campuses are located close to students who are unable to pay for board and lodging but desire a college education, and some campuses are in the suburbs serving the *adult* professional needs of employed students. His advisory board experience led Roger to review the airline's structural architecture.

Unfortunately, there is not one best way to structure an organization, nor is there a prescription that allows the designers to easily sort out the benefits of competing structures. Roger's review did not produce quick or easy answers, but he learned what some of the issues are:

- duplication of support knowledge such as code sharing and staffing for passenger flow at the hubs;
- specialization of staff support such as call centers—centralized or located at the hubs;
- orientation to overall customer needs, regardless of specific customer types;
- parochialism in attending to only local needs at the hubs, neglecting company-wide objectives;
- isolation of units by geography, by customer, by product; and
- disconnect with objectives of whole organization, e.g. feeder flight groups develop competitive camaraderie undercutting collaboration.

Technological developments can affect traditional structure choices. For one, the internet has allowed airlines scheduling, geographic, and convenience advantages well beyond one-site locations.[14]

SIZE AND LOCATION:
LOCATION, LOCATION, ... AND SIZE

We already have raised location as an architectural issue. Customer friendly companies have a combined structural attribute—size and location. InterCoast Air confronted this issue when they first considered expanding beyond Nashville. Our illustrative travelers, Susan and Mary would prefer expanded routes and locations to support their developing information systems consulting business. Leisure travelers like Richard and Lois may prefer smaller more personalized airlines. Both types of flyers are concerned about the terminals—their size and walking requirements, shopping possibilities, and dining. Like InterCoast, we all have a structural design choice—to have *more* locations, smaller in size, or, to create a *few* larger production and service sites. Both have advantages and disadvantages for customer friendliness. For example, Roger learned in his advisory board role that a large state university system can create a single campus that services 50,000 students. Or, founders and developers can choose to offer "one university geographically distributed." How "distributed" should InterCoast Air be? What are some of the issues for customer friendly leaders like Roger at InterCoast Air?

Economies of scale. By growing in size, customer friendly organizations realize advantages and efficiency of production, distribution, and support. More products are shipped faster to more sites. The growth of WalMart nationwide is a prime example. InterCoast Air found that its customers, like Susan and Mary, were expanding business travel beyond the limited sites available from Nashville. As InterCoast added first Atlanta, then Dallas, they found they were losing their vaunted efficiency. Expanding to a national service system with five hubs allowed them to regain the structural advantages of the original Nashville site. And, like United, they were able to use outsourced staff to support warehouse needs during this period.[15]

Depth and breadth of product coverage. Centralizing location and expanding size allows organizations to expand product offerings and availability in a given site. This is one obvious gain realized by the designers of so called "super stores"—Petsmart, Toys R Us, and Bath and Bodyworks. The full resources of leaders, managers, and employees focus on a concentrated product line so that competitors seem thin by comparison. Why would a customer go to a small department in a general goods department store for toys when Toys R Us will have a full range of all of the latest for kids of all ages. Roger limited the growth of hubs to five but insured frequent flights from those five sites. Other airlines had difficulty competing with the timing and frequency. And, all airlines are struggling to keep up with Internet scheduling systems and the move to more and more late booking.[16]

Support knowledge challenge. Addressing support service is an important issue, one already discussed in Chapter 3. Do we structure the organization in a way that builds bridges between locations, products and customer types or, are there silos blocking interactive communication? Many senior leisure travelers need wheelchair assistance. InterCoast hubs track and exchange data on usage. The recent Firestone tire problem surfaced early in countries such as Venezuela. Tread separation was first noticed in another location, not the primary location of the company's customers. This information was not fully shared in America, enabling a public relations disaster, and more significant—eliminating the opportunity to prevent it.

Roger insured that hub directors met regularly and that he personally linked the hub executives to the company's overall objectives. For example, InterCoast's strategic plan defined lost luggage reductions as a primary objective. This newspaper tale highlights the challenges travelers face when this objective is not met.

"To fully appreciate the annoyance caused by the loss of a checked bag, take a walk in Stacia Zukroff's shoes.

Actually, the shoes in question—black pumps that are half a size too big and don't really match the cheap skirt she hastily purchased in the hotel gift shop—are on loan from a colleague. Zukroff's shoes and the rest of her stuff are in Charlotte, North Carolina, far from the conference in San Diego where she has landed.

Or you could go for a stroll in John Kruk's shoes. They're dressy black loafers getting sopped and muddy as they tramp around the rain forest surrounding Brazil's Iguazu Falls. Meanwhile, the waterproof hiking boots he packed are nestled snugly in his suitcase somewhere in the Miami Airport"[17]

At InterCoast, data reports at first were not shared; each hub monitored its own progress. However, Atlanta seemed to have much lower loss numbers, so Roger insisted teams from Chicago and Nashville visit Atlanta to share knowledge and skills.

Scale of customer support demands. How do customer friendly organizations best structure the support demands? Roger had to address how and where to develop the hubs' support systems. The company first discussed limited individualized support located at each hub—staff to track lost luggage, traveler amenities such as clubs with showers, and equipment for the disabled. But in the end, customer service was centralized at the Nashville headquarters with the major call center located there.

In another field, the explosion of computer sales has made this issue an important and demanding problem. Customers take seriously the offer to receive technical support. But computer companies can log thousands of customer calls per day. Dell offers to pick up defective computers, offering a replacement immediately, often within days. When there are only a few customers, this wonderful service is appreciated. With thousands of customers, the ability to deliver on this intent is truly impressive. InterCoast is aware that some competitors are expanding first class amenities—reclining seats, swivel chairs, tables for dining,[18] while others are focused on "good deals" with last minute ticket purchases[19] and frequent flyer offers.[20]

Location convenience. Structure at its most basic level is location. Customer friendly companies strive to be where customers have easy access. As a Nashville native, Roger knew that airline service could have been better. His predecessor's start up proved that this was correct. With the airline now national in operation, Roger maintains feeder service from smaller communities by working in partnership with a local airline, Shortflite Jets. In a consulting business, frequent flyers Susan and Mary look for seamless transitions between local and longer flights. Companies have long addressed this issue by building close to major highways, by creating banking branch offices, airport stores, and malls that allow "one stop shopping." Internet technology enables us to address convenience in a whole different way—24 hour access no matter where you are located for schedules and ticket purchase. In some ways, this is a modern extension of the Sears Home Catalog delivered by mail to homes decades ago, giving rural customers easy access at their farm location.

Culture—standardization versus individuality. Here is a structural paradox. Customer friendly companies act in two seemingly opposite ways: to treat all customers the same and to treat all customers individually according to their national, regional, and ethnic differences. There is pressure to provide the same high level business class service (that Susan and Mary experience) to leisure travelers Richard and Lois. InterCoast Air has standardized the type of aircraft (colors and washing and repainting schedules), used training to teach staff the "InterCoast Way" of service, and follows detailed manuals for safety procedures. The company also individually plans travel for children and aging adults, reaching out to their special needs. Employees strive to deliver the same level of product quality to all customers regardless of their economic status. As another example, BMW strives to give the same service to entry-level car buyers as they do to their high-end customers. Simultaneously most leaders realize that Europeans may not buy what South Americans want, nor will customers in Phoenix have the same needs and interests as those in Boston. Business travelers on international routes want international newspapers and magazines in the clubs. It is not one or the other but both—*standardization* and *individualization.*

FORMALITY: NO SHOES, NO SHIRT, NO SERVICE

Some frequent international flyers resent the formality of airport check-in security questioning. Is this the point in the travel experience to press for easy going informality? Obviously not. Customer friendly organizations balance *formality* and *informality* in an equilibrium. This means the tight structure of product details, such as hours of operation or location of service can "float," bringing flexibility to the architecture. Roger learned of this personally on a holiday.

During a short vacation, Roger ended up with an important memorandum—renewal of the alliance with Shortlife Jets—that had to be signed and returned immediately. Because Roger received the memo while at the beach, he didn't get it until late in the day. Knowing the local post office was open until 4:30, Roger frantically raced there only to realize it was already quarter till five. Pulling into the parking lot, he noticed a person coming out and was delighted to see the post office still open.

As he ran through the door, he shouted, "Boy am I glad you're still open."

The postman said, "Yes, sir. Take your time, I'm still here."

Roger moved up to the counter and said, "Well I'm glad you're still open. What's going on?"

The postmaster said, "We had a rush around 4:30. I was planning to close, but everybody seemed to want to get their mail in so I just stayed open.

Roger found the post office's structured hours of operation were flexibly adapted to meet customers' needs. Many organizations formalize technical and managerial policies such as airline safety and security demands. To improve customer service, some companies develop rules and policies, e.g. regarding telephone response, guarantees, competent handling. In customer friendly companies, staff see customer service as more important than official policy and procedure.

In large bureaucracies, weeks may pass before staff can even meet to discuss a customer's needs. Meeting informally may be quicker and more effective for problem solving than a two-page memo sent through formal channels. For others, "friendly" means informal access which Roger saw demonstrated at one of the Inter-Coast's expansion sites.

The original hub in Nashville needed some repair and upgrading in line with runway expansion. As the construction manager started renovations and upgrades, Roger heard about adventures with contractors, including delayed schedules and incomplete attention to details. However, the construction manager did have one important customer service success to report. They needed to replace electrical components that had been eaten away by age and obsolescence. While choosing the technical approach and a replacement schedule, the contractor suggested that they call with any questions. He said, "I'm usually in from 9 to 5."

Roger's construction manager was surprised when the contractor added, "And I'll write my home number on the card. You can reach me practically any time evenings or weekends."

~~~~~~~~~~~~~~~~~~

A simple customer service offer—7-day telephone access—was effective in building confidence in the contractor and in providing follow-up service. Roger wondered how many of his staff made that offer to customers of InterCoast Air.

COMPLEXITY: TWELVE CIRCLES OF HELL

When Roger talked to the founder about InterCoast's early days, he was amazed to hear how simple and straightforward the customer friendly challenge was: two planes, three former Air Force pilots, a handful of flight attendants and ground staff—many relatives and friends. Customer friendly was a survival skill; failures were easy to spot. Too many delivery and service breakdowns and the game was over. "Commitment to friendly" was built in as a necessary element of early success. Now, organizations are so *complex* it is hard to find the levers for designing in and improving friendliness. And the complexity means additional costs that are higher than competitor start ups.[21]

Customer friendly companies "manage" complexity by dividing the organization into autonomous pieces, increasing "local" control and enabling more quick and easy changes to address customers' needs. This architectural element derives from the view that the density and complexity of formal bureaucratic processes, particularly in large organizations, undercuts customer service.

In all types of organizations, bureaucratic structure can be a barrier to getting things done. This is seen in educational institutions, industry, and certainly in health care organizations. Physicians moving from small practices to large complex organizations such as hospitals frequently are surprised at the dense policy and procedure system that must be navigated just to serve patients. Part of this density occurs naturally because of size, but customer friendly companies manage complexity, even such troublesome problems as overbooking, by offering incentives and damage control on the spot.

Roger received a letter from one of his frequent flyers who recently had been bumped from a flight.

~~~~~~~~~~~~~~~~~~

Dear CEO:

As one of your most frequent flyers, I generally support your airline. But, not being able to return home last Friday was the last straw. My flight from Dallas transported me to Detroit before what should have been my return to Nashville. Why I was sent through Detroit I am not sure, but the worst part was I was not fully checked onto the flight in Detroit. Because it was overbooked I was denied a seat on the last flight to Nashville; and, as a result, I spent a bad night in a bad hotel and missed my son's soccer game. Do you have some way to correct this very unfriendly experience?

Yours truly
William, a less frequent flyer[22]

~~~~~~~~~~~~~~~~~~

Was this one just experience or representative of many customers' cases? Sometimes a single comment can be powerful in generating follow up action.

Roger had no need to ask why they overbooked. The demands for full planes, scrutiny of per flyer cost, and uneven customer needs kept his operations research staff regularly reworking their mathematical models. InterCoast managers felt William simply was unable to penetrate the problem's complexity, as are many other flyers. "Understanding and acceptance" is not a required customer characteristic—some have it, some do not. They often are further angered by the lack of access to help and the apparent absence of rationality. For a while, return flights to Atlanta from St. Louis went through Philadelphia. Finding yourself in this situation late on a Friday does feel like one of Dante's circles of Hell.

In addition to the passenger's letter, Roger learned that one of the feeder airports had decided to hold to the existing flight levels.

Concerned about airport capacity, they will schedule no more regional flights. Roger and his team now must address passenger demand for more flights in light of "outside the company constraints," over which they have little control. The structure of their scheduling is interconnected to facility design and capacity.

HIERARCHY & AUTHORITY:
YOU MUST SEE THE KING

Customer friendliness demands risk, but authority structures are risk averse and so, easily become barriers. Employees and managers must be able to take quick novel action without consulting the full line of authority. Herb Kelleher at Southwest fought hard against snail-like decision making and bureaucracy in general.[23] A proposal for change might require approvals by various supervisors and department heads, vice presidents and committees and even a micro-managing CEO/king. By then the enthusiasm and change momentum are crushed by the review structure. Strong centralization requires checking with senior managers for permission to test new service ideas. Top managers may agree with the proposed actions, but only after an agonizingly slow review process. Centralized approval requirements add time—sometimes a lot of it—before service improves. Customer friendly companies distribute authority for service responsiveness and improvement down and across organizational levels. The following story is a good illustration of delegating.

Two travelers were returning from Germany on an international flight to Philadelphia. Having traveled by bus for several hours before boarding in Germany, they were very tired upon their arrival in Philadelphia. They had a four-hour layover before yet another flight. James had just received a new exclusive credit card, which he believed would allow him to use the airline club for Worldwide Airways. He rang the buzzer and walked in.

~~~~~~~~~~~~

James: "Hi. My wife and I have just returned from Germany and would like to visit the club for a few hours. I think this credit card allows me in. Is that correct?"

1st Attendant: "No sir, I am sorry but we do not honor that one."

James: "Yes, you are supposed to. I am sure I am right."

1st Attendant: "I could check for you, but I am sure we do not honor that particular card."

James: "Are you absolutely sure? We have been traveling for 16 hours already."

1st Attendant: "Yes, I am sure."

2nd Attendant (at next desk): "How long did you say you were traveling? 16 hours?"

James: "Yes."

2nd Attendant: "Are you a member of the Worldwide Airways Frequent Flyer Group?"

James: "Yes, I am."

2nd Attendant: "Well, why don't you and your wife be our guests for the day. We are glad to have you."

James: "Thank you very much. You've made our day."

James and his wife stayed for three hours, had two cups of coffee, some peanuts, and made two local calls.

~~~~~~~~~~

The cost to the airline is measured in cents; the benefits are measured in many dollars. James told his friends, colleagues, company travel agency, and relatives. He even used the example at the university where he taught and in corporate training. The second attendant had the authority to change standing policy at the point of service. This example graphically illustrates the airline's customer friendliness and it demonstrates that there was no need to "see the king" to seek approval. The formal structure allowed for and encouraged employee discretion. This is part of the psychological climate (see Chapter 5), played out as freedom to make policy adjustments to serve customers (discretionary judgments).

CENTRALIZATION: CONTROL RESTS IN OZ

Centralization is not a barrier in customer friendly companies, but it is in many organizations. Often, executives and senior managers are assumed to be "in the know" about how to increase customer service. But they most often do not know about front-line work issues and usually have limited understanding of how to be "customer friendly" in practice. As business travelers, Susan and Mary want centralized policy regarding late booking, changing flights, and air/

hotel/car packages. But they also want decentralized discretion to help with weather delays and equipment malfunction.

How does centralization as structural architecture affect "friendliness?"

Consider the following practical elements of operations: purchasing, pilot hiring, training, flight scheduling, and company wide planning. Roger addressed this early in his tenure.

Roger, senior executives and top managers, met in a retreat designed to rework InterCoast structure to fit the changing airline business environment. Participants raised these strategic issues: fuel costs, runway shortages, traffic volume, airplane replacement, labor shortages, and governmental regulation. How does InterCoast build customer service in the face of these challenges?

Because of the way InterCoast had grown, many key operations problems were distributed throughout the hubs. Lack of a coordinated response to recruitment, scheduling, and equipment purchase was beginning to hurt, particularly in the hotly competitive environment. The structure that had evolved—decentralization, independent growth—now was viewed as a hindrance to development. Hubs had been allowed significant discretion in scheduling, for example. InterCoast centralized purchasing, pilot recruiting, equipment replacement, and corporate planning to better coordinate development of the functions. The company believed customers are better served—with more flights, lower costs, better equipment—by a more efficient decision making process that organized and coordinated all efforts in these areas.

There are no absolute principles about the balance between centralization and decentralization. In recent years, we have emphasized decentralization by pushing decision-making down management levels and out to distantly located units. But now, information technology allows centrally organized companies to move faster based on more information derived directly from customers (see also Chapter 3). Lost luggage complaints filed by Susan and Mary and Richard and Lois can be circulated immediately to senior managers and front line employees. Thus, Roger centralizes some key activities—purchasing, scheduling—while allowing and encouraging flight crews, ticket agents and hub managers to make individual decisions in support of customers. Some empowered, customer friendly actions are made without central headquarter review. Admission to an airline club is one small example. Freedom to act flexibly is a characteristic of the psychological climate (see chapter 5), which illustrates customer friendliness in action.

STANDARDIZED: NO TWO PRODUCTS ALIKE?

Treating all customers the same is a common slogan, but standardization is a barrier to service improvement when it implies that there is "one best way." Standardization often creates mediocrity, lack of innovation, and just plain boring work. By loosening the grip of standardization, the organization sanctions creative thinking in research and development, production, delivery and support. The issue is two sided.

The customer friendly company's architecture is designed to offer quality products, delivered and supported. Variation—a deviation from quality standards—is intended to be unusual. So, what are we standardizing? These are some of InterCoast's standardization targets:

- Core products, e.g. a safe flight with on-time arrival and easy access to baggage;
- Ticket purchase and refund policies;
- Maintenance requirements;
- Production processes e.g. resulting in quality aircraft, functional information and scheduling systems;
- Delivery times, e.g. access to frequent flights and meeting of planned schedules, weather policies;
- Support experiences, e.g. security checks, rebooking of cancelled flights; and
- Interpersonal perceptions, e.g. friendly behavior from flight crews.

With the list, Roger is sure that his passengers are better served by a company-wide approach. But customer friendly organizations do not standardize services when needs and buyer characteristics are unique for many. In the airline business, as in other industries, we preserve distinctions. Specifically, we do not *standardize* but instead *individualize*, premium treatment for first class and business travelers from check-in to food service to seating space. We expect and reject standardized products and services. It is this paradox that customer friendly leaders must carefully manage. Think about the InterCoast Airline case.

At InterCoast, Roger was interested in the total quality management movement that swept through American business in the 1990s. He knew productivity gains could be made by paying careful attention to production and delivery processes. He announced standardizing to best practices in the industry as a goal of his three-year plan. In preparation for a planning retreat to assess progress, he reviewed key areas of attention in the last period. Assigning the review preparation to the quality manager, he first received a list of the targets, a mixed batch of administrative and technical issues which included: arrival and departure procedures, baggage handling, airplane turn-around procedures (for next flight), security checks, pilot takeoff preparation, new-hire training and orientation, complaint processes, perceptions of food service, ticket handling, and passenger flow in the terminals. InterCoast performance was to be benchmarked against their strongest competitors and against the industry's best. Roger's belief was that by standardizing the airline's approach to these processes, customers would be better served. An experienced and trained improvement team carefully analyzed each process. By thinking differently about the numbers, the team reconsidered what is meant by 80 percent of customers are satisfied. This means that 20 percent are not—a large number of travelers in a busy airline. At the end, Roger felt that more customers experienced the same level of high quality service (supported by the standardization) affecting customer expectations and their actual experience with the airline.

PERSONNEL COMPLEMENT:
ENOUGH PEOPLE FOR THE JOB

We all address periods of under staffing—in schools, hospitals, factories, and fast food restaurants. Roger complained about not enough pilots and too few flight crews to meet his expansion needs. The staffing structure of customer friendly companies seems just right—"not too thick and not too thin," as the saying goes. Consider the potential fallout of four scenarios listed below. One of Roger's friends, an insurance executive said the following points were made when decreases in customer service staff were proposed.

The Case Against Under Staffing........ Proposing reductions in customer service staffling levels means:

- customers will be left on hold longer or will wait longer for responses
- The number of customers on "terminal hold" will increase
- Existing staff can assume more duties and responsibilities but only for a short period (turnover increases and motivation sinks with long periods)
- using technology to replace human beings is cost effective in the short run but ultimately deadly as customers cannot talk in person and feel shabbily treated.
- Quality standard for telephone responses should be established and used to benchmark across industries and against each company's own performance?[24]

~~~~~~~~~~

Customer friendly companies employ the right number of people—experiencing only occasional shortfalls. Reduced travel after the September 11 attacks led to layoffs and labor renegotiations. Several results included longer hours and lower pay. Longer hours at reduced pay does not increase friendliness! Keeping appropriate staffing levels pleases employees, who in turn please customers.

Staffing structure is an obvious need, but it is complex to manage. How wrong can we get this balance? For Roger, the issue is current and important. Expanding passenger demand has led the team to propose more flights, but they must then recruit more pilots and crews. As the labor pool gets thinner, how do they trade off on the number of staff needed versus the quality of personnel normally hired? Hiring more pilots with the flexibility to fly different types of planes is one solution, but it brings up the specialist problem.

SPECIALISTS: WE SERVE ONLY CUSTOMER PARTS

In large organizations, we use "specialists" to improve service. Roger's pilots and maintenance crews are experts on certain airliners but not others. The expertise increases safety and boosts efficiencies from turnaround times to maintenance. But the targeted work assignments and frequent isolation inherent in a specialist structure undercuts the customer friendliness of the whole experience. Pilots flying only coast to coast are unaware of the service issues and working conflicts of pilots flying feeder routes. Many organizations combat these differences with education and training. At United, customer service representatives receive extensive training with short modules online and instructor-led.[25]

Modern, high technology products and services demand specialists that are organized in their own departments and units, e.g. computer systems, finance, aircraft maintenance, engineering, and marketing. Customer friendliness is based on mutual interdependence which can be hampered by "turf wars." In hospitals, for example, physicians must plan and solve problems with managers and nurses to achieve the friendly experience patients expect. At InterCoast, pilots from feeder and long haul routes meet as a team to discuss schedule coordination and service quality. And pilots, stewards, and maintenance experts communicate with management and other specialists at all levels in the hierarchy. In customer friendly companies, serving customers well is not restricted to a narrow definition of the specialty—or to the response "that's not my job."[26]

Roger developed a training program that allowed flight crews to move to any of the two types of aircraft at InterCoast. They were trained to know the differing requirements of cabin service and arrival, departure procedures on feeder routes and longer flights in larger jet aircraft. Roger then faced the question of domestic versus international experiences of pilots and crews. If he expanded rapidly—international routes would be new—he had to ensure that the new employees' specializations did not hinder building a team that for now focused on domestic services. While this may not work easily for pilots because of flying differences and certification requirements, the crews move beyond the barrier that present and prior specialization can present.

REWARDS AND INCENTIVES:
THANKS IN WORDS AND CASH

As their flight was about to land in Atlanta, Richard got dizzy and seemed to be having a heart attack. Although unclear what the problem was, the stewards quickly moved to help Richard and Lois. They informed the pilots and had an ambulance waiting on arrival. The quick action may have saved his life. The staff received official letters of commendation and public recognition at the next all-company meeting.

Customer friendly leaders use a structural architecture of rewards and incentives to create a culture that fosters service. Southwest Airlines is one clear example. It is not performance incentives alone, but a combination of leadership and culture that produces high performance service to the customer.[27] Sometimes, the incentives are not aligned properly. Roger found the call center reps were monitored by the length of their calls not the number of solutions.

Seven incentive issues are addressed by customer friendly architects in the next illustration, an interview with CEO Roger.

~~~~~~~~~~~~~~~

Aviation Magazine Reporter (AR): "Roger, as the leader of a company well known for its service, how do you use rewards and incentives at InterCoast Air?"

Roger: "First *I identify what behaviors are to be rewarded.*" In customer friendly organizations, staff know what is desired. The expectations are defined during the hiring process, taught during the orientation and training, "mentored in" by senior people and rewarded at first sight. Pilots help to select and train new pilots and flight crews. To insure the customer friendliness of their work they recognize, identify and teach the style and content of pilot-attendant-passenger interaction.

AR: What is your role?

Roger: "I *model and teach the desired behaviors.* Leaders, managers and senior technical staff are expected to model customer contact and support. The hub managers, and pilot leaders, just like medical school deans, chief executives of other businesses, and principals in customer friendly schools interact with patients, with buyers, with students. They offer edicts about the need to interact, but are most effective when they demonstrate how, modeling the principle and the practice. New pilots and flight crews watch how the senior pilots interact with passengers—how they greet families and they handle the stress of waiting time and delays. I have visited with passengers in the arrival and departure lounges.

AR: Do you differentiate among employees?

Roger: *I use different rewards for different employees.*" In companies with a reward system for customer friendliness, the design offers differential benefits according to the staff type and employee level. In the airline business, the reward structure might include a bonus for on-time arrivals and departures, demonstrating quality service. A senior pilot with a string of flight successes and highly demanding hours might want a day or a weekend off in place of a bonus. Some airlines like United use cash.[27]

AR: Do you recognize customer friendly contributions?

Roger: *The response to demonstrated customer friendliness is a measured one."* We don't offer extravagant trips for simply returning customer calls, but a successful two-year installation of a new ticketing system in a challenging customer environment is worthy of a trip. A hub manager with many pilots and flight crews successfully installed updated electronic records, including laptop computers for all pilots and crews. The 14-month project was demanding, calling for more than a simple thank you.

AR: How do you treat "customer hostile" employees?

Roger: *"I give feedback about wrong behaviors."* At Inter-Coast, managers pay attention to employees' rightful and wrongful behaviors. When customer friendliness is undercut by individuals or teams, the communication is direct and specific. A check-in receptionist once called across a crowded waiting room to inform a passenger that her credit card was expired. The passenger became embarrassed, and when the card was found to be good after all, she switched airlines for her next flight. The supervising manager happened to overhear, quickly reprimanding and teaching an alternative approach.

AR: How public is your feedback?

Roger: *"I deliver punishment in private."* Customer friendly architecture can and does include punishment for undercutting the friendliness intent. But the punishment is privately delivered, allowing the employee to save face and to learn, a developmental intent not a policing one. The check-in clerk was not talked to at her desk but was called into a private office. Surprising as this basic style point is, the error is often made by customer unfriendly leaders.

AR: How do you measure progress?

Roger: *"I review the costs of poor service including omissions and non-actions."* Some years ago Phillip Crosby championed measuring the cost of poor quality.[28] Poor quality and quality improvement gains have a financial impact. Customer friendly companies take time to measure the sometimes devastating effect of service—in lost repeat business, lost referrals, and widely circulated complaints.[29] The measurement process requires some resources but the impact of visible dollar losses is an invaluable tool and a key architecture component. This component ties neatly to the customer feedback information system discussed in Chapter 3. For customers, perception matters.[30, 31]

AR: What rewards do you give out?

Roger: "I use time off, flexible benefits, and gain sharing to reward employees." At a busy hub some years ago, we found that staff wanted not just bonus money, but thank you and recognition letters and an employee day at an amusement park. Inexpensive items to provide, they were troublesome in their absence. In one flight group, the pilots host an elaborate dinner for their most regular flight crews, spouses included. The dinner is somewhat expensive but the pilots feel it is essential for team building and gain sharing.

~~~~~~~~~~~~

InterCoast's incentives structure leads to higher motivation, increased productivity, and flexibility in addressing customer demands and needs. These outcomes are necessary conditions of quality service.

PROFESIONALISM:
STARCHED UNIFORM, SHOULDERS BACK

Everybody in the customer friendly organization is expected to act as a professional—to be involved in the work and to take responsibility for customer service. In some cases, this emphasis seems missing. A strike by check-in staff at British Airways left 80,000 passengers stranded while senior managers delayed action to help them. InterCoast Air is a typical example. Here, repeated patterns of behavior and reinforced cultural values are so embedded in the workforce that they are "structural" in nature ("designed-in" architecture).

Companies establish a professionalism of friendliness based on five structural elements:

- An internally-developed "body of knowledge" about how to best serve customers;
- Authority to act in the customers' best interest, based on service knowledge;
- Approval by leaders up and down the organization;
- An internal/external based "code of ethics" defining how customers are dealt with; and
- A culture of friendliness established by structure and by the other architectural elements—product, psychological climate, and leadership.

How do these become structure? By repeated public and private declarations and behaviors over many years. For example, Continental Airlines has a principles statement published on their web site outlining service values and expectations.[32]

The results of a breakdown are easy to see. At a meeting of airline executives Roger's group discussed the flight crew's reaction during the Malayasian airplane accident. The pilots apparently moved to the wrong runway for takeoff and hit a construction barrier or vehicle that broke the plane apart. With flames everywhere, passengers looked to the flight crew for help only to find they had quickly exited the plane leaving the passengers to fend for themselves.[33] This was a disappointing breakdown in professionalism.

Fortunately, neither Roger nor his colleagues knew of many instances like this. The following story is more in line with their experience.

Roger's sister, her husband, and their three children had recorded their month-long European vacation on video. On the flight home, the middle child added their departure from London and arrival in New York to the cassette. Unfortunately, she left the camera on the plane seat as they exited. No one noticed until they reached their connecting flight in another terminal. Disappointed, Roger's sister asked the check-in attendant for help. He quickly called back to the arrival gate, then reported, "They have the camera. One of the flight attendants is on her way home and will bring the camera right over. We can hold the flight for a few minutes."

A small thing perhaps, and certainly not a life saving one, but here was professionalism in action.

SYSTEM INTERACTIONS:
CONNECTEDNESS OF STRUCTURES

Airline leaders and managers were buzzing about the new competition fostered by low-cost airlines. Large carriers were beginning to react. More than one executive cited the following letter as an indicator of the challenge.

Letter [to airlines]

"United Airlines can call its new airline Ted or Fast or even Free. It likely will be out of business within a year if the carrier, like the others, does not finally change a corporate culture that penalizes people who fly coach ("United would like to introduce fliers to Ted,"

Money, November 13). Southwest has been showing competitors the right way for nearly 30 years. If United, Northwest, American, and Delta want to continue to lose market share to the so-called discount airlines, for starters, they can continue to:

- charge all travelers outragious fares, especially if they cannot stay over Saturday night;
- if travelers want to fly back the same day or need to fly in a hurry, penalize them $100 every time they change plans;
- Make it as difficult as possible for fliers to use frequent flier miles;
- Keep passengers on hold as long as possible when they call to talk to a customer service representative;
- Be sure the airline's website is cumbersome and slow so travelers have to jump through hoops to find the information they need;
- Serve bad food and charge for it;
- Assign fliers a seat, but be sure the computer also assigns it to someone else.

Post 9/11 travel concerns no longer can be an excuse for what amounts to bad customer service. As a loyal Southwest traveler who flies weekly, I am made to feel welcome—and I'm charged a reasonable and sometimes even ridiculously low fare. I don't have to suffer bad food or fight for a seat, and my questions are answered. More importantly to me, when the weather is good, my flight is on time. Will the other guys ever wise up? As things stand, a more suitable name for United's proposed airline should be "Doubtful." David K.[34]

Roger was delighted that because of InterCoast Air's customer friendly reputation, he was invited to speak at the national meeting of the popular Wright Brothers Aviation Society. Here is the text of Roger's presentation.

"The Meaning of Customer Friendly in the Airline Business"
I am pleased to be here to talk about a topic of great and frequent interest at InterCoast Air. Of course, like you, we believe in serving the passenger first and foremost. We think we have gone beyond this familiar slogan to understand how we become passenger

friendly and stay that way. Organizational learning is a hot topic so I will not bore you with another pitch about what many feel is a fad. At InterCoast Air, we have made a concerted effort to educate ourselves about the underlying architecture and the resulting behaviors of our company and employees.

This morning's speaker discussed the critical contribution of structure to the airline business. We have heard about the importance of a passenger focus, how size and location are important underpinnings of our ability to provide access and range of flight services. We also were reminded that many airlines are using modern information technology to gain customer benefits by centralizing scheduling and purchasing. And few have missed the role played by the formality and complexity of the business (from routes to regulation).

Recently, in a tight labor market, we find that expansion is restrained by a personnel shortage. We need more pilots, flight crews, and technology analysts to sustain our growth and meet increasing customer demands. In fact, a great challenge for us now is to maintain our high degree of professionalism in the face of exceedingly busy work weeks.

Before we talk more about structure, I would like to tell you about our concept of the customer focused company. At InterCoast Air, we believe that customer friendliness is a result of five architectural elements working in unison to serve the passenger. First, we believe that our product must reflect the market needs, and must be designed, produced, delivered, and supported at the highest quality level. In the airline business, a low quality product will be unreliable, unsafe, and absolutely unsuitable to our customers. We start here.

Second, we believe our corporate culture at InterCoast contributes significantly to customer friendliness. We share a common understanding that the customer is the reason we are in business. We talk about this in meetings, have it in our formal plans, and recognize employees for their commitment to the customer.

Third, we believe that good products do not happen without a strong psychological climate that encourages individual initiative and innovation. The quality of our shared working life is high. We work hard to collaborate, believing that company success (and customer friendliness) is a team effort.

Fourth, without leadership, any effort to be customer friendly is doomed. We expect all senior executives and managers to talk customer friendly, act customer friendly, and reward their people for being customer friendly.

We see these four elements plus structure as the root of our passenger friendly company. Conceptually simple but elegant, I think you'll find that the true breadth and depth of the company is covered. Now, keep in mind that structure works in tandem with these other architectural elements.

How does the modern airline company continue to use structure to maintain and improve our customer friendliness?

We have talked about the linkage between rewards and leadership at InterCoast Air. There is other interaction among the major architectural systems, elements such as product quality and psychological climate. In customer-friendly companies like InterCoast, these interactions are expected to produce friendliness by encouraging collaboration. The coordinated action of managers and professional and support staff is the root of our friendliness. Let me give you examples, focusing on our view of rewards and their interactive contribution with the other elements.

- The reward system's "structure" determines how well the products are supported, organization-wide. Thus, the product system—marketing, design, production, delivery, and support of passenger flight—depends on the tangible and intangible reward system for success. Careful maintenance and safety procedures are recognized and rewarded. When we reward innovative product design and great support in the field, passengers benefit through on-time arrivals, dependable baggage delivery, and greater cabin comfort.
- Rewards interact with employee psychological climate, helping to build teams and empower staff. We do this with the belief that more satisfied employees, working together, produce the most customer friendly actions. To be customer friendly, employees must exhibit motivation, positive attitudes, collaboration and other psychological attributes. The structure of any company including InterCoast Air— with its size, complexity, and formality of policies and procedures—can reinforce or undercut this psychological climate.
- Rewards require leaders and managers to support employee autonomy and discretion to meet customer needs. Man-

agement is responsible for the reward structure design and implementation. Leaders must first recognize the importance of tangible and intangible rewards. We offer a public and private thank you to ticket agents who have gone beyond the call of duty during a snowstorm with all of its delay headaches. Managers' support and use of the structure to recognize and reward customer friendliness is a critical aspect of InterCoast's architecture.

- Rewards reflect the base nature of the company. They certainly do here at InterCoast Air. And, they cannot stand alone absent this connection to the company's founders, its mission, and its most important values. We hear that others in the industry reward customer friendliness only "momentarily"—with one-time bonuses and raises.
- At InterCoast Air, our culture demands that we continually announce and promote our shared belief in passenger service as a foundation principle of the company's architecture. This friendliness principle binds employees and staff to our company just as others are equally committed to a hospital or a college.

I hope these examples show you that we think friendliness is created in a multi-dimensional way, at once simple but also complex.

What we do in the airline business to be customer friendly is transferable to other industries. And it is equally relevant in both the public and private sectors. The outward manifestation of customer friendly is the tip of the iceberg, with supporting architecture just below the line of sight.

SUMMARY

In this chapter, the InterCoast Air case illustrates that the organization's structure contributes to customer friendliness. The internal arrangement of organizational elements can either enhance or undercut service. Service problems are generated in some cases by too much structure, and in other cases, by too little. The "correct design" for customer friendliness allows "space" for informality, decentralization, and careful, judicious bypassing of authority hierarchies.

This chapter identified architectural elements of a customer-friendly organization's structure: Design, Size and Location,

Formality, Complexity, Authority and Hierarchy, Centralization, Standardization, Personnel, Specialization, Rewards and Incentives, Professionalism, and their interactions. Here the organization was an airline, a business that continues to attack customer service issues in many ways.[35-39]

Concerted action will enable leaders to create a structure that enhances or supports customer service. These are design questions to be confronted by *each* organization *individually*.

Product and organizational structure efforts to improve customer friendliness are architectural necessities, but they are not sufficient for success organization-wide. The organization's psychological climate must be considered as well, the subject of Chapter Five.

CHAPTER 5

THE PSYCHOLOGY OF CUSTOMER FRIENDLY, THE CASE OF THE ROYAL COURT HOTEL

In this chapter, we consider the contributions of individual and group psychology.

> Nephew: What about the registration clerk's attitude? Every time I stay at a hotel I seem to have a surly one.
> Uncle Arthur: What did your friend Sarah say?
> Nephew: Sarah is a hotel manager. She said "customer service is all about attitude and personality. That is the whole of it." She even has a Guest Friendly Program.
> Uncle Arthur: She's right, at least partly—the psychological climate exists just like the rooms, the restaurant and the written bills.

All organizations must convince potential customers of their product's quality. They must satisfy existing customers, correcting service failures quickly and effectively. And, they must convince customers to tell others about their positive experiences. Pre-purchase and post-purchase decision making and judgments are key.[1] Customer-friendly companies rely on the psychology of the workplace—people and their relations—to provide high quality service. Customer-friendly leaders believe the organization is a human social system composed of people with their individual characteristics and their relationships. Service is intangible, rendered in visible and invisible ways.[2] Hotel executives are particularly concerned about this psychological climate.

THE ROYAL COURT

Sarah is managing director of the Royal Court Hotel on the Gulf Coast of Florida. Opened in 1918, the hotel is on the register of historic places. The exterior facade is stucco with a Spanish/European decor throughout the public and private rooms. The main hotel has 310 rooms and 30 suites; a garden terrace addition built in 1956 has another 100 rooms. The hotel/resort complex is on the beach with two pools, six clay and hard court tennis courts, valet parking, golf shuttle, beach, fitness center and spa, and children's activities. The spa is rapidly gaining a reputation as a destination. where adult guests are pampered and their kids are thought of as well. Although many hotels are now allowing pets,[3-5] the Royal Court has no plans to do so. There are 18 meeting and boardrooms, including a ballroom with beach views. The hotel was renovated in 1992, maintaining the exterior and basic design but upgrading bath and conference facilities, with special attention to the addition of executive education and conference amenities. The hotel is part of an international 430-hotel chain that offers full service, select services and some extended stay facilities. Although other hotels offer casinos,[6] the Royal Court cannot.

Sarah has been managing director of the Royal Court for six years. She was trained in hotel management at the state university and studied for her MBA while working in hotel management training positions in New York and Miami. She first worked in San Diego, moving to Florida's Royal Court in 1994. Devoted to customer service she is known as a strategic manager with a real people sense. Her values are represented by what she shortens to S–3 meaning service, safety and security.

Like many other hotels in the chain, the Royal Court has two restaurants, one for fine dining, the other more casual. Both serve breakfast, lunch and dinner and have recently started a "grab and go" continental breakfast for departing guests and those spending days out.[6] The facility includes a cocktail lounge, laundry valet, concierge services, gift shop and a full business center with secretarial services. The beachfront pool staff offer full sports services from sailing to snorkeling to use of the 60 cabanas. The state of the art gym has long open hours.[7]

Guest rooms are modern with work desk and lamp, voice mail, telephone lines with data ports, high speed Internet access and cable and satellite TV. Every aspect of the room is examined for quality, from the bed comfort to office equipment to bathroom toiletries. Trends aside, there is no interest in adding self service anything.[8] Executive floors offer 24-hour butler service. Full business conference rooms hold 300-500 people with state of the art audio-video technology.

Frontline staff must correct service failures, otherwise customers search for means of retribution. At one of the executive education conference sessions, Sarah caught a few minutes of an insurance association presentation. She heard a message she absolutely agreed with. Dale L. Kurtz, director of group dental products for Sun Life of Canada in Wellesley, Mass., told insurance company officials that the key ingredient for improving customer perceptions of service is a caring attitude. Mr. Kurtz said, "Good service isn't magic or complex. It's doing the basics consistently, responsively, with a caring attitude." His statement is a good fit with Sarah's hotel management philosophy. The critical key to customer friendly is the attitude, apparent in a hotel when you meet the check-in clerk, when you call for room service, when you are checking out. Every organization has a psychological component of the architecture sometimes described in the following terms. "Climate is not an amorphous term. It refers to six key factors that influence an organization's working environment: its flexibility—how free employees feel to innovate unencumbered by red tape [empowered]; their sense of responsibility to the organization [commitment]; the level of standards that people set [expectations]; the sense of accuracy about performance feedback and aptness of rewards [structure] the clarity people have about mission and values [culture]; and finally, the level of commitment to a common purpose [dedication].[9] If climate is psychological and affects service, we can draw on behavioral science for improvement and maintenance.[10, 11]

Staff from housekeepers to registration clerks help to build the climate including the structural aspects discussed in the last chapter. Climate is surely connected to the core values of the culture discussed in Chapter 7 ("friendliness first and always"). The psychological climate can be "customer friendly or customer hostile" and underscores the important linkage of employee and working environment. As managing director, Sarah pays attention to the development and maintenance of this climate emphasizing comfort, fun and quality. We recall from the other chapters that customer friendly companies are co-produced by five systems: product, structure, psychological climate, leadership and culture. The customer friendly architect's intention in designing this climate is as follows.

Architectural Intent—Psychological Climate. Customer friendliness occurs when a consistent pattern of service support behaviors exists throughout the organization; when motivation to provide service is extraordinary; when we expect the customer to be served throughout the experience; when all customers are treated with respect; when groups collaborate to foster service; and when service leadership is a hallmark of the climate.

Psychological climate does not stand alone, separate from product, structure, leadership, and culture. But aspects of the psychological climate do stand out, as if in relief against the organization's background as a whole. For Sarah at the Royal Court, part of the climate is privacy, safety and feelings of security for the guests.

Sarah thought of herself as a designer of the hotel in an organization sense. She had heard of an approach to design by R.L. Ackoff Professor Emeritus of the Wharton School of the University of Pennsylvania.[12] In design exercises, employees and customer groups specify the characteristics of their desired organization. Sarah assembled a group that produced the following scenano. "We want a hotel with: reservations easily and permanently made; fast check in; room comfort including beds, bathroom, amenities and equipment; privacy and security; helpful recommendations; prompt and high quality room service; friendly staff; easy check out; and fair prices." In total, they went a long way toward defining customer friendly with regard to the core hotel product. But what about the psychological aspects?

The following elements constitute the psychology of service architecture, each one attended to by customer friendly leaders like Sarah. Together these "climate builders" produce the psychology of the Royal Court: Attitudes, Motivation, Norms and Expectations, Perceptions, Behaviors, Status, Group Dynamics, Leadership, Communication, Relationships, Trust, Empowerment, Commitment, Stress and Burnout. Leaders building customer friendly companies use their core resource—people—to build and maintain this climate. The psychology of individual and group relationships helps to produce and support the products and service. Leaders balance the individual and group contributors to the climate . Although both are critical, in complex organizations groups and teams ultimately carry more weight. Let's look at some of the characteristics individually and connect them to Sarah's Royal Court Hotel.

ATTITUDES—THE CUSTOMER IS LOVED

Employee attitudes are the "front line representation" of customer friendly architecture. We have already considered the part that structural aspects play—hiring, training, adequacy of staff and so on. Here the concern is for the psychological disposition toward the customer. How employees greet and respond to requests, and solve product or service failures (e.g., wake up calls not made, late breakfast delivery) is prime evidence of the true degree of friendliness. How helpful was the staff the last time you arrived at the hotel without a record of your reservation? Or, what was the attitude when you called to say there was no hot water? Some employees learn how to relate to guests on the job, taking up an understanding of the desired attitudes set; others bring it with them when hired. We do have laggards in many of our businesses who fail to see the potential impact of poor service. Consider this letter to Dear Annie in *Fortune* that makes the point for Sarah.

The Case of the Surly Staff
  Dear Annie: I'm in charge of customer service at an e-commerce company. Most of my staff is young and inexperienced. I'm trying to persuade them that it's important to be prompt, courteous and respectful of customers, but I'm not getting through. Do you know of any proof that politeness and responsiveness can actually increase sales, or am I dreaming? Boss Lady

  Dear Boss: I'm glad you asked. Last summer an etiquette-consulting company called Eticon, based in Columbia, S.C., surveyed 1,281 people across the US and found that 80 percent think rudeness in business has been increasing. Biggest beef—telephone rudeness, including "abrupt tone of voice and impolite language" (83%); "indifference or inattentiveness" to customers (39%); "long waits" for service (34%); and "long abrupt holds" (27%). Asked what behavior they appreciate most, respondents said "friendly, quick greeting" (60%), "helpful even if it isn't your job" (39%); and "appreciation of customer" (38%). Now, this is where it gets really interesting. When asked how they reacted to bad manners or lousy attitudes, 58% replied that they "take business elsewhere, even if [the competitor] is out of my way or charges higher prices." So here's an idea. Get your surly staff together and write your company's current revenues on a big blackboard. Then subtract 58%, and explain that this lower number is where you may be headed. If they don't see the light, maybe they're in the wrong line of work. That's fixable.[13]

  Sarah's hotel would not be full if served by surly staff unwilling to "lovingly" address guest's needs and complaints. We have long known no exact link exits between attitudes and behaviors— just because staff say they like customers does not always mean that they will act in customer friendly ways. But the "probability of friendliness" rises as more positive attitudes toward customers become entrenched in the company and are recognized as a part of the shared culture (see Chapter 7). Customer friendly leaders work hard to establish this desired attitude from check-in to dining.[13] How does this come about in Sarah's hotel? In customer friendly companies it is "in the water"—the psychological climate that surrounds leaders and staff in their day-to-day work life.

MOTIVATION—SERVE OR DIE

Most of us have a story to tell about an employee who went beyond minimal, past adequate, to simply outstanding service. This story circulates among hotel executives in Royal Court's international chain.

THE CASE OF THE HOTEL LAUNDRY

Every crisis is an opportunity for a hotel to shine if employees are skilled and motivated enough to rise to the occasion. At Las Brisas in Acapulco the tale is still told about the concierge who received a call from a guest because the hotel laundry had closed. Taking matters into his own hands, the concierge brought the laundry home, washed and pressed it, and returned it to the guest the next morning—all without telling management.[15]

This story tells much about the employee—his willingness to problem solve and his sense of discretion to make the decision without consulting management. It tells of his loyalty and commitment to the hotel and his desire to service guests absolutely. Sarah would like all staff to be this committed. She sets high goals but is clear about them and they are set with employee participation.

Customer friendly executives recognize motivation publicly and privately. Service friendly companies use several techniques simultaneously to generate customer service quality and continuous improvement. Rewards, additional benefits, and/or access to capital can be based on service quality (structural design discussion of Chapter 4). Constant feedback is recognized as a critical ingredient (for individuals and for teams).

The laundry story led Sarah to reflect on how she motivates hotel staff, a problem she discussed with her husband, a civil engineer with a small consulting company. He said that at a board meeting about six months ago the eight partners discussed the firm's status.

They felt that the staff had done a particularly good job of supporting them in computer aided drafting, scheduling, client contacts and billing. They agreed to reward the staff with lunch at an exclusive hotel (one of Sarah's competitors). The luncheon ceremony included bonus checks and a speaker who talked about the management of high quality partnerships. All staff were given the time off to attend the lunch. This was difficult to arrange, but the staff looked forward to it and enjoyed it immensely. They received recognition from the engineers for a job well done. This small but significant symbol builds and reinforces motivation, one element of the psychological architecture. The engineers demonstrated attention to performance, to the staff's interest in continuous improvement, to "connectedness" to the group and to pay and bonuses—all key motivational components. Sarah used the story to think about how to further motivate employees at the Royal Court. She passed this memorandum on to her regional director as a progress note.

From: Royal Court Hotel Managing Director
To: Regional Directors, Worldwide Hotel Operations

Over the past six months we have received a series of complaints about our services, from check-in to room service delivery. I have redoubled efforts to motivate the staff by taking six actions: (1) instituting a formal guest survey form, linking the data to pay; (2) initiating quarterly bonuses for improved guest satisfaction results; (3) announcing an immediate dismissal policy for unexcused absence, theft or drinking on the job; (4) scheduling weekly team meetings for each work group; (5) establishing a "quarterly review of progress" meeting; and (6) setting the date for a year-end holiday party to thank employees for their efforts. These were all presented in "my state of the hotel" speech that expressed to the managers and staff my interest in drastically improving customer service. I will keep you informed of the outcome. Sarah's action to increase motivation focused on group belonging, clear expectations for behavior, and the intention to grow as a team.

NORMS—GREAT EXPECTATIONS

Customer friendly companies establish public norms and expectations for service, signaling that high customer service is *expected*.

The expectations are sometimes detailed. For example Marriott has a 66 item checklist for how to make up a room. Marriott last year began rolling out a system called "At Your Service" that records a guest's every little desire. If you want a foam pillow or are irked by street noise, the computer remembers for your next stay at that hotel—and soon, anywhere in the chain. At Marriott's new 358 room hotel overlooking Elliott Bay in Seattle, manager Daniel Banchiu has trained bartenders to quiz guests about their stays and then to enter particular cravings, like runnier room service eggs, into the computer."[15]

Marriott's service value is embedded in the psychological climate and the company's culture. By design, this shared expectation is directed at employees' individual behaviors and at their collective work groups. The architectural structure of rewards incorporates service in the job performance standards (see structure, Chapter Four). Here it is not just the tangible rewards but the psychological climate that is the design target for Sarah and other executives. The psychology of service leads us to great and sometimes silly heights. Guests rightly complain about security (a critical issue) and want radio alarm clocks that work. Sarah read about this example, hoping her staff would not have to go to such lengths. A hotel's moment of truth occurs whenever a temperamental celebrity checks in. Little Dix Bay's came in the person of supermodel Naomi Campbell. "She called at midnight to say she absolutely had to have pure coconut butter for her face," recalls general manager Pete Shaindlin. Unfortunately, there was none on the island. "But you're never suppose to say no. So we called around and found a woman on Tortola who makes it. At 2:00 A.M., an employee boated to Tortola, got the butter, and delivered it to Ms. Campbell by 3:00 A.M.[16] How do we get managers and employees with this level of devotion to service? At the Royal Court Hotel, the senior director for human resources believes that customer service expectations are set by multiple communications. Service is a key topic in employee *selection interviews*. It is a topic at the hotel's employment *orientation*, is introduced on a regular basis in *staff and team meetings*, and is part of the *performance system* through quarterly, semi-annual and annual reviews. Sarah believes that this multiple presentation promotes and reinforces expectations throughout the network of individual and people relationships, the architectural psychology of the organization.

PERCEPTIONS—I TRULY SEE

Customer friendly leaders pay attention to the substance of the service and to employees' and customers' perceptions. At the opening of this chapter, Uncle Arthur "perceives" that clerks are surly but we do not know that that is actually the case. We do see that there is emotion in Uncle's response. The sense that customer service is provided is nearly as important as the actual service behavior and it differs by market. How is perception addressed? How do leaders like Sarah assure that employees and customers perceive the friendliness in the environment, interpreting the staff's communications and actions as intended? Are some actions and employee groups more important than others?[17]

"Friendliness" shows up in three ways: (1) through *consensus*—agreed upon ways of relating to and helping customers. Guests at the Royal Court are always greeted in the hallways and asked if they need anything; (2) through *consistency*—all employees treat customers in the same way. Everyone from managers to wait staff in all of the chain's hotels greet customers; and (3) through *transference*—employees behave the same way across different customer situations, from check-in to check-out. When guests check into the Royal Court Hotel, have dinner in the restaurant, and need help with directions to the theatre they mentally note consistently friendly behavior. The reliability of that behavior and its transference across situations lead customers to perceive that this truly is a customer friendly organization. They have the "evidence" so to speak, in repeated transactions and encounters. Sarah knows of this chain's service orientation and is establishing the practices as a regular occurrence at the Royal Court.

When my three children were small I was able to take them along on business trips. My wife and I often chose the Marriott Hotel. On our first visit we arrived in the late morning. Although the conference had filled the hotel, they found us rooms for early check-in. With children 9, 6 and 4 years old this was important. Everywhere in the hotel, staff stopped, said good morning and asked if we needed anything. We did not, but we sure appreciated the offer. At dinner in the hotel we decided to have the buffet. The children's price was $16.95—not too high. But the waiter said, "Why don't you just get the little ones what they want. There will be no charge." The food cost for all three was about $.75—rolls, applesauce and cherry pie. Following dinner, the roll-in cot was set up as requested with blankets turned down. This was much faster than the four telephone calls and the 10:30 pm delivery at another hotel while the little ones sat bleary eyed on our bed. Our experience and our perception told us this hotel was guest friendly.

BEHAVIORS—WALK THE TALK

We have considered attitude, motivation and perception—all vital to friendliness. Most critical is the actual behavior. A statement of the seemingly obvious underscores the truth: In customer friendly companies, staff behave in friendly ways. What are the examples in the Royal Court? When they see you in the hallway, they ask if you need anything. They ask if you are lost. They walk you to your destination. They telephone another department to find you the help you need. These behaviors are the true representation of cultural values and leadership intent. And, the behavior is often quite *obviously* friendly, not easily missed. The behaviors are seen not just in hotels. Here is an example from one of the hotel's business neighbors.

THE CASE OF THE BIRD WATCHING EQUIPMENT

On the recommendations of the hotel staff I went to the local sporting goods superstore to look for a pair of binoculars. We had been spending a fair amount of time at a barrier island beach not far from the Royal Court, where it was possible to see dolphins and pelicans fairly close. Unfortunately, the binoculars I had were not strong enough to give me a good view. When I went to the super store, the clerk asked me what I wanted. "A set of binoculars but stronger than the ones I have," I said. "Well here's the best pair we have." He pulled them out and placed them on the counter. He said, "These are really excellent binoculars, but tell me a little bit more about what you want." I said we wanted to see the pelicans close up and some of the unique birds in this national seashore preservation area. He said, "You really want a bird-watching specialty house that has very powerful, wide-horizon binoculars. Hang on a second, I'll get you the name and address of a place about 30 miles from here. They have a wide range of high quality binoculars. I believe they're just exactly what you want." I was amazed that I got this kind of help from the clerk. I thanked him and went to the bird-watching store. When I returned to the Royal Court I related the story to them.

Customer friendly leaders search out work activities that are producing high quality service. Although a binocular sale was lost, the customer told hotel staff, sending future guests to the sporting goods store. Teaching these behavior patterns—learning to behave in a customer friendly manner—can be done by using "customer service heroes" to create the legends of valued service. Stories of staff members who take home laundry in an emergency or boat to another island for face cream are purposely told. By illustrating and praising their behaviors, leaders increase the likelihood that other executives, managers, and employees will duplicate the behaviors. But you must publicly recognize the actions. (See chapters 6 and 7)

STATUS—VIP INVITATION ONLY

Friendly treatment can imply special status. First class and "business class" airline travel is "special"—different from coach. Think of what happens to important people when they shop or bank. Do company presidents buying BMW sedans get the same treatment as a new college student buying a Honda Civic? Often they do not, but for example, BMW management wants all customers treated in the same respectful manner, regardless of their buying power. How do we extend this "friendliness" more broadly? All of us—rich and poor, important and not—use the telephones. Sarah used the example in a training program for her staff at the Royal Court. She told them to imagine that they were a small hotel just starting out. What are the carryover lessons from the story of the telephone company?

THE CASE OF THE TELEPHONE PEOPLE

A new package of customer service, one that encompasses the dynamics of both technology and people has to be delivered for the small telephone company to thrive. Customer service is the "link" to the company's success. With this new customer service initiative, emphasis is placed on the "encounter stage" [the check-in experience at the Royal Court]. Every customer contact must be maximized. Studying today's Telco shows a definite pattern of customer contact. The Telco has several prime opportunities for direct contact: When customers come in to pay their bill. When customers call to ask questions. When new customers sign up for service. When customers ask for a new service installation. When customers respond to marketing incentives. The key is to maximize every one of these opportunities. This can be accomplished through the practice of "prestige placement." As a society, we do not really expect companies to treat us with smiling faces, politeness, and genuine interest. When customers believe they are being handled conscientiously, they will view the company favorably. So, if you can transform a request for service or a routine repair into an enhanced service experience, the customer experiences what is called "prestige placement." The practice of prestige placement lets customers know they are important and yields the highest rates of customer acceptance.[18]

The example showed Sarah's staff that friendliness could be exhibited at many different points in the hotel guest's stay—at check-in, at dinner, through special requests and at check-out. Sarah's Royal Court has a great reputation and a strong following. But she emphasized that they want to stay that way by treating all customers as VIPs.

As architects we must insure that staff at the Royal Court, at Telco and at BMW are service oriented. As part of our architectural design, we build and reinforce customer service values by awarding status to staff who provide a friendly experience. New staff are given an orientation and are mentored by senior staff (with their already recognized status and status symbols from positions to privileges to pay). New employees soon realize that status comes with "customer friendly demeanor."

GROUP DYNAMICS—RELAY RACES OR BUMPER CARS

How do employees relate to each other? Are we in team relay races, or in bumper cars? In customer friendly companies, employees help each other. In some restaurants (TGI Fridays) waitstaff deliver each other's meals to help out. Bank tellers casually consult each other. Faculty members talk about teaching challenges and share ideas at lunch. Insurance salespeople work in teams to answer customers' questions. The list of collaboration is long but breakdowns are visible too. Sarah was thinking about the level of teamwork at the Royal Court as she was clothes shopping for a weekend trip. Entering the store, she remembered reading about a "customer hostile" experience caused by individual and group behaviors. Once in the store she could not find a sales person, could not understand the sizing and pricing system and decided to call for help. The first person to respond said she did not work in that area. The second person took her time arriving on the scene only to know very little about the garments. She was directed to a locked dressing room—no keys were easily found. After waiting another ten minutes she left the store—frustration high and missing a wasted 45 minutes.[19] Sarah learned a lesson she had learned before. Can we spot customer friendly failures—which in this case was quite easy. Uninterested, uniformed staff were unwilling to provide basic service, or to insure that someone else provided service. Even attempts to get help failed. A customer and her contribution to profits walked out the door with a tale to tell. Group dynamics in the customer friendly organization translate into customer service first. There are no constraints on how one group behaves to another as long as the ultimate goal is customer service within the entire organization. Team building and intergroup confrontation are sometimes needed. What does a customer friendly process do? To Sarah, the department store problem was illustrative. Was there really no person to help out with the fitness wear? Without detailed knowledge of the retail company, we could say that training in product knowledge and teamwork was needed. An "unwillingness to help" among supposed team members illustrates the bumper car notion too well.

LEADERSHIP–BAND LEADERS' HARMONY

To establish the supportive climate, leaders like Sarah must ask: "What do guests want? followed by can the hotel afford to provide it or not? What do leaders contribute to customer friendly architecture in a psychological sense? In companies where friendliness is the norm, leaders offer vision, communication, motivation, modeling and perseverance (see also Chapter 6). The issues are raised here because leaders' actions are in part psychological—the psychological climate that is created fosters and supports friendliness. At the Royal Court, employee demeanors are shaped and reinforced by Sarah's words and actions. First, leaders articulate a vision of a customer friendly company that is psychologically engaging. Second, leaders communicate this vision up and down the organization insuring widespread psychological engagement. Third, the vision and the leader's behavior become motivational in that the vision is understood and has engaged the employee's psyche. Leaders are looked to for innovation support, new ideas and models of how to think and behave. Last, leaders must exhibit psychological perseverance in that there will be service failures to overcome.

In the following case, the leader failed in an obvious way. Sarah's friend told the story of his visit to a local bank.

THE CASE OF THE HOSTILE BANK OFFICER

I recently was purchasing a car for my college-age daughter. The woman at the bank who helped me with the financing paperwork said it would take about two days to process everything and we'll call you when it's ready. Sure enough, two days later the bank called and said the loan was set up; and we could come in to sign the papers. When we arrived at the bank, the woman who had established the loan was out for the day so the branch manager handled the final processing. As he presented the papers to my wife and I, we remarked that the interest rate was higher than originally quoted. He said, "Well what was it?" When I said it was 6.75 not 7.25, he said, "How do I know that was really the number?" He followed up by saying, "I don't really know you," (in an insulting manner). As a 16-year customer, I felt poorly treated. Coupled with surly teller service that followed this exchange, we changed banks.

Sarah wondered what the banker's vision of a customer friendly company was. He was not much of a role model for his staff. What he communicated to the customer—distrust and insult—was effective and lasting, successfully killing future business. As chief executive officer, senior manager, or bank unit head, leaders demonstrate that high quality customer service is behavior *and* state of mind. Leaders establish individual and group relations directed toward customer service by modeling service required, setting the direction and the pace.

COMMUNICATION—SAY IT AND REPEAT

The customer friendly organization relies on communication to foster internal design and production processes and it recognizes it as the key to customer relationships. Some hotels use call centers, others use guest comment and complaint cards, but the latter are not always representative of customer experiences as a whole (see Chapter 3). Complaints and report failures are important but a richer "data base" is needed. In customer friendly companies, there is an abundance of highly skilled, active listeners. Team members seek out the opinions of others using the collaborative approach to marketing, product design, production, delivery and support. Leaders use the views of service providers and customers.[20] In customer friendly companies like the Royal Court, leaders, managers and employees are all skilled at communication with customers including:

Face-to-face exchanges—a hotel manager explaining the delayed availability of your promised room;

Oral exchanges—the concierge explaining restaurant choices
and the pros and cons for your business clients;

Written presentations—directions on how to use the hotel's
services in room manuals and on the television tape; and

Listening (both empathic and active)—the hotel manager sym-
pathizing about a problem that occurred in his hotel as the
guests were waiting to depart.

Each communication mode presents the company's face to the
customer—at the first encounter and at the last encounter. A few hotels have even added translation services. Sarah thought this would
be helpful because many German tourists have found Florida. Regardless of the language, the quality of the communication does
much to determine repeat business, referrals and the absence of continued conflict over a service failure. How many customers talk to
their friends and colleagues about their experience? All of them. If
they are key segments—business travelers with centralized travel
services—a single service failure can have a dramatic effect. One
concern with large hotel chains is the central reservation number.
Guests sometimes call the main hotel number for a local restaurant
reservation recommendation. They are greeted with an inability to
respond because the call services are often based hundreds or thousands of miles away.

Businesses form formal and informal alliances. Sometimes the
owners of allied businesses do not care to try to communicate. Sarah
had thought about building a strategic alliance between the Royal
Court and several cruise lines. Until she read about the following
experience.

THE CASE OF THE BEACHED CUSTOMERS

Premier Cruise Lines, operator of the Big Red Boat, was the fifth-
largest carrier in the cruise industry. In 1998, it lost $70 million, but
last year—repositioned as a family-friendly line—it trimmed its losses
to only (only!) $20 million. Still, Manhattan-based Donaldson, Lufkin
& Jenrette, which took an 80% interest in the cruise line during a debt
restructuring, accused Premier of defaulting on mortgage payments,
seized control of the company and aborted four cruises in midsailing.
From many accounts, it wasn't pretty. About 2,8000 vacationers were

rounded up and ejected from the boats in Halifax, Nova Scotia; Nassau, Bahamas; and Cozumel, Mexico, but they were given assistance in returning home. Some Orlando hotels reportedly canceled the bookings they were keeping for Premier passengers. (To its credit, the Port Canaveral Chamber of Commerce offered would-be passengers brochures listing restaurants and hotels where they could find a discount.) Even some of the ship's crew are reportedly (it can't yet be confirmed) stranded, without paychecks, half the world away from their homes, in places such as India and the Philippines.[21]

This case is the ultimate in communication failure with customers. Not only are they physically stranded, but their trust in the company and their loyalty are completely gone, along with referrals, repeat business, and positive reports of previous trips.

RELATIONSHIPS—BEST FRIENDS, NOW AND FOREVER

In customer friendly organizations everyone understands the importance of the relationship with the customer. From first contact, through questions about product use and failure, to related follow up help, each member of the customer friendly organization works to initiate and maintain the important linkage to the customer. In revitalizing the Hampton Hotel brand, Hilton has changed course from "giving orders" about service. "We've tried to legislate service at Hampton for years (the training is now much more interactive). It'll teach our associates to connect with guests."[22] "Requiring" employees to provide service is replaced with presenting knowledge and skills about how to do so.

In stores such as Nordstroms, management encourages and supports the sending of thank you notes and ongoing dialogue. Many companies have begun to send notices of new products, of repair and service opportunities and updates on their development plans. Healthamerica, an HMO in Pennsylvania, provides members with a magazine that offers health care fitness advice, while simultaneously maintaining the customer relationship. National City Bank offers a newsletter from one of its mortgage specialists detailing home maintenance and repair advice and informing readers of new rates. All three companies believe in the importance of the customer relationship, expecting that present customers will become repeat customers, and most critically will refer friends and associates.

Customer friendly companies think of establishing customers for life, not just for a single transaction. This is especially useful for hospitals. Families that were literally started with the birth of their children can be expected to use the hospital for any number of visits over a lifetime—children, parents, and grandparents. Instead of a one-time visit to the maternity suite, these patients are viewed as lifetime partners through a whole range of health and medical care needs. This view has changed what happens to young mothers and fathers as they experience their first encounter. Candlelight dinners and nicer room furnishings are now standard practice, along with open visits for family and friends.

Many tools already are developed for building and maintaining this relationship. Fine hotels such as the Royal Court, for example, have long recognized the repeat business traveler. But it is only in the last decade or so that they have initiated frequent visitor programs. Hotels now understand the importance of ongoing relationships, but not all organizations that transport guests to the hotel have the same insight. Consider this too frequent occurrence of poor facilities maintenance imposed on auto travelers.

THE CASE OF THE DEPRESSING TURNPIKE STOPS

Royal Court Hotel guests often arrive from New York for an extended stay in January and February. They drive their cars so that they have transportation for their months in Florida. One recent arrival told this story to Sarah's concierge. "We travel on a state turnpike ... as part of the long trip to this hotel. We make frequent stops for food and restroom use, but their condition is dreadful. (One grandchild refuses to use them.) The smell is unpleasant, sinks are dirty, and paper towels lie on the floor, along with water of uncertain origin."

Turnpike travelers are captured; there is nowhere else to turn. But we are not adding lifelong relationships as a result of this too common travel experience, one that can be fixed without huge investment. Certainly the Royal Court hotel has minimal influence on public facilities, at least directly. Public restrooms are one small indicator of the customer friendliness of the state (citizens and travelers are customers). Citizens pay for the restrooms and complain about the poor experience, in part answering the question about why citizens are dismayed by public administration. Sarah and her colleagues at the American Association of Lodging Executives and the Florida Society of Travel and Tourism could unite, effectively lobbying the state government to make some changes based on the potential contribution to tourism.

TRUST—IN GOD AND THE COMPANY

Hotels are especially valuable and vulnerable when hosting business meetings, a frequent occurrence at the Royal Court. Organizers trust hotel staff to deliver and they do have concerns about the outcome. Here are some examples: rooms not ready, delayed and slow check-in, meals served poorly, "average minus" food, shifting space, no emergency preparations, staff shortages and so on. Meeting planners have confronted all types of problems from lost reservations to audio visual equipment that does not work to food shortages and space changes. With hundreds of guests—many well known members—these are embarrassing and sometimes career-ending for planners. In addressing trust, we must return to the product system (subject of Chapter 3). Trust is a core value to customer friendly architects, beginning with the analysis of customer needs and continuing through product reliability and safety. Trust is important at each of the following points in the hotel business.

Marketing—for understanding the extent of customer needs, including types and size of room, business service support, etc;

Product Design—for reliability, user ease, safety and cost, including how to insure guest security, bed and furnishings comfort, and availability;

Production Process—for quality, and consistency, including meals, arrival and departure, room preparations;

Delivery and Distribution—for access, timeliness, dependability, including concierge directions, room service;

Support Service—for technical advice and for responsiveness and correction of failure, including rooms without heat and hot water, and defective television and lap top connections.

Leading companies pay attention to the psychological aspects of each phase of the production cycle and even measure progress on unique aspects relevant to their hotel. For example, in Asia women travelers are most concerned about hotel security.[36] Sometimes there is concern that trust has been violated and that both customer and company know it. In the worst case scenario, this problem becomes public as it has for some of the travelers to Sarah's hotel. Those arriving by car are not battling just dirty bathrooms.

THE CASE OF DEFECTIVE TIRES

The loss of tread on Firestone tires has caused many accidents and deaths to drivers and passengers in Ford Explorers. The president of Ford Motor Company in particular was concerned that the relationship with customers had been violated because of a breakdown in trust. Where did they fail? First, the tire production people may not have remembered (or known) that their market valued safety above all other features. Second, the design of the tire included a defect undiscovered by the engineering teams. Third, what outcome flaws in the production process may have caused the tire to breakdown. Fourth, delivery and distribution in foreign countries resulted in problems there that were not linked to American headquarters. Last, when customers did have problems, the two companies were at first slow to fix the problem. At each point the result is a breakdown in trust with the customer. Can it ever be regained?

The message for Sarah and her staff is significant. What rests on the outcome of this particular tire problem is not just an image of friendliness but the very life of the companies—Ford and Firestone. Sarah could imagine a parallel problem for her hotel with a food poisoning or a mugging that receives wide publicity.

EMPOWERMENT & DISCRETION—TRUST THE CUSTOMER AND THE EMPLOYEE

What is the extent of an employee's ability to address a problem? At some hotels, monitoring starts when a complaint is filed. How does the employee approach the customer who has a question or a complaint? Many of Sarah's guests visit Disney World. Disney's service levels and commitment to the customer are well known to Sarah and her staff. How do they achieve such depth and consistency in employee behavior.

THE CASE OF EMPLOYEE FREEDOM

True empowerment means employees can bend and break the rules to do whatever they have to do to take care of the customer. Disney World is the epitome of customer service and empowerment. Employees are thoroughly trained and then given the authority to do whatever is necessary to handle problems on the spot to make customers happy. At Disney World if a supervisor sees a frontline person "giving away services," and he says "It's okay if a guest gets away with something. The alternative is that we could be wrong, and that could cost us a fortune. An aggrieved guest would tell everyone he knows that Disney is cheap. Occasionally, we'll take a hit, but that's OK."[23] Employees must have the trust and the discretion to manage customer needs. Many managers do not trust customers or employees making the transactions between them troubled from the start. Speed of response and continuous courtesy are the keys to establishing immediate and lasting relationships. In customer friendly companies, leaders allow and encourage employees to take action to satisfy customers. Assuming that the customer is right, employees can use their imagination and judgment to determine the best course of action. This is a significant philosophy with high psychological impact. In customer hostile companies, the response to a complaint is often the employee mindlessly stating, "I'm sorry, that's the company policy."

Contrast "that's the policy" with quick responsiveness. Hotel restaurants now address the desires of endless special dieters, but they sometimes fail on the basics. At dinner in the hotel restaurant, a guest ordered a rare steak but the one that arrived was well done. His wife's entree' was delivered with the overdone steak. When told about the problem—the waitress did not remember the correct order nor was it written clearly—the waitress removed the steak saying it would be replaced as quickly as possible. She returned in five minutes with a new one, cooked as ordered. She checked back with the diner in ten minutes apologizing and saying that there would be no charge for the man's dinner. In addition, an after dinner liquor was offered compliments of the hotel. At their business meeting the next day, the executive told the story to nine colleagues.

COMMITMENT AND LOYALTY—ONE FOR ALL, ALL FOR ONE

What makes a customer friendly company's employees dedicate themselves to the company? Sarah and the director of employee training were searching for cases to use in a hotel staff development program. One staff member said customers always complain about hotel costs. Each telephone call is billed, even local ones. Maybe a fee could be instituted for towel use.[24] This suggestion brought a laugh but was not used. Her objective was to underscore the value of commitment to the hotel and its guests. What does commitment to service look like? The Royal Court Hotel and its guests often use Federal Express providing a fine example from their start up years.

THE CASE OF THE COMMITTED FLYER

A critical part of what made FedEx work in those early days was a corps of committed ex-military pilots, many of whom, like Mr. Smith, had flown in Vietnam. They were a dedicated bunch. Captain Bourgeois still has a slip of paper documenting the night he kept a 6,000-pound load of packages from being trapped on an airport ramp in Cleveland. It was two days after Christmas in 1973, and the airport wouldn't refuel Captain Bourgeois's Falcon 20 because FedEx was having trouble paying its bills. The pilot needed 200 gallons of aviation fuel to get the plane back to the FedEx sorting hub in Memphis. So, the pilot stepped into the breach. "I made a phone call to flight operations and they said, 'Do you have a credit card?' " says Captain Bourgeois. "I didn't know if I'd get my money back, but I figured, 'Well, what the hell.'" Captain Bourgeois and the packages made it back to Memphis and Mr. Smith cut a reimbursement check for the pilot the next morning. Nearly 25 years later, the pilot, now going gray, still has the Texaco charge-card slip for $103.31 in fuel he bought that night. "That one single action is not the definitive event in the history of FedEx," he says now. "But I'm proud that I did it."[25]

This story illustrates commitment to the customer and to the company. There is no such concept as "not my responsibility," as all employees at all levels are focused on service.[26] Sarah's architectural "plan" is to build a psychological climate that fosters and reinforces this level of commitment to the Royal Court.

STRESS AND BURNOUT—I'M MAD AS HELL AND CAN'T TAKE IT ANYMORE

Providing customer friendly service can be psychologically and physically stressful. Whether it is survivable, depends on how the employee perceives the stress, their past experience in managing stress, the level of organizational support, and the tolerance levels of individuals. Architects consider all of these, addressing individual levels and past experience at the hiring point. The architect's task, however, is to craft a design that allows employees—even when they perceive and struggle with stress—to manage it with strong organizational support. Too much stress coupled with little support quickly leads to employee burnout. Burned out employees are rarely customer friendly.

What causes stress in the hotel business? A registration clerk faces high volume rate searches and is sometimes forced to work a second shift. The work of registration is too routine and too repetitive and occasionally requires the clerk to choose between telling a customer the truth and advocating for a registration (booking a family into their business oriented hotel). Registration is frequently in conflict with the room cleaning team (always late). Shift hours rotate over first, second and third. And in the end, registration clerks have no career track as the move to management is hard. Customer friendly architects like Sarah pay attention to the following elements—that individually and collectively create the stress: Job conditions—structural issues such as pay, work schedules, location; Workload—too high, too low, too routine and too repetitive; Role conflict and ambiguity—advocate for the company or for the customer or remain neutral; Interpersonal relations—collaborative, competitive, conflicted; Family work conflict—hours, deadlines, timely service, failure responses; Career path uncertainty—where does customer service take me—vertical or lateral, promotions or out the door. Customer service representatives in particular, face a number of these issues in their daily work life—sometimes having to address them in the context of one massive public problem. What Sarah did not know was that the Royal Court chain had already established an alliance with the cruise line that collapsed. She heard at the next regional meeting nightmare stories of customer complaints about unavailable rooms and conflict.

THE CASE OF THE MISSING BOATS

Few travel professionals missed the collapse of the cruise line and the sudden halting of three cruises. Imagine the stress for specially appointed customer teams as they struggle to meet the concerns of worried hotel guests and their families. One staffer, Tom, has been with the Royal Court chain for 10 years thinking of the company as a place from which to retire. First, he needed to be told of the expected job conditions and workload. Hundreds of guests and their families will call, many of them anxious and angry. Reps needed to be informed of how in-depth they could discuss the issue's technical side and how far their promises for restitution would be extended. Role conflict arises as Tom tries to determine whether he and the other reps are on the cruise line/Royal Court team or do they side "psychologically" with the parents of three children that are afraid they will not get home safely. Interactions with cruise officials or staff are strained as the leaders of the two companies struggle to assign blame, or pass it on. A few interactions with customers make Tom or his staff colleagues feel good, even when the customers are understanding and patient. The stress easily can be taken home with spouses and children feeling the effects of the daily battle to regain customer trust and fix the massive service failure. When Tom's friends and relatives gather, someone inevitably brings up the fact that they and a close friend are frequent guests of the Royal Court chain when they travel on business. The violation of customer trust is passed on at the home front as well. Last, Tom has been assigned to the customer service team. The team is charged with the task of managing a difficult situation for which the company's leaders will be grateful. But Tom has to wonder as he works, whether he will have a job or a company when the dust settles.

Tom and his colleagues must endure role conflict balancing the interests of multiple masters.[27] The cruise line case offers a full range of stress, introducing elements from workload to anxious customers to uncertain outcomes for person and company.

INTERACTIONS—AT THE ROYAL COURT HOTEL

In customer friendly companies employee psychology supports and embraces the contribution of the other systems—product/technology, structure, management and corporate culture. What is the interactive message for Sarah and the Royal Court Hotel? First, employee psychology determines the degree to which product, design, production and support teams collaborate in their work. Employee psychology contributes to the quality of production when new ideas are encouraged and ventured. The attitude extends directly to customers when addressing complaints and service failures. At the Royal Court the *products*—hotel rooms, reservation, room service, arrival and checkout ease—all depend to some extent on the employees' attitudes, loyalty, and trust of the employees. Express checkout will not substitute for surly wait staff, tardy busboys, missing towels, or cold showers.

Second, employee psychology reacts to and is shaped by *structure*. How much freedom employees have to innovate and flexibly respond to customer needs and service failures is key. Structures that reward teams and individual performance reinforce intended collaboration. Sarah hands out team awards and bonuses to departments, reinforcing the psychology of collaboration. Family friendly guest policies regarding small children (including the free buffet) offer employees the opportunity to be generous with their diners. A policy of upgrading rooms for business travelers extends a warm psychological welcome to tired travelers reluctant to stay in one more sterile hotel.

The *management system* depends on and influences employee psychology with style and with decisions. The commitment and encouragement of employees is necessary to sustain the drive for continuous quality improvement. Employees must be eager participants in building the company's customer friendly future. Sarah understands that "friendliness" begins with leadership values and modeled behaviors. To build the psychological climate of friendliness, leaders must interact with and care about customers from the time they check in until the time they leave. Sarah understands that leaders plan for and maintain the climate; it does not happen accidentally.

Finally, employee psychology is part of the framework of *corporate culture*. Individual employee psychology (one-by-one customer friendliness) is matched with a company-wide focus on friendliness as a shared corporate value. Culture does affect service.[28] A disconnect—employee non-believers—will subvert the best intentions of the culture builders. In the Royal Court, the best rooms, dinners, entertainment, and sports opportunities are rapidly undercut by maids with careless cleaning habits, busboys slow to clear busy tables, unrestrained rowdy party goers, and a leaf-filled pool. Each of those seemingly "non-critical contributions to the hotel product" are indicators of the depth and breadth of customer friendliness throughout the Royal Court.

SUMMARY

This chapter considers customer friendly companies to be co-produced by the psychology of individual people—their attitudes, commitment, motivation—and the relationships between them. Along with product and structural concerns, executive architects address the psychology of the organization to create a customer friendly climate. In this chapter, we have considered elements that help to create a psychology of customer friendliness such as motivation, service expectations, behaviors, customer status systems, group dynamics, leadership and commitment and trust. A single action is incapable of solely producing a service friendly architecture, but a package of elements does so effectively. One more element is leadership—a managerial task, the topic of Chapter Six.

CHAPTER 6

MANAGING FOR CUSTOMER FRIENDLINESS: THE CASE OF THE FEDERALIST BANK

In this chapter, we consider the contributions of leaders and managers. How do they help create customer friendly companies?

~~~~~~~~~~~~~~~~~

Uncle Arthur: "What did your banker friend Thomas say was the key to customer friendly?"

Nephew: He said: "It's all leadership and management. Without top level support, don't bother to try".

Uncle Arthur: "He's right, but only in part."

~~~~~~~~~~~~~~~~~

Throughout this book, we have analyzed the architecture necessary to create a customer friendly organization. How are leaders and managers involved? The premise is that customer service architecture must be developed and maintained *by leadership and management.* Consider Thomas, president of the Federalist Bank for the last 12 years.

Thomas was lucky to advance through the bank's ranks over a 20-year career. The Federalist Bank is a full service bank, offering commercial and consumer banking services. The bank offers secured and unsecured commercial and consumer loans, finances commercial transactions, makes construction and mortgage loans, and rents safe deposit facilities. The bank accepts deposits in the form of time, demand, and savings accounts, including fixed rate certificates.

What began as a single bank in a city of 250,000 has grown rapidly into a regional bank with operations throughout the Mid-Atlantic region of the United States. In the last fifteen years, the bank grew from one site with $150 million of assets, to major bank facilities in seven cities, 60 branch offices and $3.5 billion in assets (with $2 billion in average deposits). Observers think the bank is moving toward super regional status, gradually adding service in adjoining states. Currently, offices exist in New York, Pennsylvania, New Jersey, Maryland, Delaware, Virginia and the Carolinas. The Federalist system is based in 26 financial centers and offers full service retail brokerage out of eight brokerage offices (with 120 registered representatives). There are now nearly 250,000 household customers and more than 850 employees. Three international officers now work in the emerging international group. Insurance brokerage, life insurance and travel booking services are under consideration.

The system includes 220 ATMs that can handle individual and business accounts. For individual customers, the Federalist Bank System offers complete banking services, retail brokerage, asset management and wealth management. For commercial customers, the bank offers treasury service, corporate and investment banking, and some developing international banking services.

Current strategic issues facing Thomas and the Federalist Bank include: industry consolidation, new product development, increasing regulation, capital availability, operating efficiency, and, especially, emerging technology and Internet use. Contrast these issues with an anecdote that Thomas read in banking school. Martin Mayer, writing about embracing change, noted: "... Most bankers said the story they had most enjoyed ... was one told originally by Kay A. Randall of United Virginia Bankshares in 1973. This story was of a man honored for 50 years of service at a Virginia bank, who was asked at the party the bank gave to celebrate him what he thought has been "the most important thing, the most important change that you have seen in banking in this half century of service." The man paused for a few minutes, finally got up before the microphone, and said " air conditioning."[1] After stability, and perhaps monotony, for many years, change is here for banking.

To this point, we have suggested possible changes in product design, production processes, product delivery and support, organizational structure and psychological climate. Often, customer friendly efforts are directed at only one architectural piece with the intention that "whole company improvement" will result. Over a luncheon, Thomas heard from a physician customer who worked at the Westside Hospital that this was true in health care.

The physician told him that health care facilities have a strong interest in expanding computer support capability. Using informatics, physicians now have on-line access to extensive databases, which contain complete information on diagnostic choices, therapies such as drug options, and recommended follow-up treatments. Vast technical improvements in patient service are possible—gains in product design and quality improvement. However, the use of computers must be supported by an encompassing architecture, including financing, employee acceptance, and a willingness to undergo data-supported review of treatment decisions. Information systems require significant financial investment in both design and operation. Physicians must be willing to use computers and to be trained. Further, with the extensive data generated, targeted performance reviews are easier. What was seen at the outset as a limited, information-based technology eventually involves multiple systems of the company. Thomas saw this as a good example of the complexity of customer friendliness, transferable to his service industry—banking.

Thomas was already aware of what bank customers wanted and the list was long: easy access to loans for purchases and business expansion, fast loan processing, great interest rates, financial advice, accessible locations, extended hours, new technology convenience, friendly employees, free services for seniors, and sponsorship of community events. Bank leaders are going further, experimenting with in-bank cafes, play areas for children and home-like furnishings. How do these strategies fit architectural planning for customer friendliness?

This architectural model calls for "packages of strategies" which produce customer friendliness (through five systems) in banks, hospitals, and universities. We have not yet addressed *who* initiates this co-production and what leaders must do. But we can state the design objectives as follows.

Architectural Intent. The purpose of leadership and management is to coordinate the other core elements of the organization: product and technology, structure, psychological climate and culture. Through planning, design, development, leadership and control, organization officers build the architecture of friendliness.

We have learned from successful organization change efforts that management must be intimately involved in and lead service improvement. At the same time, bank leaders must focus on the core functions, giving customers: (1) access to cash; (2) interest on savings; (3) payment transactions; (4) loans; and (5) security, privacy and safety. Management must create the architecture to support service friendliness, beginning with information.

Consider an example presented by a Federalist Bank director at the spring meeting.

Alfred Johnston, regional vice-president of Middleboro Bank, recognized that service was critical for meeting customer needs and maintaining competitive position. He responded by creating his bank's first written *plan* for service improvement. The plan included identifying the resources needed to maintain and increase customer service (such as improved check processing). New branch buildings would be designed to accommodate private meeting spaces, product groupings and seating (*reorganized* for customer service). Bank managers identified several areas (teller services, electronic transactions) for additional training and development at a retreat focused on customer service (*leadership*). Lastly, the bank established a data system for customer feedback to individual departments (*control*). Monthly exit interviews were to be conducted by the Human Resource staff, and customer complaints were batched and analyzed.

What actions are used to initiate and produce a service friendly architecture? Management contributes to customer service through five core management functions: (1) planning, (2) organizing, (3) developing, (4) directing/leading, and (5) controlling. Consider a few examples from the Federalist Bank. Managerial *plans* include goals to increase the bank's service friendliness, such as annual targets for service improvement. *Organizing* actions include acquisition of appropriate new equipment such as automated teller machines and the *development* of customer service information systems. Managers show *leadership* by talking about customer service; by confronting cost pressures with customer service needs, and by taking the message to the public in bank newsletters, statements and advertising. Finally, managers advocate for and use performance *controls* that include indicators of service quality. All of these activities are directed at traditional banking tasks: moving money rapidly from place to place; facilitating personal and commercial transactions; screening and servicing borrowers; funding businesses; and conducting these tasks with the highest level of security. Management involvement in service friendliness is multi-directional, whether the manager is a bank executive, hospital vice president, manufacturing production manager, department store director, or college president.

To understand the architecture of a customer friendly strategy, we must examine in further detail each of these core management activities. CEOs, managers, unit directors, and department heads can build their own unique architectural response.

LEADER AS PLANNER—"PLAN OR BE PLANNED FOR"

When the Federalist Bank expanded to super regional status (serving the entire East Coast), its officers began to fly frequently, at first inside the country, then internationally. They often complained about airline service, but they did have some good experiences. Consider the airlines used by the Federalist Bank executives in their international efforts and ask, do customer friendly companies develop by accident? Or, are they carefully planned for? Some airlines focus on business travelers making reservations easy, adding extra direct flights and using the same model aircraft to aid turnaround time. Years ago, airlines such as SAS linked its choice of airplane to service requirements, as did Southwest. Although we are not always aware of them, plans and decisions are required to increase customer friendliness. Quality service created by accident is a rare event. Most often executives must have an *architectural intention* to make their companies operate at higher levels. In *each* customer friendly company, *each* manager must ask "Do I have a vision of the service future for my company (bank, hospital, college . . . ?"

Russell Ackoff subtitled one book on designing corporate futures: "Plan or Be Planned For."[2] Cost is not, and will not, be the only differentiating factor in the marketplace. Costs and pricing "flatten out" under the pressure of competition. Service friendliness and quality are then used as competitive leverage to secure and retain individual and corporate customers. Executives plan for quality service, or another company will plan their competitive death in the marketplace. Bankers are especially familiar with this threat as non-bank competitors have sprung up over the last several decades.[3, 4]

In some companies, the increase in friendliness is not "planned" in the way we would think about formal planning processes. Driven by a shared intention to "be the most customer friendly we can be," employees at all levels just take action, led and empowered by management. Thomas tried to set this tone when he took the Federalist chief executive position. "Friendliness" increases by intuition and by learning about what works. Higher levels of devotion to service friendliness emerges from action; both planned and spontaneous. When the Federalist Bank consisted of a single building in a single community, they built their service reputation through both planned and spontaneous service acts. However, in complex organizations, the interdependency of the parts requires joint planning, even if the planning is informal. As a super regional bank, being customer friendly is now a bigger and more complex challenge at Federalist.

Planning requires that managers design and describe the company's "desired service future", and the steps necessary to get there. One approach uses an interactive process involving all levels of technical and managerial personnel to measure current friendliness, define the desired level, and select the actions needed to accomplish and maintain it.[5–7] In Russell Ackoff's model, four phases of planning are formally pursued. Thomas felt that the Federalist Bank had grown enough to need a more formal process.[8]

PHASE 1. CURRENT STATUS ASSESSMENT.

In phase one, Federalist management conducted an internal and external review to establish the *standards and performance status of customer friendliness*. This meant benchmarking the level of best service in the industry (an *external* view) and understanding the shifting needs and interest of consumers. Consumers can shift their desires to lower costs, more technology, greater access and timely convenience. Inaction is not acceptable in the face of change.

Phase one also defined the present level of customer friendliness in the Federalist Bank (an *internal* view). Topics included customer wait times, automated teller technology (availability and use), product range (savings accounts to brokerage to insurance to wire transfers) and quality control (accuracy and privacy). The internal data informed bank managers about how service friendly they are. The external review helped executives to understand how the industry at large defines quality of service—the indicators used and their competitive position (e.g. interest rates, fees, teller wait time, use of branches). The external and internal reviews establish a customer friendliness "baseline."

Four questions dominate the discussions:

- are our *products* customer friendly? (bank fees, processing time, security...)

- do our *structures* support customer friendliness? (incentives, decisions processed, departmentalization)
- is our *psychological climate* fostering customer friendliness? (individual and group interactive psychology—attitudes of teller teams)
- does our *culture* express customer friendly values? (in words and deeds)

To understand their current state, the Federalist leaders need data. A sample of friendliness indicators includes: teller wait time, ATM fees, mortgage rates, mortgage application processing time, trust fees, CD rates, home banking technology implementation and ease of use. Using key data, leaders and managers plot where they stand relative to competitors.

PHASE 2. VISION–REDESIGN

How will technology and bank branches evolve? One banking expert, Divanna suggested the following: "Traditionally, the cornerstone of a bank's relationship with its customers was face-to-face interaction at a branch. Customers' use of bank branches fell along two distinct lines: use of a teller to perform simple transactions; and the use of a bank officer for more complex actions, such as securing a loan. Technologies like ATMs, multimedia kiosks, and the Internet have automated many former teller and bank officer transactions. The dotcom era offered retail banking institutions a future vision in which the number of physical branches would be substantially reduced and customers would conduct their banking in cyberspace, with customer support centralized into large, regional call centers. What many institutions overlooked was that not all customers in all market segments would opt for technological alternatives at the same rate."[9] Are bankers thinking of the customer friendly future? In phase two, Federalist Bank executives led a process that involved managers and employees in establishing a vision of the desired customer friendliness level. How would they describe the service level they wanted? This process created a vision of the level, depth, and scope of future customer friendliness and of the required organizational architecture. The vision was defined by interested stakeholders, and outlined by a unique set of key indicators. The following is one example of a future vision for banking, and was used by Federalist Bank executives in their planning.

THE CASE OF THE FRIENDLY BANK

As a banking community we need to address the deficit in customer services across the range of bank products. We must have commitment from our employees that requires us to listen to the customer, to broaden our relationships with individuals and with companies, and which expands our portfolio of products and services. We need to be creative—inventing new products and services and new channels of distribution. We wavered in our commitment to branches but have now once again found them to be a central piece of our modern strategy. Attitude is key in this forward movement. Without a commitment to put the customer first—by leaders and by staff at all levels, we will continue to lose out to the broad product firms that are encroaching on the bank's core business.[10]

Federalist Bank executives and management got the message. To remain customer friendly they will need to change, expanding traditional product lines and updating technology.

Among other strategies, Federalist's search for enhanced service and growth led them to an alliance scenario. Red Wolf Grocery Stores are prominent throughout the region. The Federalist Bank team decided to create a partnership with Red Wolf, locating new branches in the grocery stores (as Wal Mart and others look at options like this).[15] This would allow their customers to bank at the same site where they buy groceries and pharmacy products. Red Wolf was planning to expand to super stores, opening some facility space to other companies in each of their locations. Further, Red Wolf was working on an Internet service that would allow customers to shop at home and simply pick up their assembled order at the store (while on a banking visit, Thomas hoped). This became the core of their vision.

PHASE 3. GAP ANALYSIS

In phase three, Federalist leaders compare the *current scenario* (phase one) with their *most desired service future* (phase two). They asked several questions, "What are the architectural gaps? What are the operating problems?" "Are they product-related, or do they concern structural incentives, or the psychological climate?" For example, is low job satisfaction in the bank's information systems group leading to turnover and absenteeism, in turn lowering service in mortgage reviews, statement mailings, problem resolution and general satisfaction. Do the problems concern loss of professional control? Are company software engineers angry about losing control of the production process because the legal department has made demands to meet federal regulatory requirements? Below are examples of real issues presented by Lucy Griffin in the *ABA Banking Journal*:

> Think about the following scenarios for illustration purposes, all going on at once.
>
> 1. A customer comes to Teller 1 to make a deposit. The deposit consists of cash, and based on the size of the bag the customer is carrying, the total deposit will be substantial—perhaps more than $10,000.
>
> While Teller 1 is mentally running through the list of information she'll need to fill out a currency transaction report, the customer starts asking questions about cash reporting. As practiced in training, Teller 1 carefully avoids providing the customer with any information that would enable him to structure deposits, thus coming in under the reporting limit. Finally, the customer decides to deposit $8,500 in cash but the teller can see substantial cash left in his bag. She accepts the deposit and the customer leaves.
>
> 2. While Teller 1 is busy, a car dealer employee comes to Teller 2 to make a deposit for the dealership. The deposit is mostly checks, but includes $15,000 in cash. The dealership has never made a cash deposit before. Teller 2 notes the deposit with interest, obtains the required information and fills out a CTR.
>
> 3. Meanwhile, at Teller 3's window, a customer is asking questions about how to transfer funds from his savings account to this daughter's checking account at another bank in another market. The customer is looking for the least expensive and fastest way to move funds so his daughter can write a tuition check to her college."... [16]

These few scenarios are presented as an educational tool to illustrate the challenge to customer friendliness in an era of tight regulation and possibly dishonest customers. Providing great service to the client of Teller 3 is good for business. Teller 1 and 2's clients may need help too, but if they are dealing in grey areas, this may not be the type of service the bank should provide.

At the Federalist Bank, executives felt that the largest gaps were in technology application and staff attitudes toward customers. They also felt that the linkage with the many communities they serve was not localized nor deep enough. They believe the community relationship is the start of their customer relationships. The partnership with Red Wolf would change that. The gaps drive the actions and strategies selected by the bank.

PHASE 4. EXECUTION

In phase four, Federalist management teams created strategies and actions for mapping the company's path from its current situation to its desired future. With the vision in mind, management and staff identified and prioritized actions to take the company to higher levels of friendliness, systematically altering the architectural design. Actions included enhanced staffing, a product innovation group, responsibility assessments and time lines for program review. Recent leadership essays suggest execution of strategies and actions is critical.[17]

Consider the Federalist Bank example as one illustration of what other companies and organizations could do.

~~~~~~~~~~~~~~

The Vision of the Service Friendly Bank

Thomas, President of Federalist Bank, determined that banking services may be adversely affected by industry changes and pressures from state and federal fundors. He used a task force of eight executives to examine customer service in relation to the Red Wolf alliance. The task force first identified external trends likely to increase/decrease service in the next five years (e.g., baby boomers aging and retiring). They then agreed on the level of existing customer service—unit by unit, both major facilities and branches—primarily through discussions, analysis of complaints and focus groups. They found underutilized branches, a shortage of cutting edge technology, a comparative weakness in retail banking friendliness (teller shortages, dowdy branch office furnishings) and a mediocre marketing capability. The task force also identified a need for more formal data on services such as mortgage processing and Internet banking use. All of this was now connected to the Red Wolf alliance.

The group created an idealized version of what their "service future" would be if they could have it now. This included statements on the nature of their work, job responsibilities, reporting relationships, level of stress, pay, turnover, and extent of internal and public recognition. These became statements of the customer service elements in banking. The bank used this shared set of values and work standards as the guiding design for the Red Wolf project

With the vision established, the group compared the current situation with the vision. They found gaps were particularly severe in technology, workload, work definition, job satisfaction, stress, pay, career upward mobility, and turnover. The Red Wolf project needed to make a positive change in these weaknesses

To improve, the group recommended three general strategies—*development* of existing capability in the branches and *growth* in customer numbers through recruitment and through expansion to Red Wolf sites. These would be followed by a *financial* initiative increasing contributions to investment capital specifically targeting new monies for small business, for training in new technology (e.g. wireless banking) and for a doubling of the technology capability in hardware and software.

To manage their way to stronger customer friendliness, executives and managers create a plan, either formally or informally. The plan has implications for structure—for the leaders' work as architectural organizers.

~~~~~~~~~~~~~~~~

LEADER AS ORGANIZER—THE ERECTOR SET CHALLENGE

Most executives and managers will not be surprised by the statement: "Customer friendly companies have personnel, facilities, equipment, information systems, and other critical elements in the 'right place at the right time.'" Federalist Bank executives are not surprised by this "common insight" but with their rapid growth this was an important analysis. In customer friendly companies, leaders think carefully about personnel complements. Do we add retail or commercial banking staff? Physical facilities are carefully designed and periodically evaluated to ensure that the design contributes to quality service. Do we upgrade branch offices, add more, and think of a new layout entirely (more informal with thinking space for customers)?[18, 19]

For example, Richard, President of Northside Hospital, told Thomas that, in hospitals, customers are sensitive to parking, examination schedules, and the timeliness of test results. With a rapid shift to outpatient care, hospitals have reviewed the location and placement of diagnostic equipment to insure friendliness. Otherwise, waiting times are long, tests are rescheduled, and patients complain vociferously about parking problems. At Northside Hospital, continual attention to being "friendly" is a way of life that ensures the presence of key elements of production, delivery and support.

For the Federalist Bank, like many other companies, organizing infrastructure is an "erector set" challenge, involving products, facilities/equipment, finances, personnel, and integrating structure. Customer friendly leaders, in essence, are paying attention to the details of their "environment," the internal architecture and infrastructure. Federalist Bank executives confronted these topics in their customer friendly quest.

The Products and Programs Portfolio. Are there enough products and programs, and are they the correct ones? This question was the focus of Chapter 3, but is raised here as a management and leadership responsibility. A "customer friendly organization" in the year 2010 will include products and programs that currently do not exist. Federalist will expand services such as customer surveys, wireless banking and personal financial planning. A change in overall strategy may even be necessary.[20] Product profiles and evaluations can be conducted using generally accepted needs assessment and cost benefit techniques. But the analysis must actually be carried out. Customer friendly companies scrutinize and *change* products; others analyze, but do not act.

For example, banks have traditionally limited their product line. Saving accounts, loans and mortgages were the core activities. Now, with regulation changes and the emergence of non-bank competitors, activities may include insurance, brokerage, travel, credit cards, etc. These new product options necessitate a consideration of the "right balance" for optimizing profitability and supporting customer service. Too limited a product line causes customers to go elsewhere, but so does too full a product line (with flawed customer support).

Facilities and equipment. Some years ago, bank leaders called for institutional redesign, based on environmental psychology, to create attractive bank settings (i.e. colors, carpets, furnishings and room arrangements). Design and décor were viewed as contributors to customer friendliness. In many organizations, the need for redesign remains. For example, in the new Red Wolf branch office, a customer friendly inspection would consider whether the waiting room is spacious, comfortably furnished and linked to space that will allow private discussion. In the Red Wolf Project, planners needed to rethink the facility of a typical branch. Should the in-grocery branch have different furnishings and colors, physical separation from the rest of the store, with a play area for kids, and aisles wide enough for grocery carts? The key question is what do grocery shoppers want in a bank branch?

Is the bank's equipment state-of-the-art, available and in working condition? Next to the Federalist Bank headquarters is a bookstore with a lesson. Barnes & Noble's installation of radio-frequency telephones at four of its stores has improved customer service immeasurably. With a phone at their hip, booksellers can answer a call without stopping what they are doing. Furthermore, if a caller wants to know whether Barnes & Noble has a particular book in stock, the bookseller can walk right to the shelf with the phone in hand while talking to a customer. Tom wondered if using cell phones at the bank could produce equivalent results.

After reviewing the level of technology and equipment, Tom's group had several concerns—first, whether the equipment exists and second, its appropriateness, currency and condition. Years ago, banks without automated teller machines were the technology laggards. But new technologies emerge continuously. Customer friendly companies have state-of-the-art printing support, for brochures, newsletters and other customer documents. Ownership may not be necessary, but service arrangements or joint sharing is feasible. Federalist Bank uses Kinko's and Sir Speedy, located down the street, for specialty work and overflow.The bank can count on local printing help and it can monitor the printers' equipment to cue its own equipment upgrades, for example, in automated teller machines and electronic banking services.

Financial Base. Customer friendly companies have sufficient financial resources to provide the minimum needed to deliver quality service. To insure that new and current programs consider financial criteria, managers request an initial and a periodic cost benefit analysis (customer service impact), and a break-even analysis. These financial reviews help decision-makers weigh costs and benefits to customers.

Federalist Bank currently operates 60 branch offices, and expects to add new branches (like the Red Wolf Grocery Project). Tom's bank executives were not comfortable with expanding services and adding new branches until financial feasibility studies were complete. With the recent acquisitions, access to expansion capital was limited. However, managers were sensitive to the need to reach out to customers in new places—subways, train stations and grocery stores. They believed in increasing their connections to the community by sponsoring sports teams and a school band, for example.

Personnel. What is the effect of overworked, unsupervised staff? Customer friendliness is clearly hindered when too few employees deliver the personal care demanded by *product* requirements and by *perceptions* of what customer service is. Sometimes management uses a combination of methods to improve employees' customer service—training, division of labor, and coaching. Tom considered how Federalist Bank could benefit from the ideas of New York's Dime Savings Bank.

THE CASE OF BANKING PERSONNEL

Many banks try to distinguish themselves from competitors by providing better service. Dime Savings Bank (New York) takes a three-part approach to customer service: 1. Drill employees in products, services, and policies, 2. Reinforce such skills as listening, making eye contact, and rephrasing what the customer wants, 3. Keep an ongoing training process in place. One universal obstacle to good service is that customer contact people are often overwhelmed with tasks that must be handled immediately. Bay Bank (Panama City, Florida) resolved this problem through a division of labor. The bank chose five employees who had demonstrated the ability to serve customers well and moved them to a customer service department, allowing other departments to concentrate on their work without customer call interruptions. Listening carefully and asking open-ended, clarifying questions can help an employee quickly address what the customer really wants. Several banks stress this aspect of customer service in their training. One thing that can make or break a customer service program is whether it is supervised and coached properly.[21]

Another personnel problem is the absence of key specialists in a competitive technology-intensive industry. Webmasters and computer security personnel can be scarce. Without specialists in hot fields such as investment banking and computer systems, Federalist Bank's customer service is impaired. Personnel issues differ radically in geographic regions based on the availability of specialists (e.g., Boston, Massachusetts vs. Little Rock, Arkansas).

Integrating Structure. How is the Federalist Bank structure best organized? This topic is addressed in Chapter 4, but is discussed here to reinforce the leadership responsibility for creating architectural structure. For example, the Federalist Bank was reorganized into a holding company, the design of which included a matrix to build integration between functions and the program/project requirements. Now executives ask: "What structure will integrate the bank's departments and a growing array of entrepreneurial units and practices?" For Federalist, the question is, "Where in the hierarchy does the Red Wolf Project fit?"

To insure customer friendliness, leaders address structural aspects such as facilities, equipment, financial support, personnel, and product mix. For example, Federalist Bank managers, along with employees and outside consultants:

- Conducted a branch and central office "facilities review" throughout the company
- Created a technology assessment group to investigate wireless banking
- Studied personnel needs to assess requirements for the next five years
- Used an advisory group for needs assessment and for design advice to the Red Wolf grocery store alliance
- Used outside consultants to review the holding company structure and design.

Many of these tasks are not as "glamorous" as mergers and acquisitions and international banking. But they are pillars for building the bank's customer friendly architecture. You can see the result in Mary Atherton's branch office.

THE CASE OF THE CHANGED STRUCTURE

Mary Atherton, Regional Vice-President for Pennsylvania, initiated a series of quality and customer service improvement actions. A four-person task force developed the plan with the help of an outside consultant. Both limited and extensive changes will naturally lead to questions of the capabilities of current support systems and of people's performance in various roles.

Her five-point action plan included the following:

1. Increased facility space and updated equipment secured through creation of a tight needs analysis report, and a plan for systematic acquisition and use of new space at 15 branches with updated furnishings.

2. Increases in the financial base and more control over the unit's finances. Because her unit was a "financial winner," more money was "returned to the unit." Some, for example, was used for training in wireless banking.

3. Additional computer analysts made available for technical support in the second shift.

4. Two new programs, a continuing education program for assistant managers and a professional training cycle for all staff.

5. A revised reporting structure for loan officers. They now have joint responsibilities, reporting to marketing and the risk assessment unit.

Building an architecture to support customer friendliness means making structural changes when necessary, as Mary Atherson recognized.

LEADER AS DEVELOPER AND COACH—
TARGETING PEOPLE & SYSTEMS

The third management responsibility undertaken by customer friendly leaders is *development*, targeting both people and systems. Some managers at Federalist Bank believe they can improve customer friendliness without people—for example, using telephone 800 numbers and web sites. This is a seductive position, one that too easily captures executives. Can companies grow in size and sophistication while employees remain at current levels? It is not likely but often tried. Sooner or later serrvice collapses because people lack the skills and knowledge to move ahead with a more sophisticated product line and industry. Development requires macro and micro perspectives with the attention focused on the whole organization (macro) and on work groups and individuals (micro).

As CEO of Federalist Bank, Tom recognizes he is ultimately responsible for the degree of customer friendliness, visible in the bank's physical layout and in all other transactions. What leadership style will best foster customer service? Here are the well-known choices.

The Options for Leadership Style "What are the six leadership styles? None will shock workplace veterans. Each style will likely resonate with anyone who leads, is led, or as is the case with most of us, does both. Coercive leaders demand immediate compliance. Authoritative leaders mobilize people toward a vision. Affiliative leaders create emotional bonds and harmony. Democratic leaders build consensus through participation. Pacesetting leaders expect excellence and self-direction. And coaching leaders develop people for the future."[22]

Tom has taken his children to Disney World and has offered Disney vacations as bonuses for staff. He is impressed by Disney's organization and service and wanted to import some of their thinking into his bank. Below is a report on how Disney first trains, then supervises by watching staff in action and offering regular performance feedback.

THE CASE OF THE THEME PARK

Walt Disney World treats all visitors like guests in their homes and treats co-workers like guests when they interact. Walt Disney staff do not use the words "IT'S NOT MY JOB" or "go see that guy over there." They help guests with their problems; when employees do not know a solution, they personally walk guests to where they can solve the problem. Part of Walt Disney World's philosophy is to err in favor of the guest if an employee is unsure of how to solve a situation.

Walt Disney world employees follow dress codes and are not permitted to eat, drink, smoke, or chew gum in front of guests.

The overall message from a Walt Disney World visit is that guests leave feeling good. At all levels, Walt Disney World managers practice "management by walking around" and interacting with staff. In fact, cast members expect management to frequently visit them to see how things are going. When management doesn't visit, cast members remind them that they've been lax. This promotes good relations among staff and supervisors, and encourages staff to share their ideas with upper management.

Walt Disney World has "shoppers" who visit the company's various attractions and rate the helpfulness and efficiency of cast members. Cast-member supervisors and upper management then review all comments—good and bad.

Most management books say continual performance reviews are better than one performance review a year. Walt Disney World also believes a positive reinforcement system must be in place. The resort presents awards for things like perfect attendance and safety. But when warranted, constructive criticism balances praise.[23]

Tom's team began to refer regularly to the Disney experience, asking how their banks could emulate this philosophy and behavior.

Tom's lesson about the inadequacy of technology came with wireless banking. He began offering the service in one of the new markets. With little background, staff were unable to troubleshoot the inevitable problems. The systems were down just as customers were confused about the instructions for use. Customers got angry, some staff quit. The whole unit was quickly demoralized.

Customer friendly companies use staff development and training to teach "friendliness", and the variety of teaching tools is endless. For example, computer applications are exploding in sophistication and capability, with data used to increase customer loyalty while providing a base for customer performance evaluation and return on investment analysis (by customer group).

To foster employee development, Federalist Bank used these strategies and programs:

1. *job enrichment* programs to address changes in autonomy, accountability and responsibility (as branches grew larger and were placed in grocery stores).
2. *job rotation* to create new training opportunities, moving branch managers to main bank sites, giving them assignments to specialty areas such as marketing.
3. *career ladders* to recognize new fields such as information management, internet and wireless banking.
4. a *mentoring program* for aspiring managers (customer friendly role models)
5. a *training and development task force* to design and implement training programs such as consumer lending.
6. *field training* sites for customer service representatives and tellers
7. *educational leave programs* for customer service studies, emphasizing MBA programs and bank management certificate programs

One Federal Bank vice president's response to the above recommendations was an effort to meet the people development challenge.

THE CASE OF FRIENDLY HUMAN RESOURCES

Sarah Ferguson, Vice President of Human Resources, determined that industry and organizational changes had created a significant need for staff development. She created a five-part plan that included:

(1) A training reimbursement program allocating $500 to all staff for conferences and workshops

(2) Tuition reimbursement for job-related undergraduate and graduate coursework related to customer service, directly or indirectly

(3) An administrative mentoring program for staff with management aspirations.

(4) A lunch time seminar series in organization change management and continuous service improvement

(5) A task force to develop new educational ideas and approaches for enhancing customer service knowledge.

This strategic thinking bank manager used short-term resources (e.g., money) and long-term actions (e.g., training and study) to enact a staff development strategy.

Tom and his colleagues knew that technology would impact the Federalist Bank. One vice president passed on a press clip about First Internet Bank of Indiana.

THE CASE OF THE INTERNET BANK

First Internet Bank customers can now check their account balances, transfer funds from one First IB account to another, and view their last 10 transactions from their mobile phones. In addition, customers can set up new electronic bill payments, change due dates, alter amounts or cancel planned payments without going to the bank's Web site. The data has been reformatted specifically to fit cell phone windows. "Our wireless service enables customers to transact bank business when they're waiting in an airport, between appointments or simply away from their PC's," said David Becker, Chairman and CEO. "This helps maintain our leadership role in maximizing banking convenience, and it also anticipates the expected surge in wireless Internet usage."[24]

In the discussion that followed circulation of the clip, members considered the customer friendly benefits of the smart card and the virtual mall—complete with bank and online personal financial management supported by live advisors. Benchmarking these new developments to see what competitors were doing seemed important as one of several actions to take.

Several other "architectural" changes at Federalist included: the need to increase coordination and continuity between branches and the central office; the need to cross departmental boundaries (e.g., retail banking with investment banking and commercial banking) using generalists not specialists ; and the need to measure customer satisfaction concurrently, instead of relying on retrospective analysis. These are company-wide issues because they involve many architectural elements, and the effects are widespread. At the "micro level" (individuals and work groups), customer friendly companies monitor satisfaction in departments (where small groups are more affected than the company as a whole). These activities support service with department-by-department use of data feedback and targeted training.

Consider the work of this management team from Atlantic First Bank of Washington, a competitor active in the Mid Atlantic Banking Association.

THE CASE OF TEAM LEVEL DEVELOPMENT

Atlantic First's senior management team recognized the threats and opportunities facing their bank, including other banks, government regulators and non-bank competitors. After intense discussion, they created an interdisciplinary customer management task force. They assigned the group four tasks:

(1) Define customer development needs for the next five years, including existing and new customers and their technology needs.

(2) Create a plan for future customer friendliness that is exciting, measurable and complete with deadlines.

(3) Select an advisory group to oversee execution, using long term employees and newcomers

(4) Define an approach and methods for evaluating progress at
   regular intervals.

The group was given four months and staff support. As a result of
their work they selected five actions to foster service at Atlantic First:

(1) Create autonomous work groups to independently address customer needs at the bank's main sites and branches (using
   focus groups and personal interviews).
(2) use management by objectives to prioritize customer development needs—technology first, training second, new products
   third.
(3) encourage a pilot testing mentality for new service ideas (e.g.
   locating a new branch in a supermarket—the Red Wolf
   plan).
(4) create departmental level quality circles targeted on customer
   friendliness that crossed boundaries from retail to commercial to investment banking. (The bank courted customers in
   aisles and sought grocery chain business.)
(5) initiate a visiting technical specialist program to bring in new
   ideas about how to build friendliness organization-wide,
   beginning with an Internet developer, a vice president from
   Amazon, and an academic expert on banking industry consolidation.

In companies like Atlantic First, development is viewed as strategic and operational, involving people, company architecture and
most important, plan execution.

LEADERS AS MOTIVATORS—EXECUTION WITH
CARROTS AND STICKS

Managers are the architects of service friendliness. Three of
Federalists' young managers were enrolled in an MBA program,
where they inadvertently learned a lesson about incentives and management.

The three students were asked to complete an incentive study in
an organization of their choice. They chose a busy downtown bank
branch where lunch time crowds were particularly strong. Federalist
had distributed a memorandum stressing teller productivity and ser-

vice, and noting that promotions and merit raises would be based on productivity gains. The branch manager chose to emphasize teller throughput, but pushing the tellers to process the customers as fast as possible began to cause mistakes to occur. Several cash transactions over $10,000 slipped through without documentation and customers began to complain that they had little help. Deposit slips were short and tellers were surly. The regional vice president suggested that he might fire the manager if that would solve the problem. When the students investigated the root causes, they found that the manager had opted for the throughput incentive at the expense of quality service.

The problem was actually a case of incentive systems in conflict, a different architectural design problem. When Tom heard the story, he ordered a review of incentive systems' impact on bank service. Leading the company to higher levels of customer service means the executive is the architect of structure, including incentives and more.

In an article on leadership, Andre I. Delbecq identified five critical behaviors: vision, communication, people, endurance and innovation.[25] How do these translate to "customer friendliness leadership" at the Federalist Bank? First, "A leader provides a clear sense of direction." (vision of customer friendly service.). Here is the Federalist Bank's scenario:

Our bank will be at the forefront of new service technology and among the lowest in complaints and all types of unexpected errors. We will respond completely and quickly to service failures. We will work to provide our branch team with higher customer service support. And we will insure that our employees and community are aware of our commitment and accomplishments.

Service improvement could be measured in new technology, numbers of complaints and errors, response time to failure and employee/community knowledge. A vision of customer friendliness should be complete with enough detail to monitor success.

Second, customer friendly executives and managers *communicate* their desire to improve service. "A leader assures integrity and celebrates achievements." Leaders inform employees of the importance of customer friendliness, demonstrating this value by awards and rewards—public recognition for high quality service (see structure Chapter 4). For example, customer friendly executives at the Federalist Bank: designed a customer service bonus system with significant financial support; held an awards dinner to recognize customer service achievement; raised "customer service issues" at key meetings and board sessions; appointed a board level customer service committee; made selected customer service topics and employees an integral part of public information and marketing initiatives; and encouraged a joint team of branch managers and employees to define their own service recognition program. The actions are organization-wide and varied.

Third, customer friendly managers *focus on people* to improve service. ("Leaders see others as the key to success.") Federalist Bank managers cannot personally deliver customer service organization-wide, but they can develop it through encouragement and motivation. Federalist executives and managers increased customer service levels by: creating decentralized, semi-autonomous service evaluation projects (e.g., data collection and response at the Red Wolf Project); building customer service requirements into performance reviews (merit/annual increases based on service); encouraging managers to create their own monitoring system with a few key indicators (teller wait time); and creating customer service circles for problem solving (quality circles)

Fourth, management must *endure difficulties* in the push to build customer friendliness ("Leaders must know how to survive a difficult role."). Significant conflicts emerged at Federalist; for example, how to maintain service while delaying the purchase of new high-cost technology? Customer feedback creates conflicts over problems and simultaneously generates resistance to innovation. Management is at the center of the conflict, supporting service and employees through the stressful change. It is important to know how to motivate and track progress.

Fifth, management must understand innovation ("Leaders create an environment for continual strategic change.") In their strategic planning sessions, bank leaders came to understand that future service gains depend on new ideas and technologies. The Federalist management teams actively support innovation to foster continuous improvement in service. The tendency toward bureaucratization is well known and standardized protocols and government and industry benchmarking challenge innovation. Tom forwarded the example of this orientation to customer friendly behavior. To insure that the grocery store alliance would succeed, Tom needed a real leader.

After reading in Fortune Magazine about manager Louise Kitchen, cited for her commitment and ability to execute, he asked the Human Resources to find a manager like her. Ms. Kitchen's advice, as stated in Fortune, is found below:

- If you're not truly, madly passionate about an opportunity, no one else will be.
- Co-opt skeptics, don't berate them.
- Don't get resources through the chain of command. Build a community instead.
- Even in the most frenetic organizations, people will give time to projects they love.
- Don't ask for permission. Just make rapid progress and score early wins.
- A true activist doesn't need a mandate, just an opening.[27]

Federalist Bank leaders support innovation in customer service by creating "idea analysis" to evaluate and generate support for ideas that increase customer service; developing education programs for managers to help them understand which actions support innovation; surveying employees and managers to determine barriers and supports for innovation; and publicizing throughout the bank a commitment to innovation that increases customer service.

LEADER AS CONTROLLER–
ON NAVIGATION AND STEERING

In customer friendly companies, leaders evaluate and control service performance . The idea has spread from health care to banking to manufacturing. Federalist Bank executives should understand managers must control service behaviors and/or mandate adjustments when necessary. Bank managers strive to assess and influence customer service objectives, progress levels, work loads, resources or the lack of them, and achievement—comprehensive customer service control.

Tom has passed the message on to his team, and followed it with this draft set of customer service standards, captured in a pledge that will drive the Red Wolf Project.

THE FEDERALIST BANK CUSTOMER FRIENDLY PLEDGE

At Federalist Bank we pledge that:
- All promises made by the organization will be met
- All telephone calls will be answered within ten seconds
- Customers will be serviced within five minutes
- All communication with the customer will be courteous, positive, honest and genuine
- When things go wrong we will reach the customer before the customer has to reach us
- The system will fail the customer on no more than one in a thousand occasions
- Immediate action will be taken to redress any product defect or shortfall in service
- All employees will understand the product, service, and organization, know how to resolve problems, and know regular customers by name
- Staff will be able and willing to respond effectively to a customer and have the discretion to make a decision in the customer's favor
- Customer expectations will frequently be exceeded by the provision of unsolicited extras
- The fine detail of customer service will always be near perfect
- The appearance of everything the customer sees in the company will be immaculate.

Table 6.2 THE FEDERALIST BANK CUSTOMER FRIENDLY PLEDGE

At each level—mortgage group, department branch, bank as a whole—five elements of customer service control exist: baselines, standards, action, comparison and feedback. Customer friendly companies build the thinking into current operations and new projects like Red Wolf.

A customer service *baseline* is established. Bank and branch managers know the current customer service levels in their area. What is the monthly level of new deposits, of teller wait times? This data is required to create a baseline for comparison. For example, leaders inquire about the current deposit levels, retail and commercial business levels, and response times to mortgage applications.

The bank creates service standards to which all can aspire, using the baseline and industry and professional association benchmarks. These are supported by group consensus, as each group selects their own additional standards. Standards used by competitors and industry leaders in other fields should be examined. For example, Red Wolf Grocery Project planners will look at other companies such as the Winn-Dixie Stores and the Wal-Mart.

Leaders *act* to increase service—the new Red Wolf branch is opened. The bank monitors business and service levels by *data collection* on the new project, tracking modifications. Data tell Federalist managers whether customer service is on target. Focus groups and customer surveys are used in the design and first six months of operation. The architectural points throughout this book are the targets for redesign, if needed, as the Red Wolf Grocery project progresses.

Managers jointly *compare* the baseline—the company's starting point—with where they are now. The Red Wolf project was launched January 1, 2000 and was in operation nine months later. By the middle of 2001, executives had early feedback on customer reaction, from acceptance to complaints about hours of operation (Red Wolf was open 24 hours, the bank only four evenings per week, closed on Sundays). The responses led to customer service improvements: the hours were extended.

Service evaluation requires *feedback* of the data. Red Wolf project leaders developed a one-year progress report (including all aspects of operations) but its focus was customer service. CEO Thomas wanted feedback from retail customers during the annual executive retreat, with the understanding that comments should be used for development, not punitive purposes.

For the retreat, Thomas also wanted comparison information from one of the larger freestanding branches. This led to one manager's inquiry.

THE CASE OF THE CURIOUS MANAGER

Susan Baker is branch officer of Federalist Central Valley. She had been informed of customer service concerns by several potential corporate clients. Determined to answer their questions, she informed her staff that they must answer five questions in five weeks:

1. What is our company's customer service level in comparison to local and national standards?
2. What are our standards (e.g., for business loan processing, for access to capital, for new and expanding businesses)?
3. What actions have we taken to increase and maintain customer service in the past year?
4. How has customer service improved? What examples and data do we have?
5. How did we feed back this customer service improvement information to employees, staff and clients?

She informed her staff that they must answer the questions in detail and be ready with data to back it up if she decides to test audit their statements. They were also informed that she would present the report at the annual corporate-wide executive retreat.

Service evaluation methods are broad, encompassing all aspects of the company. In banking, the speed of check processing, teller wait time and staff friendliness are as important as the accuracy of account statements. Federalist managers provide the commitment and resources for service controls that employees design and use.

SUMMARY

This chapter presented leaders' and managers' customer friendly roles and behaviors. Service improvement is a manager's social and technical task, requiring a package of actions that are people and technology-related. Five management functions increase service quality in customer friendly companies:

- *Planning* leads to customer friendly visions and objectives
- *Organizing* supports customer friendly intentions
- *Developing* people and systems supports customer friendly progress
- *Leadership* guides the customer friendly commitment
- *Evaluation and control* assess customer friendly levels and feed back findings

Each action requires a greater or lesser emphasis depending on the *attributes* of an individual company. The specific methods cited here are samples used to indicate the breadth of attack required and the tools available. The management team must add to and tailor these, continually addressing customer service improvement as an architectural redesign task.

Customer service success is also dependent on how well the leadership team is able to build customer service into the corporate culture. Is customer service a core value recognized by the culture as important to the organization's viability and success? These culture issues are the subjects of Chapter 7.

CHAPTER 7

CREATING A CUSTOMER FRIENDLY CULTURE
The Case of Eastern University

In this chapter, we examine the contribution of corporate culture to the architecture of customer friendly organizations.

~~~~~~~~~~

Uncle: "What did the university administrator say was the secret to becoming customer friendly?"

Nephew: She said: "While product and incentives are helpful, and necessary, the key is building a corporate culture that is customer friendly." Elizabeth, you remember, is the provost of Eastern University, a well-regarded school.

Uncle : "She has it right, what does she mean by culture? Culture is really more of a private business concept, you know."

Nephew: "She knows. She is a graduate of a prestigious business school and may have first learned it there."

Uncle: "Well, what does she have to say, and what is the school like?"

~~~~~~~~~~

Even schools and colleges can be customer friendly, although they frequently are not. Most of us have experienced the bureaucracy and inflexibility of university structures, the attitudes of billing and financial aid office staff, or the uncertainty of book orders. Elizabeth is Provost of Eastern University, a 15,000 student private school on the East Coast of the United States. She has been Provost for three years, assuming the position after a six year stint as Dean of the Health Sciences College at a large midwestern state university.

Eastern University is located in the suburbs of a major city. It has a professional schools branch in the city with medicine, law, business and continuing adult education classes offered downtown. The university is privately controlled but dedicated to the interests of local citizens. It offers a broad-based liberal education considered fundamental to all of the school's programs. In the past 10 years, the university has rapidly expanded graduate and professional training to meet local needs. A balanced offering of extracurricular activities and social experiences has been a hallmark since its founding.

Founded in 1901, Eastern is largely state supported (65 percent). The annual budget is $1.2 billion, including $255 million in federal programs and research projects. Undergraduates compose 75 percent of the enrollment, which consists of roughly equal numbers of men and women. The annual cost for a state resident is $12,500; for a non-resident, $26,200. The university employs 675 faculty members and 2,200 academic support staff. The main campus is 320 acres with 70 major buildings, and the two libraries hold 2.2 million volumes. The university offers 70 undergraduate majors, 52 master's programs and 40 doctoral programs. Undergraduates are housed in eight large resident hall complexes with graduate students in 65 apartments.

Many universities are now using student perceptions as a feedback loop to assess quality of service and to close any gaps found.[1-3] Like many other colleges, Eastern students have long complained about rising tuition costs, poor food and housing services, safety and security, classrooms in disrepair, and a lack of new technology. The school recently has struggled with a series of "strategic

The Web of Customer Friendly Culture

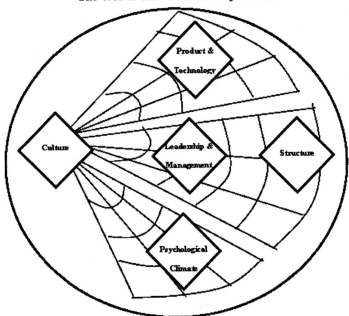

Figure 7.1 The Web of Customer Friendly Culture

issues" as well. Elizabeth believes the critical issues are building university/community partnerships; adopting and managing new technology; fund raising; competition from other schools and the Internet; and what she has labeled as "culture wars." With tuition rising, the school has struggled to maintain diversity and recruit the best students, given the increasing competition from peer schools. The issues to be dealt with are broad. For example, several weeks ago faculty confronted Elizabeth about the falling competence of incoming students. The next day the student council complained that Asians and gays were being harassed.

Elizabeth believes the key to future success is to insure that students have a "customer friendly experience" that will generate a *future* stream of referrals. She believes that the "culture of the university is crucial" because it's the web that links all other systems—courses (products and curriculum), structure, climate and management.[4-7] She often uses Figure 7.1 to illustrate her point.

Elizabeth joins many leaders in her belief that customer friendly behavior comes from shared values and beliefs—the core building block of any enterprise, public or private. In a "describe our culture" exercise, a team of faculty, students and trustees offered the following:

> Eastern University is dedicated to building a learning community, encompassing all aspects of teaching, research and service. The university strives for diversity in all endeavors, including faculty and students' characteristics and, particularly, diversity of opinion and philosophy. Commitment to access, cost containment and practical scheduling are the basis of its friendliness. The institution rewards faculty and staff for their efforts in what they jointly regard as a collaborative climate. Leaders, visible to faculty and students, see their role as building and reinforcing the institution's friendliness. Eastern considers itself a partner with the local community.

The concept of culture begins with concern for the organization's purpose and the identification of what the organization values highly: What are its goals and how closely connected are the values of its members? To become customer friendly, leaders must embed customer service in values, rites and rituals, promoting of heroes, network building, and their own leadership behaviors. The architectural effort to build a customer friendly culture continues throughout the organization's systems, each initiating a piece and also reinforcing the other systems—products, structural incentives, employee psychology, and management. We can see multi-system thinking in leaders' statements about culture building, statements relevant across industries. Elizabeth's management dean passed on this concise summary that noted a series of characteristics from training to compensation structure to teamwork to hiring practices to celebrations of success to attitudes toward employees. The list tells us that the abstract nature of culture and ideology is represented by the "concrete" structures of the company *and* the behaviors of leaders and employees. The "design work" is multi-faceted. In setting out to make her university customer friendly, Elizabeth begins with the following architectural design principle.

The architectural intent of culture building is to articulate core service values to customers, then to meet or exceed their expectations by matching behaviors to values. These primary values are represented and reinforced throughout the various elements of the organization.

Every organization has a culture. Edgar Schein at MIT was an early and leading contributor to our understanding of corporate culture. His research on culture in organizations taught us to look at three levels of culture: (a) physical artifacts (surface); (b) behaviors (deeper and representative); and (c) philosophy and assumptions (deepest and intangible.)[8–10] In a university, culture is *visible, tangible artifacts* (such as student union layout, campus setting, classrooms, signage), *behaviors and actions* (such as faculty teaching style and advising attitudes), and the *"under the surface" elements of assumptions and beliefs* (love of teaching, support of collegiality, belief in openness). Physical and behavioral support of customer friendliness rests on core values and beliefs. Thus, culture in effect is *co-produced* by:

- leaders' and founders' values and beliefs
- strategy
- decision making style
- problem solving process
- physical environment
- rituals and symbols
- rites and ceremonies
- socialization
- stories and narratives

- heroes
- sub-cultures
- counter cultures
- language and behavior—continuity and reinforcement
- environment

Culture building and maintenance is a constant cycle of establishing values, reinforcing and rewarding behaviors, and attending to deviant actions and subcultures, as illustrated in Figure 7.2.

As Elizabeth thinks about how to make Eastern University customer friendly, she must consider how support staff are rewarded; how new faculty are socialized to the desired teaching style, research and community culture (e.g., how she and other leaders can spend time with students at lunches and socials); and how some faculty do not want to spend time with undergraduate students. We can begin with values and beliefs.

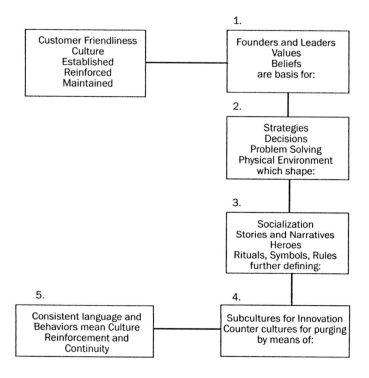

Figure 7.2 Culture building

VALUES AND IDEOLOGY—THE PLEDGE OF ALLEGIANCE TO CUSTOMERS

Organizations do not commonly use formal "pledges" such as the United States' Pledge of Allegiance. But pledges exist in unspoken forms as mutual agreements and commitments. We can see the pledge to customer service represented by employees in private companies such as Southwest where culture is the context for all behaviors and structure.

Many universities, including Eastern, already use student course evaluations to guide faculty development and contribute to tenure/promotion decisions. "Student customers," however, are rarely encouraged to evaluate the total university experience—from classes to cafeteria to bookstore to social life. The ideology of the customer friendly organization is a philosophy of service first and foremost—*every time* there is a customer transaction. Leaders and employees *believe* that outstanding customer service is the foundation of their organization's success and sustainability. In many large research universities, the scientific quest, and the grant support that goes with it, intrudes on this fundamental intent by siphoning off time and interest in teaching. In the worst case, academic medical centers now place enormous pressure on faculty to provide clinical care (to increase revenues), leaving little time for the teaching and mentoring of young physicians.

In customer friendly companies, leaders and employees believe in the basics of the architectural view presented in previous chapters. No matter the company, our:

- *Products* are of high quality, delivered on time
- *Structure* (i.e., organization design and incentives) supports high quality service
- *Psychological climate* initiates and reinforces service and mutual support
- *Management* models and leads the support for quality and service

How does this play out in an educational organization? Eastern University offers a portfolio of courses and programs fitted to today's students' needs (*products*). *Structural* incentives, such as bookstore inventory costs, are adjusted to match student requirements for books. *All* students are treated with respect (*psychological climate*). University *management* leads by modeling student-friendly behavior, for example, through accessible contact. Service friendly companies, including universities, are *founded on and managed* by a belief in customer service. Just as in private industry, implementation of the values requires standard setting, training, a reward system, and ongoing communication to reinforce the values.

Elizabeth is acutely aware that there are ongoing conflicts lurking in university values. Students value quality but many insist the university stick to its four year contract (i.e., insuring that courses are available on a schedule that allows students to graduate in four years). Some schools have aggressively pursued partnerships with private companies, cutting deals with beverage companies, renting out university facilities, negotiating naming rights, and even adding luxury boxes to stadiums and hot tubs to dorms. Many administrators and faculty see this as a commercial intrusion that ultimately erodes customer-oriented educational values.

LEADERSHIP AND FOUNDER BELIEFS–
WHAT THE POOBAHS THINK

How do values relate to leaders? At Eastern University five beliefs describe the leaders' basic assumptions.

- The university culture must engage participants intellectually, emotionally and socially
- The culture is ethical, just, and diverse in nature
- A culture of learning must be advocated and infectious
- The culture must generate energy and resources (both people and materials)
- The culture must be durable

Customer friendliness rests on these assumptions, which are widely disseminated and accepted.

Some institutions begin with a belief in service friendliness. The values and ideology may stem from founders (e.g. Walt Disney) and are expected to be carried on by successive leaders. For example, Hershey Chocolate magnate Milton Hershey founded the Milton Hershey School, a residential high school dedicated to the academic and social needs of low income and orphaned students. Many land grant universities were chartered with the understanding that they were to serve their communities and states, in particular their agricultural interests. Predominantly black universities specifically focus on African American students' needs and interests. Howard, Lincoln, and Cheney Universities are all good examples of this belief in expertly serving a particular type of customer.

Founding beliefs can also hinder customer focus. At a recent fund raising event, Elizabeth was confronted by a well known and generous donor, a graduate of the business school.

THE CASE OF THE DIRECTIVE DIRECTOR

"Provost, I noted from your presentation that the university is increasingly emphasizing graduate and professional education, and that you have been successful in this plan. I read that grant dollars from research are now four times higher than just ten years ago. But my nephew goes to school here and he told me that he has mostly teaching assistants, that much computer time is taken up by the research teams and that he has not been able to schedule an appointment with the academic star in his biology department. The professor's secretary said he is too busy to see freshmen. You know, Elizabeth, this university was founded as an undergraduate teaching institution. We have always valued teaching—at least I thought so. The founders would be highly displeased to learn of my nephew's experience."

Elizabeth began to discuss the university culture and the resistance from alumni who support the original land grant philosophy. She explained that the university was moving from a culture primarily devoted to teaching, to one that values and invests equally in research. To serve student-customers well, faculty must be encouraged to stay at the cutting edge of their fields, which means research conducted outside and brought into the classroom, sometimes with students as partners. The founders and recent alumni must come to understand the purpose and use of this "cultural shift." She further explained that alumni of womens' colleges and all male military schools experienced this type of cultural shift, in a more dramatic fashion, as these universities began to admit the opposite sex.

In a customer friendly organization, leaders like Elizabeth make five contributions to building the architecture of friendliness.[11] Customer friendly leaders create a culture in part through:

- A *vision* of high quality service—how the university's changes will impact the institution to increase friendliness and quality

- Clear and consistent *communication* of the service friendliness value—maintenance of founding values through periods of change during which new customers appear to have priority
- *People* as the key—insuring student, faculty and alumni support of traditional services and new ones (e.g. to graduate students)
- *Endurance* of conflict and failure—when alumni and others question the direction and service levels to favorite customer groups
- Stressing *innovation* to continuously improve service—creating new mechanisms to support core services, such as teaching undergraduates in a research university.

Leaders initiate and spread customer friendliness throughout the company, continuously evaluating progress and seeking improvement. The leaders create the culture and reinforce its beliefs with rewards. Academic leaders pay attention to the core products—curriculum, courses, research—and to key amenities such as facilties, food services,[12-14] sports, social events, and even the availability of music file sharing services.[15]

STRATEGY–A Chosen Path

All organizations have strategies. Some are openly defined while others are covertly practiced. Strategies are patterns of behavior, ways of acting and deciding that help form a path to the future. Strategic planning is a force for pushing strategy to the forefront of consciousness, linking *direction, destination* and *decisions.*[16] The questions are: do we want to be more customer friendly? What would we look like if we were? And what decisions do we need to make to move us forward?

University strategy is enacted in a context of contradictions. Try building a customer friendly culture with the following network of paradoxes as presented in Table 7.1.

Some customer service planning does not produce strategy because it is based on projections; is too finance oriented; comes up from the bottom levels to be aggregated; rests on untested assumptions; and is inflexible and short range. Elizabeth's board of trustees discussed how to make the school more student friendly—what some define as a *customer focused strategy.* A few administrators wanted only to talk of enrollment patterns, budget forecasts, and

Table 7.1 Paradoxical Predicaments of Customer Friendly Universities

1. Universities offer traditional products—courses and curriculum—*and* constant innovations in content and teaching process.
2. Universities have constantly increasing new technology needs *and* limited resource increases.
3. All endeavors must have education values *and* be revenue producers.
4. Universities are driven by education philosophy and incentives *and* business incentives.
5. Universities strive for collegiality *and* constructive, conflict-loaded debate.
6. Universities want increased governmental funding *and* fewer strings attached
7. Universities want leaders who are committed to education *and* who are business thinkers and do-ers

government funding cutbacks, greatly constraining the scope of the dialogue and neglecting beliefs and values.

Entrepreneurs and managers in public and private organizations had strategies long before the jargon and theory became popular. A few organizations were founded on customer service strategy (e.g., Sam Walton's approach at Wal Mart). Some leaders "announce" their strategy with actions that reveal decisions and some direction, if not a full destination. For example, we will become friendly by expanding hours, lowering costs, increasing support staff and measuring progress. The distance education programs of the universities of Maryland, Phoenix and Penn State are examples. In recent years, colleges have made registration much easier by using the Web, have added new residence facilities with private baths and have expanded social events for "night owls." Others have gone even further, upgrading food service in well-designed dining halls, adding Jacuzzis, fireplaces and café bars.

The leader identifies, evaluates and adapts the customer service strategy, relying on culture to adopt and reinforce it. The process of identifying and reviewing strategy assists leaders in learning how it has succeeded in the past. Strategy review tests the degree of fit between the existing strategy and a changing organizational environment. Culture supports and reinforces this realignment.

Some universities have taken the position that to fairly serve customers they must stand apart from commerce and industry, jealously protecting their objectivity. But Elizabeth's school believes that student-customers benefit from partnerships with local companies and nonprofits. For example, MBA students conduct projects with community-based companies.[17] Pursuing alliances, much like private company partnerships, is the driving force. Consider the principles of this partnership concept as noted by Bell.

THE CASE FOR PARTNERSHIP

A customer partnership is a living demonstration of an attitude or orientation. [The philosophical and practical elements are]

- Powerful partnerships are anchored in an attitude of generosity, a "giver" perspective that finds pleasure in extending the relationship beyond just meeting a need or requirement.
- Powerful partnerships are grounded in trust. Partners don't spend energy looking over their shoulders, but instead take a leap of faith and rely on the relationship
- Powerful partnerships are bolstered by a joint purpose. While this purpose is rarely "written down" each partner is enfolded in a vision or dream of what the association could be and a commitment to take the relationship to a higher plane.
- Powerful partnerships are coalitions laced with honesty. Truth and candor are seen as tools for growth rather than devices for disdain. Partners serve each other straight talk mixed with compassion and care.
- Powerful partnerships are grounded in grace. The spirit of partnership has an artistic flow that gives participants a sense of familiarity and ease.[18]

These principles do not directly address the hard tools of curriculum and education technology but the softer side of culture—using generosity, trust, purpose, honesty and grace to move customers seamlessly between partners—students from undergraduate to graduate and professional schools, students to internships, residents at one medical school to another and to hospitals. Each linkage takes into account the partner's needs: "These requirements are referred to as the five "Cs" of corporate college partnerships: 1. customer service and e-learner support; 2. cohort-based learning; 3. customized programs; 4. content; and 5. cost effective pricing.[19] Eastern's medical school has been involved in partnerships that encourage referrals from community-based physicians and build continuity of care between family practices and specialists. Customers recognize and appreciate these principles. And they notice their absence.

DECISION MAKING—CUSTOMER SERVICE UP OR DOWN

Throughout the university, leaders and employees make decisions enhancing or undercutting customer service. In strategy sessions, the leaders can focus on customer service or ignore it. Consider the following case reported to Elizabeth by a staff member.

THE CASE OF THE CRASHED COMPUTER

My friend bought his son, a student, a new computer as a result of a college promotion. The university had an agreement with a local office supply store to provide discounts to students [a partnership for enhanced service]. The equipment was "low end" in cost, but sold by a major manufacturer. After three months the computer refused to boot up. The student called the technical support hotline, but after an hour they said the hard drive was bad and could be returned for replacement. My friend called the manager at Super Office Supply, who suggested that the faulty hard drive be mailed to the manufacturer. When my friend asked to just bring it into the store for a replacement, the manager said he had to think it over and would call him back. He called back to say they would not replace the computer as it was the manufacturer's responsibility. When my friend protested, the manager referred them back to the university. When my friend called the school to report the experience, he was told that the computers were the responsibility of Super Office Supply. Father and son were mystified and angry.

All organizations regularly make decisions, which roll along, snowball, and eventually determine the "degree of customer friendliness" in the place. Customer friendly service can be raised at each point of the decision making process—at the point of partnership (establishing principles and responsibility), at delivery and at various points of service failure. The culture of the organization helps to determine how its leaders and staff will work each part of the problem. We aim to have each decision naturally support service, but economic and political factors enter the process, undercutting service when they are not accounted for.

PROBLEM SOLVING—SOLUTIONS OFFERED, SOLUTIONS CHOSEN

Because no college or company is perfect, customer service problems do arise (service failure and recovery, see Chapter 3). How these problems are solved (which is driven by cultural orientation) enhances or undercuts service friendliness. Within the culture, how are problems defined and interpreted? And, are the problems bound up in other aspects of the architecture? At a university, the bookstore is a common problem site of service unfriendliness as the legal books case illustrated in an earlier chapter. The problems with law books at first seemed to be a less-than-competent manager. But a deeper analysis revealed a disconnect between partners. What does the case tell us? The attempt to build a customer friendly culture at the university—based in part on bookstore service and book availability—was sabotaged by the misalignment of incentives. While they are presented here as a structural element of the architecture, the connection to a customer friendly culture is clear. What values and beliefs drive bookstore practices—inventory cost control or books for students each time, every time? Not only is the university responsible for culture in the core of the university, but the linkages to partners as well. Consider again the student's computer failure.

THE CASE OF THE CRASHED COMPUTER CONTINUED

After the student contacted the technical support hotline again, the computer company gracefully offered to replace the computer free of charge. The student's father called Super Office Supply to arrange the shipment back to the manufacturer. But the store manager said that the store would not get involved. "Why" asked the father? The manager replied, "We only guarantee for 14 days. After that you call the computer company." The boy's father was amazed and asked who he should contact to arrange shipping. The manager said, "I don't know where to call . . . as I said, it's no longer our problem."

The problem solving path reflects and reinforces the college or company culture. In customer friendly organizations, a typical solution process includes these elements,[20] illustrated by the student's defective computer and the office supply alliance:

- Problem recognition—poor quality computer and poor alliance
- Problem interpretation—computer company honors agreement
- Attention to the problem—no one at university helps
- Courses of action—immediately replace computer, discuss alliance
- Aftermath—student and father happy, Office Supply loses contract

Culture helps us recognize that problems affect service friendliness. We must consider what the ultimate effects of our solutions are. In this case, the student used the computer experience for a presentation in his management class. And, he told six dormitory mates and a girlfriend about the encounter, embellishing the story a bit each time. The "service hostility" was communicated quickly, widely and well. The effects—lost repeat business, reduced referrals, and a tarnished image –were undesirable. The damage was enhanced by a perceived cultural value of "it's not my problem." Elizabeth found out that other students had similar experiences and announced to her staff that "this university responds to service failures" (by clarifying responsibility with partners, such as Super Office Supply and the computer company).

PHYSICAL ENVIRONMENT —Comfort Added

Furnishings, office arrangement and space are some of the physical indicators of culture. One university crafted a fabulous new student union with vaulted ceilings, study and entertainment enclaves, bi-level dining, fireplaces, a nightclub, and extended hours. At a car dealership, hard chairs, dirty floors and a loud television discourage customers from waiting for their cars. Many academic departments have no waiting chairs at all for students, clearly uninviting the students from seeing faculty advisors. Consider what the location of the student ombudsman at Eastern University says.

THE CASE OF THE DISTANT OMBUDSMAN

In many American universities a student ombudsman takes complaints, troubleshoots schedule and living space problems and smoothes interpersonal conflict between students, faculty and staff. At Eastern University, an inquiry about where to find the ombudsman led to directions that included a distant outbuilding, service elevator, and a basement office, hardly a statement of support. The university president has never stopped by.

Some hospitals also have ombudsmen. At Royal Victoria Hospital in Montreal, the patient ombudsman's office is just off the main entrance lobby. Even more important, the patient (customer) representative's office adjoins that of the Chief Executive of the hospital—they share a conference room. This location also makes a statement.[21]

Culture is both "stated" and "reinforced" by physical surroundings. In customer friendly companies, leaders pay attention to the design of friendly physical space, to access and to timing. For example, at Eastern, adult professional students taking evening graduate classes in business administration discovered that the school's cafeteria closed before their arrival at 6:00 pm. While some could dine before class began at 6:30, many came directly from work. They complained, so college staff analyzed the potential costs and revenues for longer cafeteria hours. The staff found that customer levels did not justify staying open for the evening, but they were able to place a rolling cart with cold sandwiches, soups and other light refreshments at the cafeteria entrance, and allow the students to use the tables and chairs.

College administrators had just solved the food problems when students complained about short library hours on Saturday and Sunday. The college decided to extend the hours until midnight on week days and remain open 10:00 am to 10:00 pm on Saturday and Sunday. The university decided extended library hours were critical to the customer's satisfaction and success.

RITUALS AND SYMBOLS—Double Double
Toil and Trouble

How do we judge a university culture's quality, as infused by a sense of friendliness? We could use key measures adopted by U.S. News and World Report: peer assessment, graduation and retention rates, faculty resources, student selectivity, financial resources, alumni giving, and graduation rate performance. These indicators are both widely used and widely criticized. Importantly, they tell us only a little about how and where culture is created, even while they are taken as a "symbol of quality" and used in marketing.

To create a "customer friendly culture," leaders use rituals and symbols. At Eastern University, the President and the Provost preside over annual award ceremonies for support staff, recognizing student service. Faculty awards for research and teaching are common. Annual rituals, such as strategic planning and budgeting sessions, help to direct thinking toward service to students. In some colleges, students are included in the process. Designed to illustrate customer friendly values and ideology, these tools are tangible illustrations of architectural intentions. Some awards given by local, state and national groups now also include educators. In the extreme, select private companies offer awards and use work experiences and language to build and reinforce the friendly culture. Disney is a leader. Staff are called "cast members," are carefully recruited and selected, receive orientation and training including information on the history of the company and are encouraged to reach out to guests making them welcome.[22] Here is a company that invests purposely in customer service quality.

At this company, the abstract notion of "rites and rituals" translates into orientation and training, careful and pointed use of language, awards related to customer service improvement, such as most service-conscious employee, and most productive new service improvement strategy.

Rites and rituals symbolize internal public recognition and sometimes include cash rewards for customer service. This seems straightforward, but can go wrong. Before Elizabeth was appointed Provost at Eastern University, the university offered an "employee of the month" award that was largely ignored. What happened? The intended symbol was insignificant. A college staffer was named customer service employee, received a two-line announcement in the newsletter read by 1% of the employees. With the announcement, the employee received a paper certificate printed "Customer Service Employee of the Month" (cost $.14) which the recipient usually threw away. This patronizing effort did little to enhance customer friendliness. Contrast that with another organization's efforts.

At one company, the chief executive announces the award recipient at an annual banquet. The employee's picture is placed in a prominent position in the local newspaper where his contribution is publicly promoted in a short story. He is awarded an all-expense paid trip for the entire family to a resort. This higher level of award symbolizes the value the firm places on service and the investment they are willing to make. The prominence and the publicity help to establish the cultural presence of customer friendliness with a significant ritual that is widely recognized and a reward that is desired.

MORE RITES AND CEREMONIES—THE CROWN JEWELS

Awards are symbols of culture—the values and ideology of the founders, current leaders and employees. Eastern University, like many other schools and scientific societies, offers prestigious awards for faculty. Universities and colleges across the country present research grants and teaching awards. The recognition, in some cases with elaborate medals, communicates the importance of new ideas, teaching and service to the students. At first, the cultural rites and ceremonies help to publicly establish the core values. Their periodic use reinforces and renews the commitment to customer friendliness.

Nearly every school creates a comprehensive annual plan. We could ask, "Does customer service show up in the annual plan—activities, objectives, and timelines?" If not, service is unlikely to be valued in the culture. At some schools, membership on the strategic planning committee is avidly sought and widely recognized as an opportunity to influence the university's future. These annual and ongoing meetings also serve to "announce" cultural values. Customer friendliness objectives are a part of the output of the planning process, which is increasingly viewed as a major event in university life.

SOCIALIZATION—JOINING THE IN GROUP

In her first few years as Provost, Elizabeth felt she was making some progress in communicating how important student friendliness was to the college's future. Some faculty still refused to call students

" customers," but even they got the point. Each year the 600+ faculty adds about 30–50 new members (through turnover and retirement). To maintain the customer friendly culture, new members are socialized—taught how to think and feel about students/customers. No matter what business we are in, most of us try to hire customer friendly employees. However, the selection process is not foolproof. In customer friendly companies like Disney, socialization is an active and comprehensive process. New staff are taught how to serve customers, how to create q quality guest experience, how to reach out when service failure occurs, and importantly they are rewarded for their service commitment.[23]

In Disney's model, Elizabeth could see the actions taken to establish customer friendliness, such as training, empowerment, structure (rewards) and leadership. Various actions are used to underscore the service value. For Elizabeth, some key actions are:

- Role modeling by leaders
- Public group and individual support of values
- Rewards
- Stories and corporate folklore

The Provost realized that from selection through training, work experiences and recognition, employees can be socialized to the customer friendly culture.

LANGUAGE AND COMMUNICATIONS–
ALL POINTS BULLETIN
The Provost wondered how often she had heard the college President talk about service to students. Do leaders communicate with their managers and their employees that customer service is important? As the well known business authors Tom Peters and Robert Waterman noted many years ago,[24] you must "say it!"—say it in memos, say it in meetings, say it in the way you reward performance. Jack Welch, the retired CEO at GE, once noted how surprised he was to find the number of times he had to communicate the "vision" to get the point across.[25] Over time, this "message" becomes a part of the culture in companies, designed to last lifetimes.[26] The "language" of customer friendliness is at the core of communication in customer friendly cultures.

To determine the degree of friendliness in a culture, we can "listen in" on meetings, asking several questions. Is customer service listed as an agenda item? Is service discussed at critical meetings when important decisions are made about investment? Is customer service a regular topic at senior staff meetings? Does the reward system recognize customer service leadership?

In universities, and too many companies, what we hear is not friendly. Several examples illustrate.

- Teaching students "gets in the way of laboratory work" at large research universities
- Patients are "teaching and research material" at academic medical centers
- Buyers are easily "tricked" at our dealership
- Telephone users are "slammed" to change their long distance supplier
- "With the Internet information," laments one car salesman, "we have seen the last of our 'dumb customers'"

The language of friendliness is established by repetition throughout the organization. How we label customers demonstrates our core values. We look for the language indicators of customer friendliness in: formal documents—university plans and memoranda, videos—marketing, training and course presentations, letters/memos—to Departments and faculty, e-mail and attachments, voice mail—greetings and voice instructions, wait time, telephone conversation—staff and faculty, video conferences—open to the public, not just students and faculty, and face-to-face dialogue, meaning in-office transactions.

The cultural importance of using customer friendliness language is fostered through each of these channels. A quick review establishes the "hostility" or the "friendliness" of the communication, making it visible and simultaneously revealing leaders' core values.

STORIES AND NARRATIVES—THE TALL TALES AND LEGENDS

Stories circulate through organizations, becoming the folklore of our successes and failures, providing models of great effort and innovation. The resulting stories are motivational; they connect the exploits of past and present leaders. When Elizabeth was talking to a board of trustees member about her efforts to increase the customer friendliness of deans, faculty and staff, she related a story about a friend's company. Concerned that leaders and employees of his toy manufacturing company were not customer friendly, he immediately demanded customer surveys and focus groups, and he put executives on the factory and retail floors for a month. These were beginning activities aimed at increasing customer friendliness. Elizabeth thought she saw an immediate parallel to Eastern University. She would place deans in the middle of next semester's registration process.

Customer friendly companies have many tales to tell—the anecdote of the island resort hotel manager traveling miles to obtain face cream for a guest is but one example (see chapter 6). One faculty member on sabbatical heard the story of the South East Queensland Electricity Board in Australia:

~~~~~~~~~~~~~

"Providing excellent customer service is not considered a "quick fix" to a short term problem. South East Queensland continually educates employees to minimize non-value adding activities, based on several recognized principles:

1. Small and incremental efforts should be made throughout the organization
2. A broad range of quality improvement activities should be embraced
3. Customer service should be driven by objective data, e.g., market research, staff surveys, customer communication, complaints data, and customer training
4. Internationally recognized standards-based quality assurance systems should be used to ensure that contractual requirements are met
5. Both internal and external customers should be considered
6. Measurements of customer satisfaction should be used to establish a benchmark against which improvement can be gauged
7. The vast majority of customer service can be improved through well designed processes, procedures and a team approach
8. Customers are individual, and investment in training, participation, motivation, and recognition will add value to customer service
9. Every time a staff member does a job, they do it for someone else"[27]

~~~~~~~~~~~~~

Although philosophy and values are not directly transferable, these principles communicate some of the key standards Elizabeth wants to drive her university culture.

HEROES—THE RIGHT STUFF

In customer friendly cultures, leaders identify company "heroes"; executives, managers, employees anointed by virtue of their customer friendliness. Leaders spread the word that the heroes are highly customer service-oriented. At Eastern University, the first five decades of heroes were the great teachers on the faculty, many of whom did little or no research. But Elizabeth is facing a change in "Hero Membership" as the university now wants faculty that teach *and* conduct research. Customer friendly at Eastern is no longer one dimensional. The Dean of the Medical College at Eastern offered a similar story about a physician faculty member well known for his clinical care and commitment.

THE CASE OF THE CHANGING ACADEMIC MEDICAL CENTER

Dr. Martin, Professor of Pediatrics and Director of the Clinic, began his hospital rounds at 6:15 a.m. By 9:00, he was in his pediatric clinic, which was overflowing due to the cold and flu season. He and two partners worked until 6:00 pm. The other two then left, but Dr Martin was to stay until 7:00 to finish several last patients and some administrative tasks. At 6:55 a frantic mother called saying her two-year old had a severe ear ache. Dr Martin could call in a prescription, give advice for comforting the toddler during the night, or agree to see the mother. He waited with nurses until her arrival at 7:30, finishing the night at 8:00 pm—14 hours after he began. In years past this would be more than enough. But Dr. Martin returned to his lab on the way out to check on the status of his clinical trial, a study of the effectiveness of a new antibiotic for ear infections.

In academic medical centers, customer friendly heroes such as Dr. Martin are recognized for their focus on service to patients. To be successful, they draw on a wide range of resource and power sources, some personal, some organization-based. Service friendly staff like Dr. Martin are admired and supported:

- Because of their *expertise* in meeting the customer needs, e.g., clinical needs and the ability to conduct research
- Because of their *personal charisma* and interpersonal skills, e.g., in comforting a sick child and a worried mother
- Because of their *position* in the company, e.g. as Director of the Pediatric Clinic and member of the strategic planning committee
- Because of their ability to *coerce* colleagues and employees, e.g., nurses now report to the Pediatric Clinic Director and not just to the nursing Director
- Because of the *legitimacy* generated by a record of success with customers and by recognition for outstanding service, e.g., during his 14 year tenure the Pediatric Clinic has become recognized as one of the best in the state

The synergy of personal and organizational power enables customer friendly advocates to succeed and to be widely recognized as role models in the culture whatever the organization—universities, academic medical centers, hotels, hospitals, banks, and airlines.

SUBCULTURES—THE IN CROWD

Elizabeth knew that some departments were more student friendly than others, a common experience in many universities (and companies). The complexity of large organizations insures that subcultures exist in parallel or in resistance to the main culture. Leaders are challenged to encourage departments, distant divisions, and functional specialties, such as billing and collections, to promote customer friendliness. The task is to create an "in crowd" feeling that reinforces alignment of individual department values with the architectural intent to promote customer friendliness organization-wide. In a discussion of this problem at one of her board meetings, a Trustee again referred her to Disney. At Disney, she was reminded, leaders make employees "partners" in the culture.

Customer friendly leaders communicate to the organization that a service-oriented network is the key to rewards and power, e.g., "extra" benefits are based on customer service assessments. Leaders pushing customer friendly behavior insure that this cultural network consists of a select group of customer-oriented people.

Elizabeth decided to select a "kitchen cabinet" of senior faculty to use as an informal advisory board. She chose faculty that had a long standing reputation for both teaching quality and research productivity. In announcing the selections, she commented on why students want faculty who are good teachers and who are at the forefront of their fields. The message was not missed. The creation of the committee and the membership publicly announced the "in crowd" for Elizabeth's tenure.

Of course, some faculty refused to recognize the intended direction. By managing subcultures, leaders address conformity and deviance in the architecture. Cultural networks that conform are valued subcultures in the eyes of architects—many departments agreed with and readily supported Elizabeth's intentions. Their values, relationships and behaviors support and enhance customer friendliness.

COUNTERCULTURES–THE OUT CROWD

The architectural design calls for consistent customer friendliness throughout the organization—from products to incentives to staff attitudes. With strong leadership and generally good employee support, we can feel confident of consistency. But there are "deviants." In some departments, divisions or functional areas, customers are viewed differently—as enemies, as "takers," as potential victims and/or as "suckers." The long-standing stereotypes of this viewpoint are used car dealers, door-to-door pitchmen, and university finance officers. The Provost learned this when several alumni spoke to her at a fund raiser.

THE CASE OF THE HOSTILE MONEY MEN

At Eastern University, the bursar's office manages student bills and payment—any and all finance related matters.. The students are referred to as "cheats," " liars," and so on. As a university known for outstanding teaching and support, Eastern's finance office is a deviant—a hotbed of customer hostility. Students complain that the office staff will not provide clear information about procedures, deadlines, and financing options. On the other hand, staff feel that they are berated and ridiculed by students and have come to see students as enemies. Finance office staff feel these spoiled, privileged students deserve little respect.

Leader-architects work to promote customer friendly consistency but they can be resisted and undercut by a counter culture group. The finance group cannot be allowed to maintain their attitudes in the face of an organization determined to be student friendly. The rejection of mainstream values blocks the successful university-wide philosophy and tarnishes the good work of other units.

CONTINUITY AND REINFORCEMENT— BATTING 1000 OR AT LEAST 300+

Customer friendly companies design and develop a culture of friendliness, but leaders realize that, without ongoing attention, cultural decay will set in. The question, then, is what are the architectural components of cultural continuity? Elizabeth spoke with an alumus over lunch about the strategy in his learning company. As founder of a private tutorial company, the founder made customer friendliness a key focus of his working philosophy using the values in recruiting and selection and continuously expressing concern for and support of service quality. Weekly and monthly meetings reinforced this focus with constant attention illustrated by meeting agenda items and the use of service indicators shared with all employees. What does this founder know about cultural continuity? His leadership style shows us that:

- He knows the value of public praise of service.
- He clearly communicates the service friendliness intent and regularly mentions it.
- He is willing to discuss the results of service success and failure.
- He is aware that taking no action won't work. Failure to discuss service friendliness will send a message as well.

Leaders build "friendliness continuity" with a sense of behaviors and communication.

ENVIRONMENTAL CONTEXT—A BRAVE NEW WORLD

"Environmental context" is also a contributor to the service architecture and therefore to the organization's culture. Actions outside the organization influence the degree to which the organization is customer friendly. For example, university bookstores are at the mercy of publishers' printing and distribution schedules. Grumpy students facing several weeks of classes without textbooks blame the bookstore for delays and high prices, but the problem may be outside the "boundaries" of bookstore control. Costs are dictated by publishers. A university culture of friendliness is hard-pressed to extend these beliefs to a bookstore operating in a "hostile environment". Consider this example of a situation familiar to many universities across the United States. Cutbacks have a "chilling effect" on the culture, restraining resource use and risk that goes with innovation.

THE CASE OF THE MISSING STATE FUNDING

One of Elizabeth's friends is Chancellor of a 15 institution educational system in a Midwest state. The universities are distinct entities, but are all linked in a single state-funded consortium. Because the state has struggled with budget shortfalls for the past ten years, they have neglected capital improvements from basic building maintenance to new dormitories. And, costs have risen considerably with the delay. Political leaders are still reluctant to commit the tens of millions of dollars needed to catch up. Meanwhile, students attend classes with the roof leaking, the heating system sporadically down, and not enough wiring to handle the Internet needs—all customer service shortfalls.

All institutions must struggle to serve their customers in both hostile and friendly environments. Successful service architects analyze and respond to a changing environment full of politics, economics, international affairs, law and regulation. Should leaders or customers acknowledge this education funding problem, which ultimately undercuts a culture of friendliness? Elizabeth's Chancellor friend demonstrates leadership awareness of hostile environmental forces. Funding constraints are bound up in four themes that erode friendliness.

- *Complexity* of competing issues, such as access for future students, adoption of new technology, and the politics of existing vs. new students' needs
- *Connectedness*—to the economy, to perceived inefficiencies in educational institutions
- *Severity of change*—imposed by severe budget shortfalls, by mandated admissions for state students, and by the pace of new technology
- *Timing*—shortfalls during a period of emerging Internet-based education and technology, increased competition

This educational business environment is complex, connected, severe, and untimely. In some other sectors, a hostile environment is even more dramatic. Consider this health care case in an academic medical center alliance.

THE CASE OF WAR

The Western Medical School and its partner, Regional Veterans Administration Medical Center, spent six months working on a strategic plan to increase the range and quality of patient services. Leaders and employees scrutinized every aspect of the organization, proposing clinical care changes, a departmental reorganization, team building sessions and new staff. They surveyed patients about care delivery difficulties and asked for suggestions for improvement. With the service improvement plan in place, they were ready for action. But a war in the Middle East began, completely changing their priorities. VA Medical Centers are firstly responsible for war casualties, so individual strategic plans go immediately on hold.

This is an extreme case of environmental impact—the effects of international conflict and war. Since VA Medical Centers have casualty responsibility, any attention to "regular" customers must wait. Universities do not have quite this problem—although a substantial and protracted war would eventually drain both potential students and funding.

CULTURE AND OTHER SYSTEMS' INTERACTION

The creation and maintenance of culture is not independent of the other architectural systems—product, structure, psychological climate and management. Each system helps build the culture and reflects the underlying values and beliefs of the founders and leaders. Creating and maintaining customer friendliness organization-wide means each of the systems independently and interdependently must support friendliness.

What are we trying to do when we create a student/customer friendly culture? One group articulated the objective in a report titled, "A Framework for Building Safe and Serious Schools." The report centers on five areas in which schools can focus their personalization efforts: knowing our students better, trusting our students more, empowering our students in authentic ways, connecting our students in meaningful ways, and honoring all students in varied systems of recognition and reward.[28] While the leading concerns from the report are rooted in psychological climate, the implications are interactive in the architecture, affecting leadership, incentive structure, and core cultural values. Consider the contributions of the four other architectural elements at Eastern.

First, there must be commitment to high quality products—curriculum and courses designed and delivered with competence and excellence. Curriculum and course delivery failures must be recognized and addressed. (See chapter 3).

Structurally, Eastern must include incentives for high quality teaching, research, and community service. The university bureaucracy and structure must enable discretionary decision making and smooth the flow of communication. (See chapter 4)

A culture of friendliness in a university depends on a psychological climate that is especially collegial and open. So-called "culture wars" have a chilling effect on this atmosphere as both sides attempt to intimidate the other. The very essence of interdisciplinary education depends on an open climate with a balance of consensus and difference. (See chapter 5)

Finally, managers and leaders at all levels of the institution must model and reward behaviors and strategies that either reinforce or undercut friendliness in the culture (see chapter 6). This translates into accessibility of chairmen and senior professors, interactions with undergraduates, and helpful staff attitudes.

SUMMARY

This chapter addressed the relationship between customer friendliness and company culture. While "culture" is abstract, there are certain concrete indicators of cultural values. The importance of service is illustrated by discussions in meetings, by annual service awards, and by the organization's leaders (customer-friendly types or not). To build a culture of customer service, several broad actions are relevant:

- Build a corporate culture that says "customer service is important".
- Establish customer service as a core value and set specific goals for customer service improvement.
- Establish rights and rituals that recognize and support service.
- Identify and create customer service heroes.

- Establish a cultural network of people who are excessively and obsessively service-oriented.
- Monitor customer service threats and opportunities outside the organization's boundaries.

We can see from the university example that culture is a critical contributor to friendliness. However, it contributes no more or less so than other aspects of the architecture—products, structure, psychological climate and leadership. This university case concludes the discussion of the five systems and their contributions to customer service friendliness across the organization. Each leader needs to think about how to integrate improvement actions within and across the systems (an improvement package of strategies and actions). An example of how to design and use the improvement process is presented in the final chapter.

Chapter 8

THE PROCESS OF BECOMING CUSTOMER FRIENDLY THE CASE OF THE MAPLETREE LIBRARY

In many fields—public education and airline transportation for example—we are seeking to improve the customer friendliness of current operations and to establish a service oriented structure for the future . Do we have an approach and procedure for becoming customer friendly? It is clear to executives, administrators, employees and consumers that the current levels of customer friendliness in schools and airlines are weak. Similar concerns exist in manufacturing, banking, environment and health care. How do we design our future organizations to insure customer friendliness is the question.[1,2] An integrated systems-oriented approach to the design and redesign of customer friendly organizations is the topic of this last chapter. The approach is illustrated by the case of Mapletree Public Library, a type of organization present in nearly all of our communities.

Laura has been Executive Director of Mapletree Library for 12 years. She holds a BA in English from the University of Maryland and a masters degree in Library Science with a concentration in Information Systems (also from the University of Maryland). She began her career at private law libraries where resources were rich. After 3 years in a large law firm she became Reference & Development Director for a large city library. Her success in collection building and fund raising led to her appointment at Mapletree. She was not surprised to find a need for customer friendliness and for funds to support the library.

One of her first acts was to appoint a Task Force of staff and regular library patrons to create a vision of a customer friendly library. She asked them to provide a scenario of what one would look like—from facility and furnishings to types of holdings to modern technology. Their report included the following statement.

"We would like a library in a larger facility with comfortable furniture and quiet reading areas. Small rooms for study groups would be available for reserve. We want a rich set of holdings but not extensive duplication of academic and professional books and journals available at local college libraries. We want ports to connect our laptops and/or wireless connections. The staff would be knowledgeable about the latest search techniques and the Internet so that they can help with individual searches and even provide training.

We would like extended hours, a separate "café area" for coffee, tea, and snacks and a community room to host lectures. We would like circulation check out processes to be easy and Interlibrary loan to be quick. Last, we would like our library to partner with other libraries."

In reading the scenario, Laura saw that one weakness was glaring—the lack of up-to-date technology.

As we struggle to improve customer friendliness, we find that professionals in any one field, like Laura, are far from alone. Consider the following:

- many citizens and professional educators find American educational systems fatally flawed
- manufacturers face global competition forcing them to find new ways to organize and to produce goods for a world wide market
- bankers, once secure in their community relations and small town partnerships, are acquired and closed by mega banks
- governmental leaders at all levels find dissatisfaction with public service costs, performance and relations with citizens
- individual departments in all of our organizations ask how they can redesign to address the pressures for change
- patients complain of medical errors, production line service and poor communication between and from physicians

The "customer unfriendly" problem that is so visible in health care and education turns out to be a common problem across fields and professional disciplines.

Customer friendliness improvement—often allied in purpose and procedure with continuous quality improvement[3-6]—has clearly excited the private sector industrial world, with the academies and nonprofits increasingly interested the last ten years. To engage the interest, we must have clear answers to two questions:

- What are the strategic tasks for the leaders of the organization as they engage in customer service management?
- What are the protocols and working steps for project teams attacking specific customer service improvement tasks?

The position here is that a *general procedure for customer friendliness improvement* can be created. The improvement pathway has been paved with existing quality and planning models. Recognizing that there is no one best way, a general procedure for customer friendliness improvement can be tailored to fit the specific needs of individual public and private organizations across fields and industries.

The roots of this procedural synthesis are in *teaching and learning, organization change and development, and evaluation and assessment.* This systems approach[7] is based on five assumptions:

(1) redesign is a sociotechnical systems task;
(2) "future building" is both "intended/rational" and "emergent/ intuitive";
(3) redesign procedures are "rough guidance" not a mechanical blueprint;
(4) procedural adaptation is required for each unique setting; and
(5) models for building friendliness will continue to evolve.

We will use the Mapletree Public Library as our case, remembering that the process is applicable to health care, manufacturing, airlines, hotel and hospitality services, banking, and education (as illustrated in Chapters 2-7).

THE MAPLETREE LIBRARY CASE

Many organizations recognize their need to integrate new technology in order to better serve their customers. However, leaders and employees rarely think consciously about the characteristics of their company that help to produce and support successful service. For example, in manufacturing, we are interested in the characteristics of production plants that "co-produce" timely, quality products (e.g. teamwork, planning, decision making, inventory control). Most companies seek ideas on how to create and maintain a high performance organization including detailed and ongoing attention to user needs in periods of change. Libraries now confront significant changes as new technologies rapidly come into use and are both expected and demanded by customers—high school and college students, parents and faculty. We begin with this case: the Mapletree Library.

Mapletree Library serves a population of about 250,000. In existence for over 100 years, the library has a staff of 120. Their annual budget of about 3 million dollars supports 10 branches, holdings of 800,000 books and circulation of about 900,000 per year. Always busy, they serve both adults and many secondary school and college students. Lately, the library has been swamped by new "internet customers." Laura, Mapletree's Director, is interested in becoming more customer friendly by increasing use of new technologies, technologies requested by and demanded by customers.

The question for library executives and staff is: can we identify the organizational elements that help us to successfully implement new technology? (i.e. to improve our customer friendliness).At a weekly meeting the staff brainstormed a list of problems related to this new technology and to new technology in general. Their items included:

- wide ranging user sophistication and training needs
- scheduling of longer hours
- insufficient and outdated equipment
- new data base requests
- copyright uncertainties
- no financial support for technology updates
- staff resistance
- staff training needs
- purchasing "naivete"
- email and all night reference service requests

The staff agreed that they need to work on the "technology problem," or face continuing customer complaints. And, they agreed they would benefit from a greater understanding of where they are now (diagnosis) and where they are trying to get to (vision).

We will return to the case, but we first must consider some of the underlying assumptions of the customer friendly improvement process.

Philosophy and Approach

A planned approach to customer service improvement—at Mapletree and other organizations—contributes to performance in at least five ways.[8, 9]

- The desired organizational future must include quality customer service as a core value and part of a sought after vision.
- A systematic and ongoing review of the external environment identifies both national and competitors' customer service standards (benchmarks) as a base for comparison.
- A review of the present informs employees and administrative leaders about their starting point (baselines for customer friendly service).
- Investment of resources to address customer service shortfalls can result in significant cost savings (improving quality is cost containing).
- In a changing environment, one loaded with cost versus quality confrontations, organizations will need to do some things differently to protect customer service quality (planned change).

Disconnected, remedial actions to improve service quality can reduce discrete problems, such as waiting times in a physician's office, student course scheduling, car maintenance, and even hospital patient satisfaction with food, as indicated throughout this book. But each organization must individually plan its own, unique, customer friendly future by considering the whole organization as a co-producer of quality improvement.

Traditional customer service responses involve reactions aimed at attacking quality deficiencies in *existing production* and *delivery* processes. The procedures are often operations-oriented, focused on the "shop floor " (e.g., check out and cataloguing processes in a library). In contrast, planning and redesign is a preventive approach that eliminates customer service problems at the process-creation stage. Berwick identifies this as a change in "mental models" that guide our improvement strategies.[10] For example, when examining delays in hospital patient discharge, we must understand how patients are admitted to the hospital in order to improve their movement into and out of the full range of services. At Westside Hospital , competitive customer and cost pressures (external/strategic) demand speedy discharge of patients (internal/operational coordination) (see

Chapter 2). It is what Ackoff considers to be *the dissolving of the conditions that gave rise to the problem in the first place*. All organizations could do this, but they need a process that targets customer friendliness as a strategic issue *and* as an operations problem.

The customer service improvement processes described here can be used by a department, a unit, or a whole organization.By building on existing efforts, this approach bridges disciplinary boundaries and is transferable across manufacturing industries and service companies in the public and private sectors.

The approach is both simple and complex. It builds on three organizational improvement pillars:

(1) continuous quality improvement
(2) reengineering; and
(3) vision building and strategic planning.

The procedures are both "shop floor"-oriented *and* strategic in perspective, different yet consistent with the way many think of quality service planning and improvement action. Continuing with our Eastern University Case (see Chapter 7), an example in university education illustrates.

Imagine three university faculty meeting for lunch to discuss the dismal state of teaching and learning . Each agrees that faculty could do much more to improve teaching (to help their student customers). One of the three suggests that they each make a statement of what they would do—as individuals. Their answers capture the need for (1) an incremental approach to improvement; (2) to radical reengineering of teaching approaches; and (3) to new visions.

Professor Thomas. I believe in the *continuous quality improvement* of our well-tested, traditional approach to teaching. I think faculty should be constantly refining and updating their lectures. In-class work should include a variety of occasional films, pop quizzes, and regular writing requirements with detailed feedback. By continuous incremental improvement of the fundamentals we should approximate excellence across the faculty and better serve our student customers.

Professor Franklin. I disagree. Traditional approaches have not worked. It is only through a complete *reengineering* of our approach to teaching will we achieve excellence. For example, I would organize the students into project teams emphasizing active learning. In-class work would include limited lecturing with much interactive "question and answer," discussion and debate. Outside work sessions would be required. Students would produce group projects and receive both individual and group grades, improving our customers' learning experiences.

Professor Martin. Wrong, we need an entirely new *vision* of teaching. I propose we put courses on the internet, using distance learning technologies to take courses to the student. Students would use simulations, learning much from compact disks at home. We would have a world-wide market with an international student base and self-pacing to fit individual needs (through programmed texts).

~~~~~~~~~~~~~~~~

Obviously each of the professors could elaborate their individual approaches to the redesign task. This brief anecdote illustrates the three components—*continuous incremental improvement* of current methods, *radical reengineering* of classroom approaches, and a completely new *vision* of the educational future. The point is that all three are needed for a successful redesign, a redesign that enhances customer friendliness.

How does Mapletree Library successfully embrace new technology for its customers—through gradual adoption, large "leaps" into new technology or a rethinking of the concept of library (given the web and extensive internet use of posted resources).

ROOTS OF THE PROCEDURAL SYNTHESIS

The combined approach is based on several common purposes. Each of the procedures—quality improvement, reengineering and visioning—are used for the following three purposes: organization change and development, teaching and learning, and evaluation and assessment. The intent is ongoing development of organization structures and processes (change) which requires both teaching and learning and periodic review of progress.

There is already much history. Over the past 20–30 years, but particularly the last ten years, specific methods and tools have been developed.

Quality improvement work led by Deming,[11] Juran[12] and Crosby[13] has been emphasizing the search for quality—increased customer friendliness—as an organization-wide philosophy and approach.

Reengineering has both extended and adapted total quality management and systems thinking, with a definitive emphasis on radical results—changes to core business processes that enhance services to customers in dramatic ways. Rather than an incremental, continuous improvement of existing processes, designers are asked to think of bold change. Reengineering is a "blowing up" of existing business processes[14-19] but not usually a redesign of the whole organization.

Whole organization visions move the stakes up a level, expanding the purview. As one example, Ackoff's work on idealized design, first offered in the 1970's takes a systems and whole-organization perspective.[20-22] Participants are asked to consider the question: if we could redesign our whole organization right now—to be more effective in this environment—what would it look like? Rather than incremental change, this approach pushes for a radical redesign that will serve as a change incentive.

Our brief review can begin with any of the three streams. Here we start with Ackoff's work on idealized design because it incorporates some of the continuous improvement and reengineering thinking. In 1970, Ackoff published *A Concept of Corporate Planning* presenting his approach for creating new organization designs through strategic planning processes. He would use his approach to strategic planning to help Mapletree Library adapt to new technology demands. His follow up works have elaborated this model over the past 35 years.[23] At the same time, quality management was unfolding with leading writer-practitioners Deming, Juran and Crosby offering both the philosophy and the procedure of continuous improvement. Hammer and Champy's work on reengineering for example is both more recent and a derivative of these original streams of quality improvement and visioning.

We will not further consider the history other than to remark that their concurrent development reflects the general dissatisfaction with the status quo of *customer unfriendliness*. We recognize the need to develop formal procedures for moving forward into a vastly changed future at both the operating level—where products are made and delivered—and the strategic decisions of the whole organization (culture, values and grand design level).

All of these customer friendly improvement efforts point to five assumptions that are the underpinnings for this model.

1. *Redesign is sociotechnical in nature.* Customer friendly organizations are comprised of: (1) the *technology* or core business e.g. library circulation, reference and cataloguing, medical therapies, industrial engineering, banking services (the technical aspect of sociotechnical) and (2) the values, culture and psychology of the workplace (the *social systems* side). Most often we think about customer friendly improvement in terms of new techniques and products, (see Chapter 3) paying much less attention to the nature of the social system we will need. We cannot redesign manufacturing, medical care, or teaching processes without considering the psychological impact on providers/employees and customers. At Mapletree Library the anxieties and resistance of the staff (psychology)are as important as the type of Internet service (technology). .

2. *Future building is both intended/rational and emergent/intuitive.* We often set out to purposely plan for our desired customer friendly future—an intended, rational process. But the future of our organizations "emerges" from a complex set of external environmental threats and opportunities and internal decisions and actions (many that are intuitive and not easily explained). Thus we purposely plan *and* we flexibly take advantage of new options and imaginative ideas. We have moved from grand plans—blueprints—to a sense of flexibility and adaptability based on experience. Most recently we believe that logic does not prevail over emergent creative processes. At Mapletree Library we can create a "technology adoption plan" but we will need imaginative "on the spot" ideas from staff (combining intended with emergent).

3. *Redesign procedures are "rough guidance" not a mechanical blueprint.* The most recent strategic planning and futures literature suggests that a tight set of steps walked out in mechanical fashion is not flexible enough to address the emergent/intuitive flow of ideas and options that make great companies. Thus redesign processes should be viewed as a "skeleton" with much room for additions, eliminating the confinement and innovation-killing "boxes" present in many planning processes. The step-by-step procedures of the past have failed because organizational life is not so mechanized. Taken as "general direction," redesign plans help to guide us, but without detailed prescriptions. Mapletree's executive staff and board must create their own unique process, inventing new procedural actions

as they go forward in a constantly changing world, realizing that plans may be changed over time.

4. Procedural adaptation is required for each unique setting— creative innovative use of the model. Organizations are all unique. Future design processes must be created to fit each individual culture. Some are very formal and bureaucratic, requiring extensive minutes and follow up reports. In others the process is informal with little written (fast moving decisions seemingly flow from "breakfast meetings"). No single model can be used in all organizations because companies and non-profits and governments are all unique enough to require tailor-made processes. Laura, Mapletree's executive can not simply follow a "cookbook plan" as their organization is different from others.

5. The model is still evolving. We are far from a consensus on a process for development of customer friendly organizations. What we are seeing is some increasing recognition of the interconnectedness of quality improvement, reengineering, visioning, and strategic planning, i.e., customer service improvement[24], is realized by a number of concurrent strategies. We have not created a definitive model of change because we are still building our knowledge of the philosophy and methods of redesign. Mapletree's executives will not find a "one best way" to embrace technology. And the process successfully used by another library may not suit them.

With these assumptions in mind we can consider a general model for customer friendly improvement, one with six steps.

This approach defines an organization-wide process used to improve customer friendliness preceding or concurrent with project efforts at the team level. Through planning, the organization defines customer service quality improvement as a strategic concern that must be addressed in an organized, purposeful way.[24-26] Competitors, and regulators demand quality improvement, and as external actors, they encourage each department, unit, and organization to plan for customer friendly improvement on both an organization-wide and an individual subunit basis. Strategic level work follows a general procedure with the steps shown in Table 1. The process encourages and requires leaders to confront the service friendliness problem in a strategic way; meaning strategic for the organization as a whole and for the level of

Table 8.1 Steps to customer friendly improvement

1.0 Define & Describe Present Levels of Customer Friendliness
1.1 external conditions
1.2 internal strengths and needs
2.0 Define & Describe Desired Future Customer Friendliness
3.0 Critical Gap Analysis (between current and future)
4.0 Define Grand & Leading Strategies
5.0 Identify Resource Requirements
6.0 Establish Operational Start-up: Actions, Responsibilities, & Evaluation

the department e.g., a strategic future for improved quality in engineering, production, marketing, human resources, or accounting.

For the Mapletree Library, better technology implementation best emerges from a process involving four well known tasks:

- *diagnosis* to examine the state of technology support in every area of the library's organization architecture
- *planning* to take a uniquely tailored set of improvement actions throughout the organization (the architectural systems: products, structure, psychological climate, leadership, and culture)
- *action* to implement multiple methods in multiple areas of the library's operations
- *evaluation* to assess the impact organization-wide

Importantly, the underlying concept is what academics have labeled "double loop learning." By this we mean leaders question operations level customer service *and* they question the rationale for offering the service at all.[27] That is, how available and reliable is Internet service at Mapletree Library, and is there a driving need for the service in order for the library to continue to receive its constituency's support? The change process addresses customer friendliness issues organization-wide (total management) as well as the project work targeted by individual units and teams (specific problem and project-oriented interventions—such as how to pay for more computers).

In a sense there is a strategic imperative in our Mapletree Library case. How do we create libraries with diversity in their approach to adapting to new technology? And, importantly, how would we fix those that are struggling with technology disasters? Recently commentators have suggested the need for a new vision of libraries, for a new vision of the public library, for innovative use of technology, and for library reorganization to address change.[28-31] In years past, libraries could acquire and begin to use new technology in a graduated fashion—not the "fast forward" pace of today. The option to ignore the technological imperative will be even less viable in the future. Library leaders are confronted by at least six enviromnental pressures (external to their organizations) to improve their use of technology: technology breakthroughs in—capability, availability, cost, rapid adoption of Internet use by schools, recognition of technology capability as a key job skill, the capability of privatization as an alternative (outsource), accountability for and stewardship of scarce resources, and declining/increasing levels of public funding.

In short, societal forces—across fields including libraries—are mandating attention to technology and to the change it fosters. The wide ranging impact of the information revolution has been noted.[32] New ways of organizing and leading will be needed by both public and private sector companies.[33] Threats of corporate oblescence,[34] pressure to change human resources[35] and the recognition of transitions in adapting to technology[36] have been cited. We must look inside the library organization to see how supportive we now are of technology development and how we can design/redesign our libraries to be more "technology friendly." Let us look more closely at the steps in the process.

1.0 DEFINE AND DESCRIBE THE PRESENT

To improve customer friendliness, we must have strong knowledge of the organization's structures and processes (*internal operations*) and the environment in which it exists (*external conditions*). The purpose of this Step is to define where the organization is starting from—its current degree of customer friendliness. First, planners look outside the organization for external customer friendliness standards (such as competitors and industry data). For example, what are the technology capability and service levels in other libraries? The outside look is referred to as benchmarking.

Second, planners evaluate internal customer friendliness strengths and weaknesses (internal performance trends). What is the quality of the support system e.g., in terms of response time for a student asking a reference librarian for help with an Internet search? Here, we ask for an assessment of the strong and weak aspects of the organization, while simultaneously building baselines and potential points for action. Let us look more closely at these two procedures.

1.1 External Conditions. Trends and issues outside of the organization (the "environment") are searched and analyzed as to their likely impact on the organization (an environmental scan).[37] The underlying assumption is that the external environment—both perceived and real—plays an increasingly major role in the organization's success or failure via its degree of customer friendliness. Environmental pressures and trends could mean that the organization should literally be offering different products or services during the coming three to five to ten years. Mapletree Library must embrace technology and Internet services or risk losing the support of the community. Each organization's environment is unique, consisting of changes in such areas as economics, politics, demographics, law and natural resources (e.g., aging population means more library users; heating cost increases tighten the budget).

Organizations engage in scanning at levels that vary in sophistication and depth. For example, one city library's "environmental scanning activity" is conducted by a small group. The director of purchasing, one reference librarian and the Deputy Director for Operations meet for lunch about once a week to talk about "what's going on out there." This is not as dependent on extensive, formalized data sets as it is on a "sharp eye" wielded by the people within the organization. This group does not use an analyst's research on economic projections, measures of technological development and change, or data and demographic trends. Instead they use their own "intuitive sense" of what's happening in the environment, plus information culled from colleagues, customers and competitors. Mapletree Library's staff uses their state and national associations and their network of colleagues at other libraries.

At the other end of the scanning spectrum are the groups who use sophisticated, analytical and data-based methods for plotting various trends and changes in the environment. These reports are developed one or more times a year and are presented as a formal environmental assessment (usually in a formal strategic planning process). Some industry groups even publish them as reports for the members (e.g., American Hospital Association). While Mapletree library is too small to have such a formal in house group, they can expect information from the American Library Association.

1.2 Internal Analysis. A second part of defining the present is a review of the "internal" aspects of the organization or department, e.g the Mapletree Library's current operations and structure. Along with external environmental drivers of change, there are internal elements that define the nature of the organization in the present (see Chapter 2). Future design takes into account both the external and internal systems—the essence of the systems approach to organizational analysis. This approach integrates research on organization design and change with a model of the organization that is based on the work of F. E. Kast and J. E. Rosenzweig published initially in 1970.[38, 39] We have used the model in a series of researches and consulting assignments over the past 20 years and as a basis for graduate courses in organization behavior, management policy, management information systems, health care quality and consulting/problem solving.[40–47] It has been the analytical guide for internal strengths and weaknesses reviews in strategic planning processes of dozens of organizations[48] and is based on a recent book.[49]

A systems model of organization directs us to five areas of inquiry inside an organization (such as Mapletree Library): (1) culture (e.g., values and beliefs); (2) technologies (e.g., search and circulation); (3) structure (e.g., departmentalization); (4) psychology and sociology (e.g., group dynamics); and (5) management (e.g., planning and control). These subsystems—as an integrated whole—are the organization and are the critical elements of all organizations e.g production, manufacturing and service companies, hospitals, schools. Those experienced at implementing new technologies recognize that barriers are present in each of these areas of the organization. To search for organizational characteristics and interventions supportive of successful technology implementation, we can use the model as a guide, examining each of these subsystems for barriers and opportunities. A systematic mapping enables library executives and staff to develop strategies for addressing concerns throughout the organization.

As a whole, these subsystems and their interrelationships are the organization to be planned for—the target of the customer friendly future redesign work. Each participant is first asked to identify the core competencies.[50] The design/redesign group systematically examines each of the subsystems, searching for significant customer service competencies and weaknesses of the architecture of the whole and the parts meaning: the product/technical system; the structural system; the psychosocial system; the managerial system; and the cultural system (goals and values).

When participants think of the core work of the organization—book circulation in a library, medical care in hospitals, counseling in a social service agency, legislative activity in an association—what is done very well? Mapletree Library would inspect hardware/software, incentives, staff willingness to adopt new technology and leader commitment to moving forward.

The analysis strives for as complete a description of the customer friendly organization as possible—identifying strengths and weaknesses. "Needs" is the identifying term as in *what do we need to do* that the organization is not now doing, and *what do we need to do differently.* The latter often stimulates discussion of redesign and organization change issues to improve friendliness.

Whole parts of the organization can be considered strengths or weaknesses. For example, one newer library defined their customer service strengths as their hardware and software , their support staff, and their financial position. The librarians were viewed by students and colleagues as the best in the area. Technician staff were dedicated and skilled. A strong financial base enabled them to invest in continuing education for the staff. Weaknesses (in management) included staff scheduling, staff turnover, and board relations. Access to and support of the newest technology was also cited. All of these became targets for change in a newly envisioned customer friendly future, one that builds on strengths and attacks weaknesses. Mapletree Library used a short survey to begin to discuss the friendliness of the present structure. Used in any field, the survey probes each element of the organization with a score indicating degree of friendliness. The scoring is used less for an absolute indicator of scientific truth and more for a stimulant for discussion. The belief is that no matter how customer friendly we now are, we can always be better. And, we certainly want to know whether staff feel we are customer unfriendly. In this way the survey helps to complete our picture of the present.

2.0 Define & Describe Desired Customer Friendly Future

Step Two is the creative design or redesign of the desired customer friendly future of the organization. Building on Russell Ackoff's idealized design process, the step requires participants to design/redesign their organization (or department) in any way they want in order to maximize customer friendliness. According to Ackoff, futures planning involves a series of psychological barriers that must be cleared. In his view, "Probably the most important property of an idealized design [is that] . . . it reveals that the principal obstruction between us and the future we most desire is ourselves. This obstruction can be removed by a set of mobilizing ideas; an idealized design can provide such a set of ideas."[51] In this Step participants take the position that the organization does not exist (it does not really exist in the case of a new organization). If it could be designed or redesigned in any way at all, how would the participants create it in order to improve customer friendliness?

The purposes of Step 2—creative design/redesign—are several. Customer friendly improvement teams at Mapletree engage in the design work, asking:

- participants to think creatively about their organization's purposes, structure, and work process from the starting point without existing constraints on services.
- participants to focus on what they would change—further surfacing issues for organizational attention and development (friendliness improvement opportunities)
- participants to inject innovation and creativity into organizational structures and processes that may have been in place for years or decades.

The intention is a "zero-based" redesign concept—an opportunity to start fresh creating a whole architecture addressing customers' needs. For Mapletree Library—with a 75 year history—traditions and customary procedures have long been assumed. The process addresses the problem that prevailing organization structures and processes are too often taken as starting and fixed points. The process requires courage from participants because we are called upon to do something new, to push into a forest where there are no well-worn paths and from which no one has returned to guide us. The "first cut" scenario produced by the Mapletree Task Force is a good start. With redesign to improve customer friendliness at some level a necessity for all organizations, how do we go about it?

There are three properties of an idealized design which are conditions to be met by the design team. An idealized design for a customer friendly future must be: (1) Technologically feasible, (2) Operationally viable and (3) Capable of rapid learning and adaptation. Why are these conditions important? "The product of an idealized design is not an ideal system, because it is capable of being improved and improving itself. Therefore, it is not perfect or utopian system. Rather, it is the most effective ideal seeking system of which its designers can conceive. It is that system with which its designers would currently replace the system planned for if they were free to replace it with any system they wanted."[52] The three properties are requirements that insure that proposed designs for the organization's future are not utopian (divorced from the realities of daily operations including constraints of the marketplace). When applying this approach, the first outcome is usually dissatisfaction with continuing as is. This leads to efforts to define a more desirable state. The idealized design becomes a statement of invested aspirations.

Importantly, the idealized design/redesign is not a creative stand-alone step. Beginning with vision-building effort is daunting without data and without sensitivity to the external and internal systems. This step is driven by the group's previous thinking about changes in the external environment and about the strengths and needs in the five internal organizational systems—which are, in summary, pressures for greater customer friendliness.

Idealized design is the philosophical match of continuous quality improvement. In both, the point is to strive for higher quality performance by constantly redesigning all aspects of the organization from culture to service delivery systems to reporting and reward structure to quality of working life and management style. Mapletree Library staff will look at all aspects of their operation, an openness that requires leadership from Laura.

There are seven tasks in this "visioning" procedure, regardless of the level of the organization. The customer friendliness improvement team must:

1. Develop a generalized *vision* of a desired customer quality future that is exciting and challenging to all staff.
2. Describe the dominant customer service improvement *goals and values* of the future.

3. Describe the *expected customer quality levels* of every aspect of the organization—both technical and administrative operations.
4. Redesign the *structure* to enhance the customer friendliness of the administrative service.
5. Describe the desired *psychological climate* that would maximize customer service quality in the future.
6. Describe a customer service-oriented, quality enhancing *management*, including its planning, leadership, and control activities.
7. Develop an *integrated vision* of the higher quality organization that is broad yet detailed enough to motivate the project level teams.

Answering these questions leads to the development of a vision of the quality future that is both directional and specific. As Ackoff put it: "Design is a cumulative process. It is usually initiated by using a very broad brush. Therefore, the first version is a rough sketch. Then details are gradually added and revisions are made. The process continues until a sufficiently detailed design is obtained to enable others to carry it out as intended by its designers."[53] This sequence ensures that the creative process begins with a vision of the quality of the whole organization, but it also forces the quality team to address specific needs, from technical processes such as Internet search and cataloguing to management control, e.g., frequency and design of middle management meetings. The result is a designed future (improved customer services) that is derived both from broad vision and from operational specifics.

For example, how would the Mapletree Library of the future be different—more technological with a greater range of products and services? The design group is then asked to sketch each subsystem focusing on how these become an integrated and *different* whole, especially their impact on the customer friendliness of operations. This redesign effort includes the products and services, structure, psychological climate, leadership and culture (see Chapter 2).

3.0 CRITICAL GAP ANALYSIS

In Step Three, redesigners conduct a comparative analysis of the customer friendly present with the newly designed customer friendly future. Analysts look for differences—a gap or gaps—between the current structure and functioning of the organization and the vision of the future. For example, the intention to create a participative, empowered work force (characteristics of the future) is compared to the current management approach (top down, solitary decision making) and lack of a structure of teams and groups for employee input. System by system analysis leads to a set of "gaps" to be addressed during the implementation of the redesign. What are the differences between the "technologically weak" Mapletree Library of today in comparison to the "technologically strong" Mapletree Library of the future?

4.0 DEFINE LEADING STRATEGIES

In Step Four, a strategy or set of strategies is selected to represent the "direction—destination—decisions" that are driving the redesign.[54] For example, a library branch office was identified as redundant following construction of a large main facility. In an effort to consolidate buildings and people, the new "super regional library" saw "closure" as the strategy best representing the direction (leaner), destination (fewer branches) and decisions (transfer of employees and equipment).

Laura knew that some years ago a neighboring library determined that the facility was too small to support the expanding technology activities of the community and region. A growth strategy was announced with the intention of adding facilities, equipment and staff. Strategy is used here as a way to organize *perspective* about the future, to begin to develop a *pattern of behaviors* and *decisions* and to *position* the redesigned organization for success—meaning in our case greatly enhanced customer friendliness.[56, 56]

5.0 IDENTIFY RESOURCE REQUIREMENTS

Redesign implies and requires the addition of new resources or the redistribution of existing ones. Each customer friendly redesign effort must identify the resource requirements in terms of: production process, personnel, facility, equipment and supplies, and finances.To successfully implement the new design, needs such as training must be identified as well as staff requirements, space, equipment and an overall budget. The resource requirements defined in Step 5.0 are refined in the final step, linking the changes to daily operations.

6.0 OPERATIONAL START: ACTIONS, RESPONSIBILITIES AND EVALUATION

Step 6 links the vision of the desired future, chosen strategies and initiating actions to operations and budgeting. There are five parts to the linkage. First, the planning group must set program objectives. Second, the planning group must subject the programs proposed to detailed operations-oriented analyses. Third, the group must define what the year-to-year outcome expectations are and how to know when yearly progress is successful (performance indicators). Fourth, responsibility analyses and then responsibility assignments must be made in order to insure that persons in charge are directly connected to the proposed programs and actions. Fifth, the proposed programs and strategies and actions must be connected to the budget.

This Step—linking redesign to operations—establishes the ties between the "designed desired future" and the near-term work of year-to-year operations. There are three ties to be made: links between the redesign and the budget; between the redesign and the existing structure; and between the actions and the timing of the budget cycles.[55] The task is to link the vision and plans to actions and budgets.

At Mapletree Library, the underlying assumption is that "technology supportive" organization behaviors are co-produced by multiple aspects (or subsystems) of the organization . Thus, the library user experiences new high quality technology not simply because of skill in search and circulation services but as a result of staff and managerial actions at every point of the process from first contact at the reference desk to follow-up. At Mapletree, library leaders pushing technology improvements identified strategies and action in five organizational systems, creating an organization-wide intervention. Laura's team summarized their work in five points below.

Task Force Report of the Customer Friendly Improvement Team

We propose the following series of actions to enhance technology at the library and therefore to better serve our customers.

1.0 TECHNICAL INTERVENTIONS. The product and technology system of the library involves the core professional work of library science including selection and organizing of materials; circulation; search and reference; and educational programming.

The team's study question was: How do we propose to improve technology use in the core work of the library? Although many staff still feel that outcomes such as search or book availability still drive satisfaction, we are increasingly recognizing that the total library experience (i.e. degree of customer friendliness) contributes to user loyalty and support. To improve technology implementation in this subsystem of the organization we could employ the following:

- complete a needs assessment to identify customers and their unique technology requirements
- use co-design teams to create a vision of a richer technology future vision
- expand internet assistance
- benchmarking of best practices from other libraries, public and private
- quality management of existing technology
- form a task force to study the needs of underserved, low access populations
- follow up calls to selected technology users
- user feedback through surveys and focus groups
- create an industrial library "peer consulting" group (volunteers)
- expand convenience characteristics—e.g. hours of operation; privacy; cleanliness; signage

These are technical interventions that, while helpful, will not by themselves create total technology implementation. Four other targets offer opportunities identified by the team.

2.0 STRUCTURAL INTERVENTIONS. The structure of the library involves formal departmental design, job and role descriptions, and policies and procedures defining work flow and authority relations. Along with core library services such as search and circulation, the structure of the library can enhance or undercut technology use. The team's study question was: how can the structure of library administration support and enhance technology adoption? Five examples of structural system interventions follow.

- increase incentives and rewards for technology use
- alter reporting relationships, e.g., technology representatives report directly to senior management levels
- improve structural visibility, e.g., create an Internet department
- enhance communication about technology e.g. direct telephone lines, mailings, email

- integrate operations using technology throughout e.g. cross departmental and use of List Serves

For example, the last target, integration, has been addressed with planning boards that mix members from different departments and levels,[56] These boards have service unit structures and service directors that coordinate technology services for a student or adult user group. The team recognized that both technical and structural methods are necessary but not sufficient. The "psychology" of the organization is a contributor to technology improvement.

3.0 PSYCHOLOGICAL INTERVENTIONS. The psychological climate of the library is the individual and group psychology of staff including motivation, satisfaction and group relations. The improvement team's study question was: How does the "psychology" of individual staff and work teams relate to technology? We are looking for staff to foster and communicate technology support. They are "expected" to be technology-oriented which they learn about at employee orientation and through training. Employees are empowered to act to improve technology use and constantly seek improvement individually and in teams. Methods for this system include: increased orientation and technology training, empowerment of staff to take technology adoption action, promoting expectations for new technology skill development, increasing intergroup collaboration because teams are key to adoption, and organizational learning to continuously improve technology use. Training, expectations, teamwork and the philosophy of continuous improvement of service create a "technology friendly psychology." But managers must lead and they must take specific actions as well.

4.0 MANAGEMENT INTERVENTIONS. Management activities coordinate the relations of the other systems—through planning, organization design, leadership and evaluation and control. The effort to improve "technology friendliness" in the technical, structural and psychological climate of the organization must be led and supplemented by management. The team's study question was: Does management plan for and lead us toward technology implementation? Interventions in the management system are: increase contact with library users regarding their technology needs and experiences, create a strategic plan targeting technology acquisition strategy and goals, obtain staff and user feedback about current and future technology through multiple measures, engage in joint purchasing alliances to gain advantage of lower costs for new equipment, distribute feedback regarding customers' technology experience to departments, form a grantsmanship committee to secure additional resources, and leaders role-model technology support and use. Management is expected to be in a dialogue with library users, using feedback to help staff to craft a vision of the technology future that includes external trends, current strengths and weaknesses, developmental strategies and resource and responsibility commitments. Why? Library users of the technology can provide feedback that will tell us about improvement opportunities; gaps in communication and progress toward the strategic goals of securing state of the art technology capability and use (and customer loyalty).

5.0 CULTURAL INTERVENTIONS. Culture is a collective way of thinking about the core values and assumptions of "work life" in the library—in shorthand "the way things are done around here." Culture is the web that links all systems using both tangible physical objects and actions and core values to create a "technology friendly whole." Edgar Schein believes that culture is represented by various levels—surface, visible objects such as furnishings and the placement of the technology, behaviors at a deeper level and core values and assumptions as the innermost core of the culture.[57] We improve culture support for technology implementation at Mapletree by addressing all levels. The study team's question was: Does the culture of our library organization support and enhance technology adoption?

Leaders could improve technology support by taking the following actions. conduct a "technology culture audit" to assess the current support for technology, improve the visibility of technology values, e.g., posters, program announcements, mission statement, include symbolic statements in communications, e.g., mailings with technology promotions, establish ongoing dialogue with library users regarding technology needs, create an alliance philosophy—"trust your customers like lifetime partners."

Team members believe that the essential dimensions of customer service can be translated to the technology problem. Presented below are the dimensions of service with a notation in parentheses regarding the organization system involved.

1. *Reliability:* the ability to provide the technology that was promised, dependably and accurately (technical)
2. *Assurance:* the knowledge and courtesy of employees and their ability to convey trust and confidence in the technology support (psychosocial and cultural)
3. *Tangibles:* the physical facilities and equipment and the appearance of personnel (technical and structural)
4. *Empathy:* the degree of caring and individual attention provided to technology users (psychosocial and cultural)
5. *Responsiveness:* the willingness to help technology users and provide prompt service (cultural and managerial)[58]

Achieving full organization support of technology requires multiple initiatives and a process for organizing the intervention.

SUMMARY

The following systems principles are the drivers for this approach to organization-wide technology implementation. Whole organizations, not just staff contribute to high or low technology adoption. We consider both equipment and psychology in the improvement process at Mapletree.

Whole means that both social and technical aspects of the organization are considered as appropriate targets of technology improvement action."Technology friendly" designs require attention to structure (e.g., library organization components and policies) and process (e.g., decision making and group dynamics). Technology improvement strategies are viewed as synergistic, meaning the whole is more than the sum of the parts, and that multiple initiatives rather than single actions are called for to produce adoption (multisystem actions).

Technology adoption is influenced by the external environment; therefore, external opinions and measures (benchmarks) of quality improvement are important.Organizing for technology implementation is dependent on the situation—each library must create its own unique technology service improvement plan.

Implementing new technology in libraries will require more money. This has been recognized. The Carnegie Foundation is making available $15 million to 25 major urban libraries for development. And recently one Senator announced support for a bill to provide 1 billion dollars over 5 years to repair and upgrade the nation's library infrastructure—including renovation and expansion. But money is not the sole answer. To effectively integrate technology we must think about the complex nature of library organizations. Multi-system strategies that recognize the sociotechnical nature of change can provide both a conceptual and practical base for building a technology friendly library.

Mapletee is our last case but we could have included many other organization types. This synthesized procedure for design/redesign is a first step toward development of a consensus process on how to create the architecture of customer friendly organizations. Leaders have recognized the need to redesign their public and private organizations from US Airlines to Comcast to Frediemac, but are confronted by a bewildering set of process choices. Many of these alternatives have a common systems core. We need to extend our thinking about this core process and its desired contribution to meeting future change needs. Customer friendly organizations would benefit all of us regardless of field and industry.

Notes

NOTES FOR CHAPTER 1

1. Reese, J. (1996). Starbucks: Inside the Coffee Cult. *Fortune.* 134(11); Dec 9; 190-200.
2. Deming, W.E. 1982). *Out of Crisis.* Boston, Ma: MIT Press.
3. Juran, J.M.'(1989). *Juran on Leadership for Quality.* New York: Free Press.
4. Davis, S.L. (1997). *Unbridled Power: Inside the Secret Culture of the IRS.* New York: HarperBusiness. In J.H. Birnbaum. Unbelievable. *Fortune.* April 13, 1998.

NOTES FOR CHAPTER 2

1. Paige, L. (2000). Emergency Marketing. *American Medical News.* 43(33); 317.
2. Ziegenfuss, J.T. (1982). Do your managers think in organizational 3-D? *Sloan Management Review.* 24(1).
3. Scott, W.G. (1961). Organization Theory. *Acad. Mgmt Journal.* 4(1); 7-26.
4. Ackoff, R.L. (1981). *Creating the Corporate Future.* New York: Wiley.
5. Ackoff, R.L. (1999). *Re-creating the Corporation: A Design of Organization for the 21st Century.* New York: Oxford University Press.
6. Ackoff, R.L. op.cit. see note 4.
7. Emery, F.E. (Ed.) (1969). *Systems Thinking.* Harmondsworth, UK: Penguin.
8. Ozbekhan, H. (1977). The Future of Paris: A Systems Study in Strategic Urban Planning. *Phil. Trans. Royal Society London.* A 28; 523-544.
9. Checkland, P.B. (1981). *Systems Thinking, Systems Practice.* New York: Wiley.
10. Ackoff, R.L (1974). *Redesigning the Future.* New York: Wiley.
11. Waring, Alan. (1996). *Practical Systems Thinking.* New York. International Thomson Business Press.
12. Jackson, Michael C. (1991). *Critical Systems Thinking: Directed Readings.* New York: Wiley.
13. Jackson, Michael C. (1991). *Systems Methodology for the Management Sciences.* New York: Plenum Press.
14. Jackson, M.C. (2003). *Systems Thinking: Creative Holism for Managers.* New York: Wiley.
15. Wolstenholme, Eric F. (1993). A case study in community care using systems thinking. *Journal of the Operational Research Society.* 44(9), 925-934.
16. Ulrich, Werner. (1994). Can we secure future-responsive management through systems thinking and design? *Interfaces.* 24(4), 26-37.
17. Farmer, S.; Luthans, F.; Sommer, S. (2001). An empirical assessment of internal customer service. *Managing Service Quarterly.* 5; 2001; 350 -358.
18. Meyer, C. (2001). While customers wait, add value. *Harvard Business Review* 79; 24.
19. Emery, F.E.; Trist, E.L. (1960). Socio-technical Systems. In C.W. Churchman and M. Verhulst (eds.) *Management Science, Models and Techniques.* Vol 2. New York: Pergamon.
20. Emery, F.E.; Trist, E.L. (1973). *Towards a Social Ecology.* New York: Plenum.
21. Ackoff, R.L. (1975). *On Purposeful Systems.* New York: Wiley.
22. Kast, F.E.; Rosenzweig, J.E. (1970). General Systems Theory: Applications for Organization and Management. *Acad. Mgmt J.* 15; 452-456.
23. Kast, F.E.; Rosenzweig, J.E. (1985). *Organization and Management: A Systems and Contingency Approach.* (4th edition); New York: McGraw Hill.
24. Ziegenfuss, J.T. (1985). *DRGs and Hospital Impact: An Organizational Systems Analysis.* New York: McGraw Hill.

25. Ziegenfuss, J.T; Perlman, H. (1989) Decreasing medical malpractice: an organizational systems approach. *Health Care Management Review.* 14(4); 67-75.

26. Ziegenfuss, J.T. (1992). Are you growing systems thinking managers? Use a systems model to teach and practice organizational analysis and planning, policy and development. *Systems Practice.* 5; pp 509-527.

27.Ziegenfuss, J.T. (1996). A methodology for use of systems thinking and redesign in graduate health care management education. In W.W. Gasparski et al (Eds.) *Praxiology: International Annual of Practical Philosophy and Methodology.* Vol. 4; New Brunswick, N.J.: Transaction.

28. Jacques, C.M.; Bauer, L.C.; Ziegenfuss, J.T. (1993). Characteristics of strong departments of family medicine: results of a Delphi survey. *Family Medicine* 25(6); 256-261.

29. Ziegenfuss, J.T. (1993). *The Organizational Path to Health Care Quality.* Ann Arbor, MI; Health Administration Press.

30. Ziegenfuss, J.T.; Lartin-Drake, J.; Munzenrider, R.F. (1998). Organization change in a university hospital: a six year evaluation report of the Horizons Project. *Systems Practice & Action Research.* 11(6); 575-597.

31. Ziegenfuss, J.T.; Bentley, M. (2000). Implementing Cost Control in health Care: Strategies Driven by an Organizational Systems Approach. *Systems Practice & Action Research.* 13(4); 453.

32. Ziegenfuss, J.T (2002). *Organization and Management Problem Solving: A Systems and Consulting Approach.* Thousand Oaks, Ca.: Sage Books, 2002.

33. Institute of Medicine, Committee on Quality of Health Care in America (1999). *To Err is Human: Building a Safer Health System.* Washington, D.C. : National Academy Press.

34. Institute of Medicine, Committee on Quality of Health Care in America. (2001). *Crossing the Quality Chasm.* Washington, D.C.: National Academy Press.

35. Zeithaml, V.A.; Parasuraman, A.; Malhotra, A. (2002). Service quality delivery through web sites: a critical review of extant knowledge. *Academy of Marketing Science J.* 30; 362-375.

36. Zhu, F.; Wymer, W.; Chen, I. (2002). IT based services and service quality in consumer banking. *Intl J. Service Industry Mgmt.* 13; 69-90.

37. Yucesan, E.; Groote, X. (2002). Lead times, order release mechanisms, and customer service." *European J Operational Research.* 120; 118.

38. Lighter,D.E.; Fair, D.C. (2004). *Quality Management in Health Care.* Sudbury, MA: Jones and Bartlett.

39. McLaughtlin, C.P.; Kaluzny, A.D. (1999). *Continuous Quality Improvement in Health Care.* 2nd edition. Germantown, Maryland: Aspen.

40. Crosby, P. (1979). *Quality is Free.* New York: McGraw Hill.

41 Walsh, J.; Godfrey, S. (2000). The internet: a new era in customer service. *European Management J.* 18; 85.

42. Peters, T.J.; Waterman, R.H. (1982). *In Search of Excellence.* New York: Warner Bks.

43. Collins, J.C.; Porras, J.I. (1994). *Built to Last: Successful Habits of Visionary Companies.* New York: HarperCollins.

44. Andrews, T.L; Rogelberg, S.G. (2001). A new look at service climate: its relationship with owner service values in small businesss . *J. Business and Psychology.* 16; 119.

45. Bienstock, C.C.; De Moranville, C.W.; Smith, R.K. (2003). Organizational citizenship behavior and service quality. *J. Services Marketing.* 17;357.

46. Bougie, R. Pieters, R; Zeelenberg, M. (2003). Angry customers don't come back, they get back: The experience and behavioral implications of anger and dissatisfaction in services. *Acad. Mktg. Science J.* 31; 377.

47. Chase, R.; Dasu, S. (2001) Want to perfect your company's service? Use behavioral science. *Harvard Business Review.* 79;78.

48. Rotfeld, H. (2001). Misplaced marketing: a service economy whose employees say "customer service is not my job" *J. Consumer Marketing* 18; 39.

49. Pugh, S.D. et al (2002). Driving service effectiveness through employee customer linkages. *Acad Mgmt Exec.* 16; 73.

50. Shortell, S. M. et al (1994). The performance of intensive care units: does good management make a difference. *Medical Care* 32(5); 508-525.

51. Schein, E.H. (1985). *Organizational Culture and Leadership.* San Francisco, Ca: Jossey Bass.

52. Martin, J. (1995) *The Organizational Culture War Games: A Struggle for Intellectual Dominance.* Palo Alto, Ca: Stanford Business School.

53. Wilkof, M; Ziegenfuss, J.T. (1995). Culture Audits: A Tool for Change. *Health Progress.* 76(4); 34-38.

54. Argyris, C. (1974) *Theories in Practice.* San Francisco, Ca.: Jossey Bass.

55. Ziegenfuss, J.T.; Bentley, M. op cit see note 28.

56. Disney Institute. (2001). *Be Our Guest: Perfecting the Art of Customer Service.* New York: Disney Editions.

57. Cummings, T.G.; Worley, C.G. (2005) *Organizational Development and Change.* 8th edition. Mason, Ohio: Thomson Southwestern.

58. French, W.L.; Bell, C.H.; Zawacki, R.A. (2000) *Organization Development and Transformation.* 5th edition. Irwin:

59. Freiberg, K. (1996) *Nuts: Southwest Airlines Crazy Recipe for Business and Personal Success.* Bard.

Notes for Chapter 3

1. Iacobucci, D. (1994). Customer satisfaction fables. *Sloan Management Review,* 35(4); 93-96.

2. Gilmour, P. (1994). Customer Service: Differentiating by market segment. *International Journal of Physical Distribution & Logistics Management,* 24(4); 18-23.

3. Maynard, M. (2003). The End of Detroit: *How the Big Three Lost their Grip on the American Car Market.* New York: Doubleday.

4. Welch, D. (2004). Bummer for the Hummer: Sales are Way down. Can GM make its hulk less of a gas hog and comfier inside? *Business Week.* February 23; 49.

5. Roderick, D. (1999). Getting ready for the superjumbo era. *Time.* 154(19). Nov. 15.

6. Korth, K. (2003). Platform reductions vs. demands for specialization. *Automotive Design & Production.* 115(10); 14.

7. Freeman, S. (2003). Media and marketing—Advertising: Dodge's Rocky courtship of Women; Male focused Durango ads risk offending an audience the car maker badly needs. *Wall Street Journal.* Nov 14; B2.

8. Chong-Wee Keng Neo, L. (1993). Customer service in Singapore: Luxury or necessity? *International Journal of Retail & Distribution Management.* 21(1); 21-25.

9. Wall Street Journal. (2003). Toyota Motor Corp.: Hybrid Prius Subcompact Car may be launched in China. *Wall Street Journal.* Aug 11; B4.

10. Hawkins, L. (2003). GM Revamps Hybrid Strategy, Delays Saturn SUV. *Wall Street Journal.* Nov 6; D2.

11. Welch, D.; Kerwin, K. (2004). Detroit tries it the Japanese way; shared platforms and parts save time and money, but the Big three are years behind. *Business Week.* Jan 26; 76.

12. Wall Street Journal. (2004). Ford Motor Co.: European unit seeks to cut component costs by up to 13%. *Wall Street Journal.* Mar 3; 1.

13. Boudette, N.; White, G. (2003). GM hopes bigger Saab lineup will help fill up showrooms—No 1 auto maker considers compact and SUV to stem losses at its Swedish unit. *Wall Street Journal.* Apr 9; B3.

14. Wall Street Journal. (2003). Nissan motor Co.: Auto Company to Roll Out. *Wall Street Journal.* Nov 25; 1.

15. Ackoff, R.L. (1981). *Creating the Corporate Future: Plan or be Planned For.* New York: Wiley.

16. Kaulio, M.A. (1998). Customer, consumer, and user involvement in product development: A framework and a review of selected methods. *Total Quality Management*, 9(1); 141-149.

17. Goffin, K.; New, C. (2001). Customer support and new product development: An exploratory study. *International Journal of Operations and Production Management*. 21; 275.

18. Truett, R. (2006). Ford readies 6-speed automatics, new engines. *Automotive News*. 80(6214), July, p. 23.

19. National Institute of Standards. *Malcolm Baldridge National Quality Award*. Gaithersburg, MD. National Institute of Standards.

20. Anonymous. (2003). Green and safety laws may spell end of the road for manual gears. *Professional Engineering*. Aug 13. 16(14); 10.

21. Whitfield, K.E. (2003). Honda's elemental strategy: flexible and fast. *Automotive Design & Production*. 115 (7); 20.

22. Destafani, J. (2003). Lean by design and by necessity. *Manufacturing Engineering*. 131(3); 59.

23. Turrettini, J. (2003). Made to order. *Forbes*. 172(4); 78.

24. Budmir, M. (2003). BMWs speed through production thanks to robotic measurer. *Machine Design*. 75(10); 88.

25. Cole, D.E.; Baron, J. (2003). Automotive manufacturing's changing face. *Manufacturing Engineering*. 131(3); 136.

26. Editor. (2003). Design engineering: a crust you can trust. *The Engineer*. Oct 10; 49.

27. Gibney., F. (2000). The revolution in a box. *Time*. July 31, p. 30.

28. Wheatley, J. (2000). Super Factory or Super Headache: GM's new plant may build a lot of cars Brazil can't swallow. *Business Week*. July 31, p. 66.

29. Behara, R.S. (1995). Customer satisfaction measurement and analysis using six sigma. *International Journal of Quality & Reliability Management*, 12(3); 9-18.

30. Zaun, T. (2003). Police raid Mitsubishi Motors to probe allegedly defective truck. *Wall Street Journal*. Oct 27; A18.

31. Behara op cit see note 29.

32. Tracey, M. (1998). The importance of logistics efficiency to customer service and firm performance. *Journal of Logistics Management*, 9(2); 65-81.

33. Susman, G. (1976). *Autonomy at Work*. New York: Praeger.

34. TGI Fridays.

35. Ogden, H.J. (1996). Customer satisfaction with delivery scheduling. *Journal of Marketing Theory and Practice*, 4(2); 79-94.

36. Gilmour , P. ; Heskett, J.L. (1994). Customer service. *Intl. J. Phys. Distribution and Logistics*. 24(4), 18-23.

37. Kirkpatrick, D. (1998). Dell delivers; HP eats crow. *Fortune*. May 25.

38. Harris, K.E. et al. (2006). Online service failure: consumer attributions and expectations. *J. Services Mktg*. 20(7); 453.

39. Mattila, A.S. (2006). The power of explainations in mitigating the ill-effects of service failures. *J. Service Mktg*. 20(7); 422.

40. Maxham, J.G. (2001). Service recovery's influence on consumer satisfaction, positive word-of-mouth and purchase intentions. *Journal of Business Research*, 54; 11.

41. Davenport, T.; Klahr, P. (1998). Managing customer support knowledge. *Calif. Mgmt. Rev*. 40(3); 195-208.

42. Juran, J. (1988). *Juran on Planning for Quality*. New York: Free Press.

43. Deming, W.E. (1982). *Out of Crisis*. Cambridge, Ma.: MIT Press.

44. Crosby, P. *Quality is Free*. New York:

45. Juran, J.M. (1989). *Juran on Leadership for Quality*. New York: Free Press.

46. Vasilash, G.S. (2003). Quality by the numbers at Ford. *Automotive Design & Production*. 115(5); 40.

47. Anonymous. (2003). Chrysler improves quality one part at a time. *Quality*. 42(10); 46.

48. Miller, M. (1994). Customer services drives reengineering effort. *Personnel Journal,* 73(11); 87-91.

49. Juran, J.M. op cit see note 45.

50. Tysse, J.W. (1990). Customer Alliances II. In *Creating Customer Satisfaction.* The Conference Board.

51. Berry, L. (1997). Listening to the customer: The concept of a service-quality information system. *Sloan Management Review,* 38(3); 65-76.

52. Gerber, B. (1995). Customer service data: Amassed but ill-used. *Training.* 32(5); 16.

53. Karimi, J., Somers, T., & Gupta, Y. (2001). Impact of information technology management practices on customer service. *Journal of Management Information Systems,* 17; 125-158.

54. Gerber op. cit. see note 52.

55. Hui, S., & Jha, G. (2000). Data mining for customer service support. *Information and Management,* 38; 1.

56. Bailey, E. (1990). *Creating Customer Satisfaction.* New York: Conference Board.

57. Ibid.

58. Day, G.S., & Hubbard, K.L. (2003). Customer relationships go digital. *Business Strategy Review,* 14; 17.

59. El Sawy, O.A., & Bowles, G. (1997). Redesigning the customer support process for the electronic economy: Insights from storage dimensions. *MIS Quarterly,* 21(4); 457-483.

60. Hui op cit see note 55.

61. Berry op cit see note 51.

62. Fitzgerald, P. (1996). Chemical companies are increasingly benchmarking best practices outside the industry. *Chemical Marketing Reporter.* 15; 249.

63. Matta, K. (1998). The information requirements of total quality management. *Total Quality Management,* 9(6); 445-461.

64. Vasilash, G.S. (2003). Advance composites for an advanced Corvette. *Automotive Design & Production.* 115(8); 42.

65. Wheatley op. cit. see note 28.

66. Peters, T.; Waterman. (1984). *In Search of Excellence.* N.Y.: Warner Books.

67. Ziegenfuss, J.T. (1987). *Patient Client Employee Complaint Programs: An Organizational Systems Model.* Springfield, Illinois. Charles C. Thomas.

68. Harrison, M.I. (1994). *Diagnosing Organizations.* 2nd Edition. Thousand Oaks, Ca.: Sage. 76.

69. Berry, L. Pasauraman, P. . (1997). Listening to the customer—the concept of a service quality information system. *Sloan Management Review.*38(3). Spring; 65-76.

70. Petersen, D. E. Beyond Satisfaction. In *Customer Satisfaction.* The Conference Board.

Notes for Chapter 4

1. Nadler, D.A. et al (1992). *Organizational Architecture: Designs for Changing Organizations.* San Francisco, Ca.: Jossey Bass.

2. Kaplan-Leiserson, E. (2003). Strategic Service. *Training and Development,* 57(11), 14.

3. Stringer, K. & Harris, N. (2003). Paved paradise: The new airport parking lots; competition brings travelers cheaper, fancier option; a car wash and oil change. *Wall Street Journal,* Nov. 12, 2003, D.1.

4. Flint, P. (2003). It's a blue world after all. *Air Transport World,* 40(6), 36.

5. Carey, S. (2003). United to install in-flight e-mail by end of year—In bid to court business travelers, carrier begins to outfit U.S. fleet; pricing will start at $15.98. *Wall Street Journal,* June 17, 2003, D.1.

6. Stringer, K. (2003). Hard lesson learned: Premium and no-frills don't mix. *Wall Street Journal,* Nov. 3, 2003, B.1.

7. Carey, S. (2003). Business-oriented Midwest Air adds low-fare leisure service. *Wall Street Journal*, May 29, 2003, D.3.

8. McCartney, S. (2003). Airlines lavish full-fare fliers with new perks; some travelers in coach will now get first-class treatment; elite-for-a-day on Continental. *Wall Street Journal*, Sept. 16, D.1.

9. Mason, T. (2003). Virgin Atlantic set for flat-bed battle. *Marketing*, June 19, 1.

10. Glader, P. (2003). Takeoffs & Landings. *Wall Street Journal*, June 27, W.9.

11. (2003). US Airways' in-flight cafes take off. *Foodservice Equipment & Supplies*, 56(7), 20.

12. Michaels, D. (2003). Wine glut bodes well for fliers; airlines keep vintages on board, squeeze suppliers on price. *Wall Street Journal*, June 17.

13. (2003). E-Tickets on Northwest, US Air. *Wall Street Journal*, July 23, D.7.

14. Donnelly, S.B. (2004). Friendlier skies. *Time*, 163(4), 39.

15. (2003). United outsources staff for U.S. warehouses: Journal of Commerce Online Edition. *Journal of Commerce*, July 17, 1.

16. (2003). Crowded out. *Economist.com*, July 31, 1.

17. Clark, J. (2000). Luggage on a Different Flight? Your're not alone. Here's What to do. *USA Today*. Dec 1.

18. Johnson, K. & Michaels, D. (2003). Some airlines soup up first class, others kill it. *Wall Street Journal*, Oct. 30, D.5.

19. McCartney, S. (2004). The middle seat: Airlines experiment to woo travelers back from discounters. *Wall Street Journal*, Jan. 28, D.1.

20. McCartney, S. (2004). The middle seat: Your flight to Maui is hobbling the airline industry. *Wall Street Journal*, Feb. 4, D.1.

21. Foran, J. (2003). The cost of complexity. *Journal of Revenue and Pricing Management*, 2(2), 150.

22. Krames, J.A. (2003). Performance culture. *Executive Excellence*, 20(11), 16.

23. Freiberg, K. (1996). *Nuts: Southwest Airlines Crazy Recipe for Business and Personal Success*. Bard

24. Albrecht, S. (1994). *Service, Service, Service*. Holbrook, Ma: Adams.

25. Johnson, H. (2004). Editor's choice: United Airlines. *Training*, 41(3), 69.

26. *Nuts*. Op cit see note 23.

27. (2003). Airlines brief—UAL Corp.: United Airlines will reward workers in cash for goals met. *Wall Street Journal*, Dec. 31, 1.

28. Crosby, P. (1979). *Quality is Free. The Art of Making Quality Certain*. New York: McGraw Hill.

29. Diaz, A., & Ruiz, F. (2002). The consumer's reaction to delays in service. *International Journal of Service Industry Management*, 13, 118-140.

30. Sultan, F., & Simpson, M. (2000). International service variants: Airline passenger expectations and perceptions of service quality. *Journal of Services Marketing*, 14, 188.

31. Benady, D. (2003). When the pilot loses the plot. *Marketing Week*, July 31, 2003, 22.

32. Continental Airlines—*Customer First*. (Satisfaction Statement—effective June 14, 2004). Web Site

33. Lee, M; Cunningham, L.F. (1996). Customer Loyalty in the airline industry. *TransportationQuarterly*. 50, Spring; 57-72.

34. *Woodyard, C.* (2003). United Would Like to Introduce Fliers to Ted. *USA Today*. McClean, Va. Nov. 13. Follow up: David, K.—Letter to Editor.

35. Stringer, K. (2003). Cranky Consumer: Coping with loss; We test the lost-and-found at airlines and rental cars; hotels put discretion first. *Wall Street Journal*, Nov. 18, D.1.

36. McCartney, S. (2003). Continental Air makes elite eliter. *Wall Street Journal*, Sept. 18, D.10.

37. Sweetman, B. (2003). Something for everybody. *Air Transport World*, 40(6), 42.

Bitner, M.J., Brown, S.W., & Meuter, M.L. (2000). Technology infusion in service encounters. *Academy of Marketing Science Journal*, 28, 138-149.

38. Prasad, A., & Steffes, E. (2002). Internal marketing at Continental Airlines: Convincing employees that management knows best. *Marketing Letters,* 13, 75.

39. Scott, E.D. (2003). Plane truth: A qualitative study of employee dishonesty in the airline industry. *Journal of Business Ethics,* 42, 321.

NOTES FOR CHAPTER 5

1. AI-Sabbahy, H. Z. (2004). An investigation of perceived value dimensions: Implications for hospitality research. *Journal of Travel Research,* 42(3),226.

2. Bebko, C. (2000). Service intangibility and its impact on consumer expectations of service quality. *J. Services Marketing* 14(9).

3. Allen, R.L. (2004). Operators must be responsible for pampering adult guests but not for diapering their kids. *Nation's Restaurant News,* 38(14), 19.

4. Alisau, P. (2004). Going to the dogs (and cats). *Hotel and Motel Management,* 219(7),60.

5. Foley, D. (2003). Roll the dice. *Communication News,* 40(12), 14.

6. Shaw, R. (2004). Know customers before redefining foodservice operations. *Hotel and Motel Management* 219(9), 18.

7. Binkley, C. (2003). Hotels pump up their gyms to lure execs seeking pecs. *Wall Street Journal,* Nov. 13,2003, Dl.

8. Goldenberg, B. (2004). Customer self-service: Are you ready? *Customer Relationship Management,* 8(5), 20.

9. Goleman, D. (2000) Leadership That Gets Results 196. *Harvard Business Review.* March-April, p.81.

10. Davidson, M. (2003). Does organizational climate add to service quality in hotels? *Inti J Contemporary Hospitality Mgmt.* 15; 206.

11. Chase, R.; Dasu, S. (2001). Want to perfect your company's service? Use behavioral science. *Harv. Business Review* 79; 78.

12. Ackoff, R.L.; Magidson, J.; Addison, H.J. (2006). *Idealized Design.* Upper Saddle River, N.J.: Wharton School Publishing – Pearson Education.

13. Fisher, A. (2000). Truth and Consequences - And the Perils of Surly Service. *Fortune.* May 29, 2000, p.292.

14. Barth, S. (2004). Mitigate the urge to litigate. *Lodging Hospitality,* 60(2), 30.

15. Fitch, S. (2004). Soft pillows and sharp elbows. *Forbes,* 173(10),066.

16. *Editor* (1998) How far will hotels go? *Travel & Leisure,* June, 1998, p.101.

17. Hartline, M.D. et al Guest perceptions of hotel quality. Determining which employee groups count most. *Cornell Hotel and Restaurant Administration Quarterly* 44; 2003; 43-52.

18. Editor (1996) *Rural Telecommunications* 197.

19. Feiertag, H. (2003). Customer service: Are salespeople ever going to get it right? *Hotel and Motel Management,* 218(17), 14.

20. Chow-Chua, C.; Konnaran, R. (2002). Managing service quality by combining voice of the service provider and voice of their customers. *Managing Service Quality.* 12; 77-86.

21. (2000) Cruise Ships Strand Passengers. *Sunday Patriot News,* October 1.

22. Higley, J. (2004). Hilton unveils 127 point plan to recharge Hampton brand. *Hotel and Motel Management.* 22, 19(3), 1.

23. Tschol, J. (1991) *Achieving Excellence through Customer Service.* New Jersey: Prentice Hall.

24. Higley, J. (2003). Free amenities? Don't ask by phone-it'll cost you. *Hotel and Motel Management,* 218(19), 8.

25. Blackmon, D.A. (1998). FedEx Pilots Trade Their Old Loyalties for a Tougher Union. *Wall Street Journal* Oct. 9.

26. Rotfeld, H. (2001). Misplaced marketing: a service economy whose employees say "customer service is not my job!" *J. Consumer Marketing* 18; 39.

27. Chung, B.; Schneider, B. (2002).Serving multiple masters: role conflict experienced by service employees. *J. Services Marketing.* 16; 70-87.

28. Liu, B. et al; (2001). The relationships between culture and behavioral intentions toward services. *J. Service Research.* 4; 118-129.

NOTES FOR CHAPTER 6

1. Mayer, M. 1998). *The Bankers.* New York: Plume.

2. Ackoff, R. L. (1983). *Creating the Corporate Future. Plan or Be Planned For.* New York: Wiley.

3. Newman, D.J. (1993). A 12 point tune-up for your bank's marketing machine. *Texas Banking* 82(11); Nov., 13, 21.

4. Russo, A. (1999). Ten cost-Slashing tips for Community Banks. *Amer. Community Banker* 8(6); Jun., 20-24.

5. Ackoff, R.L. (1970). *A Concept of Corporate Planning.* New York: Wiley.

6. Ackoff, R.L. op cit see note 2.

7. Ackoff, R.L.; Majidson, J.; Addison, H.J. (2006). *idealized Design: Creating an Organization's Future.* Upper Saddle River New Jersey: Wharton School Publishing.

8. Editors. (1994). Three Banks—Three Planning Approaches. *Bank Management.* 70(2); Mar./Apr. 1994; pp 65-67.

9. Divanna, J. A. (2004) *The Future of Retail Banking.* New York: Palgrave Macmillan.

10. Durkin, M; Bennett, H. (1999). Employee commitment in retail banking: identifying and exploring hidden dangers. *Intl. J. Bank Mktg.* 17(3). 124-137.

11. Business Wire. (2000). First Internet Bank Launches Wireless Banking: Customers can now perform Key functions form their Cell Phones. Indianapolis; Nov. 1.

12. Editors.(2000). Retail Banks had Better Get "Smart" Now. *American Banker.* Nov. 2, 2000.

13. Business Wire. (2000). Key Corp Chooses Live Person's Real-Time Technology for its Online Personal Finance. Nov. 1.

14. Ptacek, M.J. (2000). First Union gets ready to push Virtual Mall Site. *American Banker.* Nov. 2.

15. Canada Newswire. (2000). Wal-Mart Canada to open new store in Scarborough Town Centre. Nov. 2.

16. Griffin, L. (2004) Compliance Clinic. *ABA Banking Journal.* April .

17. Goleman, D. (2000). Leadership That Gets Results. *Harvard Business Review* Mar./Apr. 19; 80.

18. Griffin op cit note 16.

19. Divanna, op cit note 9.

20. Barker-Benfield, S. (2000). Bank of America Changes Florida Strategy. *Florida Times–Union*, Nov. 3.

21. Lunt, P. (1992). How seven banks service low income markets. *ABA Banking J.* 84

22. Hellrigel,D.; Slocum, J.W. (2007). *Organizational Behavior* (11th Edition). Thomson Southwestern.

23. McGough, L.L. (1992). Customer Relations in Walt Disney World. *Association Mgmt.* March 1.

24. Smyth, J. (2000). Online Banking gets Physical. *Irish Times* Nov. 3.

25. Delbecq, A. L. (1986). Five Leadership Patterns for Contemporary Healthcare Systems. In *Emerging Issues in Healthcare.* Englewood, CO; Estes Park Institute.

26. Editors. (2000). Measuring People Power – Global Most Admired. *Fortune,* Oct. 2.

27. Editors. (2000). The Loudest Activist, Louise Kitchen, Enron. *Fortune,* Sept. 4, 2000; p 180-181.

NOTES FOR CHAPTER 7

1. Watson, S. (2003). Closing the Feedback Loop: Ensuring Effective Action from Student Feedback. *Tertiary Education and Management.* 9(2); June, 145.

2. Adee, A. (1997). Linking student satisfaction and service quality perceptions: the case of university education. *European J. Marketing.* 31(7); 528-540.

3. Hampton, G. (1993). Gap analysis of college student satisfaction as a measure of professional service quality. *J. Profess Services Mktg.* 9 (1).

4. Kast, F.E.; Rosenzweig, J.E. (1972). General Systems Theory: Applications for Organization and Management. *Acad Mgmt. Journal.*

5. Kast, F.E.; Rosenzweig, J.E. (1985). *Organization and Management: A Systems and Contingency Approach.* (3rd edition). New York : McGraw Hill.

6. Ziegenfuss, J.T. (1985). *DRGs and Hospital Impact: An Organizational Systems Analysis.* New York: McGraw Hill.

7. Ziegenfuss, J.T. (2002). *Organization and Management Problem Solving: A Systems and Consulting Approach.* Thousand Oaks, CA: Sage.

8. Schein, E. (1985). *Organizational Culture and Leadership.* San Francisco, Ca. Jossey Bass.

9. Schein, E. (1999). *The Corporate Culture Survival Guide. Sense and Nonsense about Culture Change.* San Francisco, Ca.: Jossey Bass.

10. Martin, J. (2002). *Organization Culture: Mapping the Terrain.* Thousand Oaks, Ca.: Sage.

11. Delbeq, A.L. (1986). Five Leadership Patterns for Contemporary Healthcare Systems. In *Emerging Issues in Healthcare.* Englewood, CO.: Estes Park Institute.

12. Buzalka, M. (2003). Why cash is king at San Diego State. *Food Management.* 38(11); Oct 2003.

13. Lawn, J. (2003). New demands drive campus dining programs. *Food Management;* 38(6). June 2003; p 8.

14. Sheridan, M. (2003). 2003 Ivy Awards: Princeton University. *Restaurants and Institutions.* 113(12); May 15, 2003.

15. Wingfield, N. (2003). College students to get free access to Napster service. *Wall St. Journal .* Nov 7.

16. Ziegenfuss, J.T. (2006). *Strategic Planning: Cases, Concepts & Lessons.* (2nd Edition). Lanham, MD: Rowman & Littlefield/University Press.

17. Anon. (2003). Baylor MBA students get hands-on consulting experience with AA.com. *Baylor Business Review.* 20(10; Spring, 30.

18. Bell, C.R. (1994). *Customers as Partners: Building Relationships that Last.* San Francisco, CA.: Berrett-Koehler.

19. Meister, J. (2003). The latest in corporate-college partnership. *Training & Development.* 57(10); Oct.

20. Hellriegel, D.; Slocum, J. (2004). *Organizational Behavior.* 10th Edition. Thomson Southwestern.

21. Ziegenfuss, J.T.; O'Rourke, P. (1995). Patient Ombudsmen and Total Quality Improvement: An Examination of Fit. *Joint Commission Journal on Quality Improvement.* 21(3); 133-142.

22. Disney Institute. (2001). *Be Our Guest: Perfecting the Art of Customer Service.* New York: Disney Editions.

23. Ibid

24. Peters, T.; Waterman, R. (1982). *In Search of Excellence.* New York: Warner Bks.

25. Welch, J. (2001). *Jack: Straight from the Gut.* New York: Warner.

26. Collins, J.C.; Porras, J.I. (1994). *Built to Last: Successful Habits of Visionary Companies.* New York: Harper Business.

27. Navaratnam, K. (1994). Customer service in an Australian quality award winning public sector service industry. *Intl J. Public Sector Management* 7(2); 42.

28. Hoffman, D. Levak, B.A. (2003). A Framework for Building Safe and Serious Schools. *Education Leadership.* September, 30.

NOTES FOR CHAPTER 8

1. LeBoeuf, M. (1987). *How to Win Customers and Keep Them for Life.* New York: Putnam.

2. Griffin, 1. (1995). *Customer Loyalty.* New York: Lexington Books.

3. Berwick D.M. (1998). Crossing the boundary: changing mental models in the service of improvement. *International Journal for Quality in Health Care.* 10(5), 435-441.

4. Carman JM, Shortell SM, et al (1996). "Keys for successful implementation of total quality management in hospitals." *Health Care Management Review* 21(1):48-60.

5. Alemi F, Moore S, et al (1998). "Rapid improvement teams." *Joint Commission Journal on Quality Improvement* 24(3): 119-29.

6. Ziegenfuss, J.T. (1993). *The Organizational Path to Health Care Quality.* Ann Arbor, MI: Health Administration Press.

7. Ziegenfuss, J.T. (1998). Design and Redesign of the the Organizational Systems Future: A transdisciplinary Process crossing Work Domains. *World Multiconference on Systemics, Cybernetics & Informatics: SCI 98 .* July 12-16, 1998. In Ziegenfuss, J.T. & Sassani, J. *Portable Health Administration.* London: Academic Press/ Elsevier.

8. Ziegenfuss, J. T. (1989). *Designing Organizational Futures: A Systems Approach with Cases for Public and Non-profit Organizations.* Springfield,Il.: Charles C. Thomas.

9. Bryson JM. (2004). *Strategic Planning for Public and Nonprofit Organizations:. A Guide to Strengthening and Sustaining Organizational Achievement.* San Francisco, California, Jossey Bass, (3rd edition).

10. Berwick op. cit. see note 3.

11. Crosby, P. (1979). *Quality is Free.* New York: McGraw-Hill.

12. Deming, W.E. (1986). *Out of Crisis.* Cambridge, MA: MIT Press.

13. Juran, J.M. (1988). *Juran on Planning for Quality.* New York: Free Press.

14. Hammer, M. (1990). Reengineering Work: Don't Automate, Obliterate. *Harv. Bus. Review.* 90(4), July-Aug , 104-112.

15. Hyde, A.C. (1995). A Primer on Process Reengineering. *The Public Manager.* 24 (21), Spring , 55-68.

16. Cooper, R.; Markus, M.L. (1995. Human Reengineering. *Sloan Management Review.* 36 (4), Summer, 39-50.

17. Ghoshal, S.; Bartlett, C.A. (1995). Changing the Role of Top Management: Beyond Structure to Process. *Harv. Bus. Review.* 73(1), Jan-Feb , 86-96.

18. Levine, D.I. (1995). *Reinventing the Workplace: How Business and Employees Can Both Win.* Washington, D.C.: Brookings Institution.

19. Champy, J. (1995). *Reengineering Management: the Mandate for New Leadership.* New York: HarperCollins.

20. Ackoff, R.L. (1970). *A Concept of Corporate Planning.* New York: Wiley.

21. Ackoff, R.L. (1981). *Creating the Corporate Future.* New York: Wiley.

22. Ackoff, R.L. (1989). The Circular Organization Design: An Update. *Academy of Management Executive.* 3, 11-16.

23. Ackoff, R.L.; Magidson, J.; Addison, H.J. (2006). *Idealized Design: Creating an Organization's Future.* Upper Saddle River, N.J.: Wharton School Publishing.

24. Bryson, J.M. op cit see note 9.

25. Collins, J.C.; Porras, J.I. (1995). Building a Visionary Company. *California Management Review.* 37(2); Winter, 80-100.

26. Hamel, G.; Prahalad, C.K. (1994). *Competing for the Future.* Boston: Harvard Business School Press.

27. Elliot , R.L. (1996). Double loop learning and the quality of quality improvement. *Joint Commission Journal on Quality Improvement.* 22(1), 59-66.

28. McClure, CR.; Bertot, J.C. (1977). Creating a Future for Public Libraries: Diverse Strategies for a Diverse Nation. *Library Trends.* 46(1); Summer, 36-51.

29. Line, MB. (1997). The Public Library in the Future: A British Reaction to Buildings, Books, and Bytes. *Library Trends.* 46(1),68-82.

30. MacAdam, B. (1998). Creating Knowledge Facilities for Knowledge Work in the Academic Library". *Library Hi Tech.* 16(1); 91.

31. Harris, R.M; Marshall, V. (1998). Reorganizing Canadian Libraries: A Giant Step Back from the Front. *Library Trends.* 46(3); Winter,564-580.

32. Makridakis, S. (1995). The Forthcoming Information Revolution: Its Impact on Society and Firms." *Futures.* 27(8); October, 799.

33. Malone, T.W. et al. (1996). Organizing for the 21st Century. *Strategy & Leadership.* 24(4); 6.

34. Sankar, Y. (1999). Organizational Culture and New Technologies. *J. Systems Management.* 39(4); 10.

35. Swierczek, F.W. (1991). The Management of Technology: Human Resource and Organizational Issues. *Intl.. J. Technology Management.* 6(1,2), 1.

36. Kwiatkowski, W. (1989). Managing the Introduction of New Technology. *Management Services.* 33(9); Sept.; 8.

37. Meeker, H. (1993). Hands-On Futurism. How to Run a Scanning Project. *Futurist.* May-June; 22-26.

38. Kast, F.E.; Rosenzweig, J.E. (1972). General Systems Theory: Applications for Organization and Management. *Acad. Mgmt. J.* 15(4) Dec.; 452-456.

39. Kast, F.E.; Rosenzweig, J.E. (1985). *Organization and Management. A Systems and Contingency Approach* 4th ed. N.Y.: McGraw Hill.

40. Ziegenfuss, James T. (1985). *DRG's & Hospital Impact. An Organizational Systems Analysis.* New York: McGraw Hill.

41. Ziegenfuss, J.T. (1988). Increasing Innovation Organization Wide: A Systems Approach and Case Example. *Sixth World Productivity Congress Proceedings* Vol. II. pp. 1223-1238. Montreal, Canada: Canadian Council for Productivity and World Confederation of Productivity Science.

42. Ziegenfuss, J.T.; Perlman, H. (1989). Decreasing Medical Malpractice: An Organizational Systems Approach. *Health Care Management Review* 14(4):67-75.

43. Ziegenfuss, J.T. (1991). Organizational Barriers to Quality Improvement in Medical and Health Care Organizations. *Quality Assurance & Utilization Review* 6(4): Winter, 115-122.

44. Jacques, C. M, Bauer, L.C. ; Ziegenfuss, J.T. (1993). Characteristics of Strong Departments of Family Medicine: Results of A Delphi Survey. *Family Medicine* 25(6):256-261.

45. Ziegenfuss, J.T. (1992). Are You Growing Systems Thinking Managers? Use a Systems Model to Teach and Practice Organizational Analysis and Planning, Policy and Development. *Systems Practice* 5(5):509-527.

46. Ziegenfuss, J.T. (1995). A Methodology for Use of Systems Thinking and Redesign in Graduate Health Care Management Education. In *Praxiology: International Journal of Practical Philosophy and Methodology.* Vol. 4, Social Agency: Dilemmas & Education. Fall.

47. Lartin-Drake, I M , Gillis-Donovan, J.G.; Curran, C.R.; Kruger, N.R.; Ziegenfuss, J.T. (1996). All Together Now: The Circular Organization in a University Hospital. Part II. Implementation. *Systems Practice* 9(5); 403-419.

48. Ziegenfuss, J.T.(2006). *Strategic Planning: Cases, Concepts & Lessons .* 2nd Edition. Lanham, Md.: Rowman & Littlefield/University Press.

49. Ziegenfuss, JT. (2002). *Organization and Management Problem Solving: A Systems and Consulting Approach.* Thousand Oaks, CA: Sage.

50. Prahalad, C.K.; Hamel, G. (1990). The Core Competencies of the Corporation. *Harv. Bus.Review.* May-June, 79-91.

51. Ackoff 1981, op. cit. see note 21, p. 123.

52. Ackoff 1981 op. cit. see note 21, p. 107.

53. Ackoff 1981 op. cit. see note 21, p. 113.

54. Ziegenfuss, J.T. op.cit. see note 48.

55. Mintzberg, H. (1994). The Fall and Rise of Strategic Planning. *Harv. Bus. Review.* Jan-Feb., 107-114.

56. Mintzberg, H. (1994). *The Rise and Fall of Strategic Planning: Reconceiving Roles for Planning,Plans, Planners.* New York: Free Press.

57. Schein, E. (1985). *Organizational Culture and Leadership.* San Francisco, CA: Jossey Bass.

58. Griffin op. cit. see note 2, p 119.

Index

ABOUT THE AUTHOR

James T. Ziegenfuss, Jr., Ph.D., is Professor of Management & Health Care Systems in the Graduate Programs in Health & Public Administration, School of Public Affairs, Pennsylvania State University.

Professor Ziegenfuss teaches courses in strategic planning, health systems, quality management, organization behavior, and organization/ management consulting. He holds the Ph.D. in Social Systems Sciences from the Wharton School of the University of Pennsylvania and Masters degrees in Psychology (Temple) and Public Administration (Penn State) and the B.A. in English (Maryland). At the Penn State Medical College he is Adjunct Professor of Medicine (1988–), co-directed the physician fellowships program in quality and has been Evaluation Coordinator for the six-year organization change project sponsored by Robert Wood Johnson/Pew (Redesigning Patient Care Systems).

Before joining the faculty, he worked full time in organization analysis and planning, including consulting evaluations, strategic planning at the single and multi-institutional levels, organizational change projects, and research and development of health care systems.

Dr. Ziegenfuss has written over 100 articles for journals and conferences and has authored eleven books including, *The Organizational Path to Health Care Quality*, (1993), Relearning Strategic Planning (1996); *Organization & Management Problem Solving: A Systems & Consulting Approach* (Sage 2002), with J. Sassani MD (editors), *Portable Health Administration* (Elsevier 2004) and most recently *Strategic Planning: Cases, Concepts & Lessons* (Rowman & Littlefield/University Press, 2006). His monograph, "Country and Community Health Systems: The Futures and Systems Redesign Approach" was presented in Madrid and was top prize in the Latin American 1998 international manuscript competition. The paper was translated to Spanish and published by the Pan American Health Organization in 1999. Dr. Ziegenfuss received the distinguished service award from the American College of Medical Quality in 1999 for his contributions in education and research and has been Associate Editor of the *American Journal of Medical Quality* since 1989. His monograph, "Building Citizen Participation: The Purposes, Tools and Impact of Involvement" won second prize in the international competition in 2000 and was published by the Center for Latin American Administrative Reform. In November 2004, he received the Regents Award for Senior Health Care Executives for leadership and management (American College of Healthcare Executives). At the annual meeting in Baden Baden Germany in 2005, he was elected Fellow of the International Institute for Advanced Studies in Systems Research & Cybernetics for his innovative research contributions to health care systems and medicine.

Professor Ziegenfuss' current teaching, research and consulting interests are in the fields of strategic planning, quality management/ customer service, and organizational development. An active consultant to public and private organizations, his education, research, and consulting works have been supported by more than 75 organizations including medical schools, associations, hospitals, banks and non-profit organizations.

Contact: Telephone: 717-948-6053
Email jtz1@psu.edu